THIS IS RHYTHM

Ella Jenkins with children at the St. Vincent de Paul Center in Chicago, 1987.
Photo by Charles Osgood. Courtesy the *Chicago Tribune*.

THIS IS RHYTHM

ELLA JENKINS, CHILDREN'S MUSIC,
AND THE LONG
CIVIL RIGHTS MOVEMENT

GAYLE F. WALD

The University of Chicago Press ✳ CHICAGO AND LONDON

The University of Chicago Press, Chicago 60637
The University of Chicago Press, Ltd., London
© 2025 by Gayle F. Wald
Published 2025
Printed in the United States of America

34 33 32 31 30 29 28 27 26 25   1 2 3 4 5

ISBN-13: 978-0-226-82481-9 (cloth)
ISBN-13: 978-0-226-82482-6 (e-book)
DOI: https://doi.org/10.7208/chicago/9780226824826.001.0001

Library of Congress Cataloging-in-Publication Data

Names: Wald, Gayle, 1965–, author.
Title: This is rhythm : Ella Jenkins, children's music, and the long civil rights
    movement / Gayle F. Wald.
Other titles: Ella Jenkins, children's music, and the long civil rights movement
    Identifiers: LCCN 2024039151 | ISBN 9780226824819 (cloth) |
    ISBN 9780226824826 (ebook)
Subjects: LCSH: Jenkins, Ella. | Folk singers—Illinois—Chicago—Biography. |
    Women folk musicians—Illinois—Chicago—Biography. | African
    American women entertainers—Illinois—Chicago—Biography. | African
    American women—Illinois—Chicago—Biography. | African American
    lesbians—Illinois—Chicago—Biography. | LCGFT: Biographies.
Classification: LCC ML420.J348 W35 2025 | DDC 782.42092 [B]—dc23/
    eng/20240905
LC record available at https://lccn.loc.gov/2024039151

♾ This paper meets the requirements of ANSI/NISO Z39.48-1992
(Permanence of Paper).

A long time ago,
An enslaved people heading toward freedom
Made up a song:
Keep Your Hand On The Plow! Hold On!
The plow plowed a new furrow
Across the field of history.
Into that furrow the freedom seed was dropped.

"Freedom's Plow," Langston Hughes, 1943

I think we who create music . . . know that it survives you.
I want to serve children, and not just for today, but for
a lot of other generations. Whoever sings a song is not
important, it's just the song itself.

Ella Jenkins

CONTENTS

PART III: CHILDREN'S ARTIST

INTRODUCTION
THIS IS ELLA JENKINS

In a classroom in Chicago's South Side in 1956, Ella Jenkins, a thirty-two-year-old "rhythm specialist," leads a group of Black middle-grade students through "Tah-boo," a rhythmic chant of made-up words. "This is a game of follow the leader," she instructs them. "Whatever I say, you say it back to me. Remember, it's awfully important to listen."

As she speaks, Ella cradles a large conga drum that hangs from a neck strap made of braided fibers. Her voice is clear, with a soft but firm timbre. It is a Northern voice, a city voice, but listening closely, the children might detect the barest traces of her Alabama and Mississippi roots.

"Tah-boo," she chants. She stretches the minor-key phrase out over four syllables, to *tah-boo-oo-oo*, the tone rising higher and then fluttering.

Tah-boo-oo-oo. The children echo it back.

"Ee-pah," she sings. The first syllable, the *ee*, is fast and sharp. The *pah* is an exhalation that flickers like the *oo* of "Tah-boo."

Ee-pah-ah-ah. The children sing it back the way they hear it.

"Ee changah changah changah yeagah," she intones. *Changah* has a soft, gently percussive sound. The *yea* in "yeagah" rhymes with "say." *Ee changah changah changah yeagah*, they repeat.

The sounds of "Tah-boo" evoke Africa, but the call-and-response dynamic between Ella and the children is universal, a pre-mother tongue known to all of its participants. It is simple, but also complex; playful, but also profound. It teaches children about music and yet musical proficiency is not its goal. It is unique to the moment—to this classroom and these children at this time—and yet repeatable in its essentials everywhere, and with different groups of people. Ella's call says *Are you here? Do you hear me?* The children's response says *We are here. We hear you.* Through this musical conversation, Ella and the children enter into a relationship of mutual recognition. The feeling of connectedness will endure even after they finish singing.

Nearly thirty years later, on a Pittsburgh soundstage in 1985, sixty-one-year-old Ella Jenkins, the acclaimed "First Lady of Children's Music," is teaching Fred Rogers and Chuck Aber, his *Mister Rogers' Neighborhood* castmate, how to do "Head and Shoulder." Much has changed in the world and in Ella's life over these three decades, but she is still sharing call-and-response songs and chants like "Tah-boo," this one involving the body. Like the clapping game "Miss Mary Mack," the game of "Head and Shoulder" challenges participants' sense of rhythm, requiring them to tap different body parts—head and shoulder, knees and ankles, and ankles and toes—in time with the chant. Ella's a cappella version of "Head and Shoulder" is jazzy, with a swinging, syncopated melody that sounds like something out of the Ella Fitzgerald songbook. A few bars in, she is joined by the in-studio band, the pianist Johnny Costa supporting her with airy, melodic riffs.

Head and shoulder baby, one—two—three
Head and shoulder baby, one—two—three

Head and shoulder head and shoulder head and shoulder baby
One—two—three

Ella nimbly performs the chant's choreography. Aber follows, mostly keeping up with her rhythmic movements. But from the beginning, Rogers stumbles and fumbles. By the time Ella arrives at the "knees and ankles" verse, bending over deftly to touch her legs and then snapping back up to clap her hands on the offbeats, he has lost the rhythm entirely. For a moment he gives up, throwing his head back and laughing, but then he rejoins her for the chant's ending. After the director, Paul Lally, calls "Cut!," a chastened Rogers blurts out to the producers and crew, "I didn't do it well at all! I was terrible! I just couldn't do it." Lally teases him good-naturedly. "You could never be that dumb again, never, Fred," he says, as everyone cracks up. But Ella, who never thought to pause the chant while they were taping, has a different take. "You were wonderful," she tells Rogers. "Just like the blues! You could never get it the same, *never* get it the same."[1]

Her words are not false praise. What she sees in Rogers's attempts at "Head and Shoulder" is at the center of the practices and beliefs that have taken her from community centers and classrooms to guest spots on national television. By teaching Rogers and Aber a Black girls' game from the Bronzeville neighborhood of Chicago where she grew up, Ella has offered them a lesson in Black diasporic music. It is an invitation, a call, and Rogers's response demonstrates his willingness to engage, to play the game despite its unfamiliarity. "Head and Shoulder" is ultimately about synchrony between people, as participants aim to align their bodies and voices. On the playground where it passes from peer to peer, newcomers learn the chant by mimicking the moves of experienced players. As the newcomers make mistakes, their awkwardness eventually yields to familiarity. Some will be gifted at the game, some will not. But everyone participates. This is why, even though his movements are unwieldy and mostly off-beat, Ella calls Rogers "wonderful." There can be beautiful music even in mismatched rhythms.[2]

Such moments illustrate the iridescent genius and generous spirit of Ella Jenkins, the most significant and prolific American children's musician of the twentieth century. Between 1957 and 2017 she released forty albums, including the best-sellers *You'll Sing a Song and I'll Sing a Song* (1966) and *Multicultural Children's Songs* (1995). Her music is in the Library of Congress's National Recording Registry and in the score of Alvin Ailey's modern dance classic *Revelations*. She remains the only Black woman and the only children's musician to have received lifetime honors both as a recording artist (a 2004 Grammy Lifetime Achievement Award) and a songwriter (a 1999 Lifetime Achievement Award from the American Society of Composers, Authors and Publishers [ASCAP]). Ella's work drew an extraordinary array of twentieth-century artists and public figures into her orbit, including musicians like Billie Holiday, Pete Seeger, Odetta, Big Bill Broonzy, Sun Ra, Cuban drummer Armando Peraza, and German composer Carl Orff; civil rights figures like Martin Luther King, Bayard Rustin, and Chicago mayor Harold Washington; and artists and writers like dancer Alvin Ailey, sculptor Richard Hunt, and Langston Hughes, whose writings deeply influenced her philosophy of rhythm. And while she is best known in the United States, in a career spanning more than six decades she has traversed the globe as an educator, making music that defies borders.

This Is Rhythm tells the story of how a rebellious Black girl, the daughter of a domestic servant who migrated to Chicago from Mississippi, became a musical presence in the childhoods of large numbers of Americans across several generations. It is a tale that travels with twentieth-century US popular music, encompassing Chicago blues and jazz, the 1950s vogue for Cuban dance music, the post–World War II folk revival, the development of civil rights "freedom songs," and the birth of rock and roll. It weaves together strands of Cold War internationalism and interculturalism, democratic pluralism, African diasporic consciousness, and anticolonialism, along with feminism and environmentalism. And it bends around the social transformations of American childhood and children's education, including the postwar invention of "youth" culture and the 1960s emergence of preschool.

Yet above all, Ella's life and work is a story of civil rights activism, using children's music as a tool of community-building and anti-racism.[3] Ella's sense of mission rendered her as much an educator and community activist as a musical performer and recording artist. She used musical performances to model more perfect social worlds, teaching audiences matched timing (synchrony) and call and response (antiphony). She redefined the "classroom" to include any place where people might gather to sing together. Across a changing and varied repertoire, she used songs and chants to develop deep listening, fostering skills like empathy, turn-taking, and communication.

Ella's career posed the question, *What does civil rights sound like for children?* She answered it with deceptively simple songs that taught them to see beauty and value in themselves and others, and that ranged fearlessly over genres, periods, and national traditions. The social and physical powerlessness of her audiences meant that she approached every musical encounter with profound care. She also took personal risks in teaching children about Black freedom struggles, both domestic and international. Few people would have dared to smuggle chain-gang songs, spirituals-cum-civil-rights-anthems, and lessons about African independence movements into programs for white children in small towns in the Upper Midwest in 1962. But Ella did. She believed that by carrying her own sonic Black girlhood to such places, she could open children of all backgrounds to its vibrant rhythms.[4]

Perhaps no other "self-taught" musician has had as profound an impact on American children's music. With her conga drum, Ella fashioned herself as a female griot, openly contesting two assumptions: that musical instruction was the sole purview of the conservatory-trained and that folklore was primarily a domain of "collectors" and ethnographers. "Though I never studied music when I was growing up," she said, "I was a 'good blues' child."[5] Blues was indeed her first musical language, learned at the feet of her beloved Uncle Floyd

"Flood" Johnson, a Louisiana-born migrant who played harmonica to unwind after a day's work at a steel mill. But "'good blues' child" also suggested Ella's heritage as the daughter of African American migrants who carried Southern musical traditions with them on their journeys to the North. Living in Bronzeville, Ella wrote, "one could not help but absorb" the vibrant tapestry of sounds, all bearing echoes of the resilient rhythms of Africa: from Black girls' clapping games to the sounds of Sunday church worship to the pulsating energy of popular performers such as the "hi-de-ho" man Cab Calloway.

In the early 1950s, when Ella first began calling herself a "rhythm specialist," recorded music for children consisted mostly of blandly entertaining "kidisks": nursery rhymes and lullabies, Western-themed cowboy songs, Disney recordings, and the songs of animated characters like Tubby the Tuba. Alongside this commercial children's music, since the 1940s a small cadre of prominent folk musicians—including Lead Belly, Pete Seeger, Cisco Houston, and Woody Guthrie—had performed children's music and recorded it on the independent Folkways label. Through their songbooks and writing, composer Ruth Crawford Seeger and music educator Beatrice Landeck promoted an American children's folk canon. Yet before Ella, few professional musicians *composed* for children, and those who did, including Guthrie, were not generally considered "children's musicians."[6]

With "Tah-boo," the first track of her first album for Folkways, *Call-and-Response Rhythmic Group Singing* (1957), Ella dropped the needle on a radically different way of doing children's music—and became the first musician in the United States to establish a career performing and recording for young audiences. Where other children's albums presented songs for listeners to emulate, Ella's album involved children in its production, featuring their voices alongside her own. Instead of entertaining children with polished performances, it portrayed music as a participatory activity requiring no special tools or training. And rather than promote music as a means to an end, Ella's songs proposed that the *doing together* of music was an end in itself.[7]

Call-and-Response Rhythmic Group Singing was equally revolutionary for grounding children's music in the sonic practices and traditions of the Black diaspora. While studying Afro-diasporic music, especially Cuban rhythms, in her twenties, Ella discovered a source of sonic self-knowledge as an American woman of African descent. She drew on this knowledge, and on a US Black woman's sonic "idea of Africa," to activate children's interest in places, peoples, and cultures they had been taught to regard as primitive.[8] In songs like "Moon Don't Go" and "Another Man Done Gone," Ella communicated the spirit of Black people determined to find their freedom. While not ideological, the album promoted humanistic ideals of brotherhood, equality, and fairness that Ella saw at the center of the modern civil rights project. It was in this sense like the other sorts of sonic activism—from the collective singing of "We Shall Overcome" to protest songs such as Charles Mingus's "Fables of Faubus" or Nina Simone's "Mississippi Goddam"—that were an indelible part of that movement.[9]

In the decades following her Folkways debut, Ella expanded her repertoire, adding songs associated with different cultures and traditions. She moved from the "made-up" sounds of "Tah-boo" to songs incorporating words in Spanish, Navajo, Swahili, and Japanese. Without ever retiring her conga drum or rhythm sticks, she took up the baritone ukulele, a four-stringed Hawai'ian instrument that afforded her greater melodic opportunities. (It was not a typical "folk" instrument, but it served her interests well.) As she developed expertise with preschoolers and with disabled children, she made albums that adapted call and response to their distinct needs and abilities. She came up with new arrangements of folkloric material or composed her own songs, taking care to retain the copyright. Often these original works were inspired by travels that took her to every continent, including Antarctica.

Her career sustained Folkways until it was sold to the Smithsonian Institution in 1987 following the death of its founder, Ella's dear friend and occasional sparring partner Moe Asch. Yet Ella's artistic and financial contributions to the label have been obscured. In 1995 Smithsonian

Folkways head Anthony Seeger challenged an audience to name the label's best-selling artist, knowing that most people would guess Lead Belly, Seeger, or Guthrie. After a beat, he supplied the "surprise" answer: "Ella Jenkins has sold tens of thousands of records for Folkways," he said, "and she is still selling them today."[10]

Beyond pointing to Ella's importance to Asch's business, Seeger's question hinted at the underestimation of her music, which, because it is simple and directed at young listeners, is assumed to lack depth or sophistication. But simplicity and unpretentiousness were aesthetic choices that communicated Ella's commitment to music as a means of community-making. As Grammy-winning family musician Dan Zanes observed, her "courageous minimalism" allowed Ella to "create conditions" in which everyone could feel part of the music. "That's a very different experience from watching someone perform," he said. "It was social music in its simplest, purest form."[11]

Generations of educators have gravitated toward this social quality of Ella's recordings and performances, embracing both the messages of her songs and her participatory methods. Just as she taught children to be in love with singing, so she taught early childhood educators to trust in their own music-making capacity, even if they struggled to sing in tune. Her analog recordings became treasured resources, retaining their vibrancy and relevance with children of the digital era. "To this day, you can walk into not just preschool classrooms but elementary school classrooms that still have Ella's vinyl," said eminent children's and folk musician Cathy Fink.[12]

Ella, in turn, often identified as an "educator" rather than a "musician," associating the latter term with formal training and knowledge of Western notation. "I think I have a good ear," she said. "I'm not a professional musician as far as studying music, but I say I make music, you know, and I understand music. I feel music." At other times, she would call herself a "natural" musician, identifying with Black folk singers like Elizabeth Cotten and Bessie Jones. "If you grow up in non-affluence," Ella observed, "you learn to rely on your creativity."[13] Music was recreation, but it was also a means of sustenance and survival.

None of Ella's successes with adults would have been possible, though, without her peerless rapport with and respect for children. Over the years, observers have tried to pinpoint the source of her gift for connecting with them, sometimes calling her a "magician." Ella's open-heartedness and seemingly perpetual good cheer did lend her the air of a kind of living musical saint. The sisters Rosalind Henderson Mustafa and Kathie Anderson, who knew Ella when they were growing up, described her as "a very light, free spirit," with "no darkness or sadness about her . . . [nothing] . . . maudlin or negative." Fred Rogers similarly spoke of the "light" that Ella brought into the television studio during each of her eight visits to *Mister Rogers' Neighborhood*. And music therapist Louise Dimiceli-Mitran noted that Ella "didn't seem to ever get worn out" by children. "She seemed to have the same flame burning inside of her that they have burning."[14]

Bernadelle Richter, the woman Ella lovingly called her "dearest friend," and who was her manager and life partner of more than sixty years, understood how hard Ella worked to be a light for others. And she had a simultaneously more prosaic and remarkable explanation for Ella's "magic." "A lot of people who work with children are afraid of them," she said. "They don't know how to relate to children. Ella has never been one of those people. She never talks down to children."

I first met Ella in 2017, when I visited her at the North Side of Chicago assisted-living facility where she had been living for several years, after her daily care became too difficult for Bernadelle to manage. The three of us had lunch in the small on-site cafeteria. Around us, people of various ages and abilities navigated the serving lines and the drink stations. I sat with Ella, who used a wheelchair, while Bernadelle got her a bowl of soup and a cup of coffee. Theirs was the choreography of longtime companions who anticipate each other's rhythms.

It was not difficult to understand why people grasped for superlatives to describe Ella. Although at ninety-two it was hard for her to retain new information or remember people, I found her charming, curious, unassuming, insistent, and subversively witty, especially on issues of race, gender, and sexuality. (Sometimes Bernadelle would try to shush her when she felt that Ella's jokes were too bold.) The conversation had a kaleidoscopic quality, with rich anecdotes refracted through the lens of Ella's capacious memory. At one moment she would recount a story about receiving "whippings" from her mother, and feeling that as a girl she was punished more harshly than her brother. At another moment, she would recall the time that Big Bill Broonzy took her to join the musicians' union, Local 208, in the 1950s when Chicago shops were still racially segregated. She wisecracked about the acquisition of Folkways by the Smithsonian, quipping, "I hope they don't hang me up like one of those airplanes" in the National Air and Space Museum. Sometimes when she remembered her life she would break out into song. A mention of her musical mentor Armando Peraza had her tapping out rhythms on her lap with her long, expressive fingers.

After that, I returned regularly to Chicago to talk to Ella, more often than not with Bernadelle by her side, helping to keep her comfortable and fill in details that escaped her recall. Yet as Ella came to entrust me more and more with telling the story of her life, her cognitive impairment advanced, and thus she also increasingly struggled to remember me. She would greet me warmly, as though she knew me, but I would have to remind her who I was and why I was there. Once, after I again told her that I was writing her biography, she regarded me and, with a twinkle in her disarming olive-green eyes, deadpanned, "Anything you write about me, I'm sure it will be important." She mustered tremendous energy and concentration to communicate. She wanted to tell her story, and she wanted her story told.

During the COVID pandemic, we stayed in touch through FaceTime calls. After it was safe to visit her in person again, she agreed to sit for an extended series of interviews—about twelve hours over three days in November of 2021. During these demanding sessions, Ella was remarkably cogent, sharing some of her most intimate memories, including of meeting Bernadelle. There were some memories she preferred not to dredge up—and which Bernadelle understandably worried would unnecessarily agitate her. These included painful incidents from her childhood and traumatic experiences of racism and misogyny. And yet during one of these conversations, Ella teared up while volunteering a story—unknown even to Bernadelle—about being the object of a racial slur in California in the late 1940s. I was profoundly moved, not only because Ella had invited me to bear witness to this painful memory but because I felt that she had shared it precisely to communicate aspects of her experience that were beyond my own. Sensing this, I chose that moment to ask Ella whether it made a difference to her that I am white and Jewish. "You can't walk in someone else's shoes," she responded. "You can't trade places."

I was not able to get Ella to elaborate; by the time I asked, her mind had moved on. But the moment confirmed for me Ella's fundamental desire to be known, both to herself and to others. The drive was apparent in her lifelong practice of self-archiving. In her papers I discovered typical items relating to her career—like flyers, clippings, and business correspondence—but also well-thumbed copies of Mary Baker Eddy's *Science and Health with Keys to the Scripture*, attesting to the formative significance of Christian Science on her personal philosophy. There were also table-tennis rackets, trophies, and books about the sport, the evidence of lesser-known talents that played important if indirect roles in her career.

The most notable materials reflected a powerful autobiographical impulse. "For years and years I was writing something all the time," she recalled. "I kept track of things." Her papers included dozens of lists, which I came to understand as a kind of rhythmic, repetitive gesture of stock-taking. There were lists of important people in her life; of places she had lived; and even of her political activities, particularly during the late 1940s, when she worked with the Chicago branch of the Congress of Racial Equality. There were carefully crafted scrapbooks, one documenting the late 1950s and 1960s folk revival. There were poems on topics ranging from the lack of job opportunities for African Americans to the pleasures of airplane travel, in which the quotidian world gave way to clouds and light. And there were prose works with titles like "Things to Remember," "My Rebel Days," "Highlighted Memories," and "Experiences That Stand Out." One professional biography began with the line "Ella Jenkins, single . . . ," the ellipsis covering aspects of her life that Ella chose not to share, perhaps as much out of self-protection as out of "privacy."

Like Ella's ellipsis, I have honored Ella's occasional preferences *not* to "tell all." Sometimes she struggled to remember, but sometimes she preferred not to say too much. I see respecting her wishes as an embrace, not an abdication, of my role as a biographer. It is a form of acknowledgment and appreciation of the ways Black women of Ella's generation were simultaneously silenced and the subject of endless raced and gendered discourses that distorted their humanity.

Ella was most happy talking about her life when she was sharing it with children. At some point, in response to their curiosity about her own childhood, she wrote a memoir in the form of a poem, which she set to music and titled "A Singer of Folk Songs":

When people ask me
Who I am
I tell them this
I tell them this
My Mother's from Mississippi
And my Father's from "Alabam"
I tell them this
My Brother was born in St. Louis Missouri
And so was I
We both liked school
As well as my Mother's apple pie
My Uncle "Flood" from Louisiana
Played the harmonica blues
And my Aunt, Willie Mae,
Bought me some "Buster Brown" shoes
I grew up in Chicago
In a poor neighborhood

But being poor
Didn't mean
I wasn't any good
I graduated from high school
And from College too
And I found out soon
There were many things
I could do
Now I'm a singer-musician
I enjoy it a lot
But I had to work hard
For all that I've got[15]

As the poem suggests, Ella lived a life that was not foreordained. Coming up from poverty and amid the stain of racial segregation, she invented herself as singer-musician, launching a career that afforded her remarkable creative freedom and personal autonomy, if not riches or celebrity. At a time when few African American women traveled internationally, she circled the globe. While embracing the notion that her romantic choices were "nobody's business," as the blues singers put it, she built a life with a white female partner who supported her career materially and emotionally. And, through song, she facilitated children's consciousness of democratic pluralism, modeling through percussion what Cuban drummer Dafnis Prieto has called "a comfort with different patterns or rhythms living together."[16] When she passed away on November 9, 2024, it was at the storybook age of 100. Her life, in a sense, was the ultimate "call and response": love given and love returned. A game that never grew old.

A NOTE ON CHILDREN'S LETTERS

One of the idiosyncrasies of Ella's career, familiar to professionals in the field of early childhood education, is that children whom she influenced may now have few or no conscious memories of her, save perhaps for an instinctive knowledge of the proper response to the musical query "Did you feed my cow?" ("Yes, ma'am!") Luckily, over the years Ella saved many children's letters, drawings, and poems, most compiled and sent to her by thoughtful teachers. The chapters of this book are prefaced by some of these letters, idiosyncrasies and all. The letters constitute an archive of Ella's relationship to children, presented in their own words.

PART I
CLAVE

Clave (/ˈklaːveɪ, kleɪv/; Spanish: [ˈklaβe]): a rhythmic pattern used as a tool for temporal organization in Cuban music. In Spanish, a key, clef, code, or keystone.

Dere Ms. Ella Jenkins, I enjoyed your trip to my room. I had never met a lady that can play the harmonica as good as you. Ms. Ella Jenkins, I thank you for coming. Some famous people like you wouldn't come even if we beg. But you came and that was nice of you.

Your life story was interesting to me. Ms. Ella Jenkins I know we just met today but if it doesn't bother you, could you write me the song Long in your spare time and give it to [my teacher]? Your life must be wonderful you sing, play the harmonica, travel a lot, speak lots of languages and your famous to all little kids all over the world. You must be proud of yourself!

Truly your new friend,
Antonio

(CHICAGO, 1985)

1

BRONZEVILLE

1924–1938

A daughter of the first Great Migration of African Americans, Ella Louise Jenkins was born on August 6, 1924, in St. Louis, Missouri, about halfway between her mother Annabelle Walker's birthplace of Coffeeville, Mississippi, and her family's ultimate destination of Bronzeville, on the South Side of Chicago. The first songs she heard as an infant were sung by Southerners who regarded her with special tenderness because she was born in the North, a land of hope. The aspirations of an oppressed people searching for their freedom were baked into her DNA.

She came into the world as a sister to Thomas Harrison Jenkins, born in January 1923. Had Annabelle given birth to Thomas or Ella back in Mississippi, the babies might have been delivered by midwives, skilled Black women who served communities that were neglected by the medical profession. But Barnes Hospital, in accordance with its founder's wishes, served the citizens of St. Louis "without distinction to creed." For Ella, this detail had an almost providential quality, both encapsulating modernity's promise for Black female migrants like her mother and anticipating her own life's journey as a poor girl who grew up to earn a college degree, travel the world, become a popular recording artist, and pioneer the field of children's music.

Annabelle was born in Coffeeville in 1903 but grew up in Grenada, Mississippi, a larger town about twenty miles to the southeast, just across the Yalobusha River. Place names like *Yalobusha*, a Choctaw word meaning "tadpole place," were a testament to the area's Native inhabitants, whom the US government forcibly expelled from their territories after the passage of the Indian Removal Act of 1830. Yet Native people continued to inhabit the land and influence its culture. Annabelle's mother, Virginia Parson, was part Choctaw and, along with her older sister Willie Mae "Big Mama" Walker (born in 1900), Annabelle had an additional four half brothers from Virginia's marriage to a Choctaw man with the surname Hudson. Although Ella didn't know all of her Hudson cousins well, she grew up hearing her mother and aunt speak of them as having "good hair."

Like the overwhelming majority of Black women in Mississippi in the early twentieth century, the women in Annabelle's extended family farmed cotton, worked in domestic service, or did both, for subsistence wages. And because their labor was paramount to the survival of their families, they received little formal education. Annabelle was called to the fields to work before she could complete fourth grade. By her teenage years she had begun to daydream about getting out of Grenada—and out of the South. She pictured herself in Chicago, its bustling thoroughfares illuminated by electric streetlights.

Instead, Annabelle landed in St. Louis, a North-South "border city" on the Illinois Central Railroad line. St. Louis was a popular destination for Mississippi migrants, but her decision to settle there may also have had something to do with a man with a name out of the Bible. Obadiah Jenkins (born October 8, 1895) was a native of the northern Alabama town of Huntsville. He was compactly built, standing 5'5", and had a kind demeanor. Unlike Annabelle, he grew up in relative prosperity, the son of Thomas Jenkins, a lay leader of St. Bartley

Primitive Baptist Church, the oldest African American congregation in the state. The Jenkins family owned their home, and Obadiah—who had been educated through the eighth grade—grew up sharing a roof with his parents, five siblings, and grandmother Bettsie.

Obadiah was twenty-two when Congress declared war with Germany in 1917 and, like many Black Southern young men, he heeded the national call for "Negro" enlistees, arriving in France in winter 1917/18 as a member of the 302nd Stevedore Regiment of American Expeditionary Forces. Overseen by white officers, he loaded and unloaded cargo and did other manual labor, working ten or more hours a day, seven days a week, with rare days off. After two years he received an honorable discharge and arrived back in the United States in July 1919. By 1920, he was living with extended family in St. Louis's Twenty-Second Ward.

According to the *St. Louis Star and Times*, Obadiah Jenkins and Annabelle applied for a marriage license in August of 1922.[1] Both of them liked the idea of deriving their children's names from the names of beloved relations, since, as Annabelle would say, with a "family name" you always knew where you came from and to whom you belonged. Their son carried forward the given names of Obadiah's father, Thomas, and his oldest brother, Harrison. When their daughter was born, they came up with a creative twist on Louella, the name of Obadiah's younger sister, calling the baby Ella Louise.

As a young married couple, Annabelle and Obadiah struggled to make ends meet. Annabelle did domestic work and Obadiah took jobs as a laborer. Like many African American veterans of the Great War, he found his national service afforded him little protection from racism or discrimination in his own country. He had served in a segregated army and returned home to a segregated workforce. Among Southern Black migrants in St. Louis, traumatic memory of the vicious 1917 "race massacre" in East St. Louis, the Illinois city across the Mississippi River, were still fresh. White mobs had wantonly murdered Black men, women, and children, many of them recent migrants. In some cases, the mob burned people alive.[2]

Ella would never know why her father struggled with alcohol, but she understood that Black men in his position often turned to drink to dull feelings of shame and rage. Obadiah's alcoholism may be one reason why, while Ella was still a toddler, Annabelle sent her and Tom to live with their grandmother and cousins in Mississippi. It is unclear whether Annabelle was then working as a "live in" servant; if she were, then she would have had no other option. At least in Grenada, she might have reasoned, her children would be well fed and doted over, with plenty of opportunities for fresh air.

Grenada is about sixty miles west of the Mississippi Delta, an iconic region sometimes described as the "Birthplace of the Blues." It is hard to imagine that the soundscape of Ella's time there did not include some form of blues, whether by way of popular commercial recordings, traveling musicians, or amateur music-makers, although the proper church people among her relatives might have disapproved of it as the "devil's music." On the other hand, that area of north-central Mississippi was full of other sounds. As scholar William Ferris has noted, the musical traditions of Mississippi included "one-strand instruments, bottle-blowing, fife and drum, hymns, spirituals, the banjo, the fiddle, and prison work chants."[3]

In addition to the droning of insects and the muffled racket of trains carrying cotton and cane syrup to places where they became fabric and molasses, Ella primarily remembered the music that accompanied her relatives' rituals of work and prayer. She recalled accompanying the adults to the fields where they picked cotton. As they worked the grown-ups would sing a rhythmic song: "O Lordy, pick a bale of cotton / O Lordy, pick a bale a day." Ella was fascinated to hear them improvise, so that no two versions of the song were ever exactly the same. Sundays reverberated with the sounds of all-day services at the local Baptist church, where the intermingling of voices drew worshippers together as a community. During his sermon, the preacher would ask, "Do I have a witness?" and the congregation would respond, "Yes, Lord. Yes, Lord!" In the midst of lively collective singing, people would "get happy" and run to the front of the tabernacle. The adults responded to these moments with shouts of encouragement and choruses of Amens.

By the time Annabelle was reunited with her children, she had left Obadiah and relocated permanently to the Bronzeville neighborhood of Chicago. Just as Ella did not grow up hearing tales of her parents' romance—where and how they met and fell in love—so she would know little about its dissolution. Adults did not speak of such things. And yet she understood that sometimes men and women could not get along. In the evenings, she heard neighbors quarreling through thin kitchenette walls.

Annabelle brought her children to Chicago at an opportune if fragile moment: the "Fat Years" between the end of World War I and the onset of the Depression. The number of Black Southern migrants in the industrial city had doubled between 1910 and 1920, and it would double again between 1920 and 1930. Migrants like Ella's family regarded the city as a bountiful Black Metropolis, complete with Black schools and banks; Black doctors and dentists; Black shopping districts and nightlife establishments; and parks where Black children had free rein to play. And yet, as observed by Richard Wright, these migrants' lives were precarious and defined by the persistence of white supremacy. Wright, himself a migrant who landed in Chicago from southwest Mississippi at around the same time as Ella and Tom, wrote that many migrants "were driven and pursued, in the manner of characters in a Greek play, down the paths of defeat," while others "somehow survived."[4]

Annabelle was determined that her family would be among the survivors. At one point, the three of them lived in a second-floor flat—a cramped space above a store—with four other adults. In such tight quarters, Tom and Ella learned to share beds and to perform what Tom called "gymnastics around the eating table."[5] Privacy was an afterthought. On weekends, they overheard adults from other apartments fighting in the hallways, using cuss words they dared not repeat in front of their mother. They observed with interest the intermittent visits of local numbers runners, who jotted down bets on small colored scraps of paper. Compared to the laboring men they were more used to seeing, the runners, who wore starched shirts to conduct their business, appeared as dapper professionals.

Bronzeville was bounded by Cottage Grove Avenue on the east and the Rock Island Railroad on the west, Twenty-Second Street on the north and Fifty-First Street on the south. The farther from downtown Chicago you went, the higher the street numbers became and the better off the neighborhood. Ella and Tom learned to measure their affluence in terms of their address. On "moving day," which was May 1, they would help Annabelle load their possessions into a van, following their mother's annual quest for better housing. The children always hoped the van would point south, toward a "high end" address. Before they left their old flat, Annabelle would make Tom and Ella scrub the floor so it was spotless for the next occupants. If the previous inhabitants of their new apartment had not been so conscientious, they would have to get on their knees again. Thus Annabelle taught her children: "We may be poor and we may have very little, but you can be clean."[6]

The Fat Years that the family briefly enjoyed ended with the stock market crashes of 1929. Black male laborers were among the first to feel the effects of the cratering Midwest economy, but young Black women like Annabelle were also early casualties of the Lean Years, as white women economized by laying off their domestic servants. Although their family sometimes lacked food and heat, Ella and Tom took pride in their mother's ability to stretch their allowance of government aid. The children, too, found creative means of making do with little. They would play a game they called "save along," which had a simple rule: "If there was something you especially liked, you would eat it slowly, a little bite at a time."[7] Through the alchemy of play, they even transformed their experiences of constant moving into a source of amusement. As in the game of "memory train," in which players must try to recall a long list of items to bring on an imaginary journey, they turned their frequent moving into a pleasurable ritual of remembering. Their addresses included the 3400 block of S. Wabash; 3948 S. Indiana, near the South Side Boys' Club; 4135 S. Indiana; a basement apartment at 4103 S. Prairie; and 5100 S. Parkway.[8]

Yet while these addresses trended upward over time, Ella's family's ascent to the "higher end" of Bronzeville was not linear. They survived by living periodically with relatives or boarders and by hosting Saturday-night rent parties, at which Tom and Ella were "shush-shushed out of the way" while the adults found respite from their worries in food, drink, and dancing.[9] Sometimes even such creative strategies of survival were not enough. Around 1930 Annabelle accepted a live-in domestic position with a white family in the northern suburb of Winnetka, in New Trier Township, and was forced to place Ella and Tom in a social service agency, the Sunshine Home for Deserted Children. Located at 3520 S. Wabash Avenue—near their first flat in the "low end" of town—the Sunshine Home had been founded by African American women reformers to support the destitute and orphaned offspring of migrants. Ella, about six at the time, was too young to grasp the cruel irony of the Sunshine Home's name. In adulthood she carried forward few memories of this time of separation (or preferred not to remember it), allowing only that she looked forward to her mother's days off, when Annabelle would visit bearing treats of sweet rolls and cookies.

The cost of the separation for Annabelle is powerfully insinuated in the 1930 US federal census, which finds "Annabelle Jenkins" enumerated as a twenty-six-year-old divorced "servant" in the suburban Chicago home of Emory Andrews, an ink company executive, along with wife, mother-in-law, and two sons, aged twenty-four and sixteen. With Annabelle counted as an unprotected female laborer within a white family's "household," her own family ties, including her

FIGURE 1.1. Ella, ca. 1929. Personal collection of Ella Jenkins.

motherhood, are effaced. As for Ella and Tom, the same 1930 federal census contains no record of their whereabouts.

Sometime after she retrieved Ella and Tom from the Sunshine Home, around 1931 or 1932, Annabelle came down with a sudden illness, which the doctors diagnosed as breast cancer. They said her case was grave. Ella and Tom knew only that their mother was unwell.

But Annabelle made a sudden, even miraculous, recovery. Ella and Tom had been allowed a visit when their mother looked quite ill, but "then the next time we saw her she was better," Ella remembered. Annabelle attributed her revival to the intervention of a new religion called Christian Science. During her hospitalization, an acquaintance arranged for her to be visited by a practitioner (or healer) of the thriving new religion. The practitioner prayed for Annabelle, reading passages from the Holy Bible and from *Science and Health with Key to the Scriptures*, a text written by Mary Baker Eddy, the founder of

Christian Science. Annabelle emerged from the experience with a new outlook on health, both physical and spiritual. For the rest of her life, she remained a devout believer.

Annabelle was among thousands of Chicagoans—including many Black South Siders—attracted to Christian Science and other "New Thought" religions during the Depression. To cope with and make sense of the newness of their environments, Black migrants searched for new spiritual homes. They found refuge in the many South Side "storefront" churches that promulgated varieties of Pentecostal Christianity, or in membership in the Moorish Science Temple of America or the Nation of Islam, sects that stood outside of traditional Black Protestantism.[10] If Annabelle was initially drawn to Christian Science by virtue of her recovery from illness, her decision to convert and to bring her children up in the faith was a powerful act of self-determination, an act of agency that contrasted with her social powerlessness as a poor Black woman.

Initially, most converts to Christian Science were white and middle-class, and a disproportionate number were women, drawn to the egalitarianism of a religion that permitted women to occupy important institutional positions. With the growth of Chicago's African American migrant population after World War I, however, the number of Black converts soared.[11] The congregation Annabelle joined in the early 1930s, the Eighth Church of Christ, Scientist, met in an enormous domed temple at 4359 South Michigan Avenue that was completed in 1911, before the neighborhood was majority African American.[12] But after the Eighth Church began admitting Black members, white congregants left for other churches, just as they left neighborhoods when African Americans moved in.

The Eighth Church attracted a substantial middle-class membership, another reason it appealed to Annabelle. Congregants included Basil O. Phillips, photography editor for *Ebony* and *Jet*; Theodore Stone, an opera singer and pianist who contributed music columns to the *Defender*; and musician and educator Geraldine Glover, who would later marry Associated Negro Press correspondent Adolph

Slaughter. Ella and Tom attended Sunday School with Harold Bradley, who would become a pathbreaking professional football player and a noted musician-artist. Such associations with Bronzeville's Talented Tenth befit Annabelle's social and economic aspirations. As she told Ella, "Christian Scientists, they don't go down the ladder; you have to work up to them."[13]

Annabelle's friends and relations might have wondered what she saw in this austere white woman's religion, which lacked the expressiveness and warmth of the Baptist churches of her youth. But Sunday services at the Eighth Church, which focused on readings of Holy Scripture and Eddy's commentary, reinforced and gave spiritual sanction to Annabelle's educational and social aspirations for her children. Following the faith's emphasis on reading, at home she would perch on a dining-room chair with Ella and Tom arrayed on the floor at her feet, guiding them through their daily reading of *Science and Health*, despite her own limited literacy. Mrs. Eddy's Victorian prose style set a standard of eloquence that the children were expected to emulate, which may explain their family's unusual practice of formal address. Instead of calling Annabelle "Mama," in the manner of most Black girls and boys, Ella and Tom called her "Mother" and referred to each other simply as "Brother" and "Sister" (the latter sometimes affectionately abbreviated to "Sis")—customs that lasted through their lifetimes.

At the core of Christian Science was Eddy's metaphysical critique of the mortal body, which led the faithful to turn to prayer in the face of illness. After her conversion, Annabelle never took Ella or Tom to visit doctors or dentists. When one of them was injured or sick—as when Tom cut his leg while playing on a fence—she would call a practitioner, who would come to the house and pray; occasionally, she would use what Ella called "folk medicine"—natural remedies learned from her childhood. Most of the time prayer produced the desired outcome. But once, at school, Ella accidentally broke a glass bottle of milk and suffered a deep and bloody gash in her right palm that required stiches. Annabelle did not stand in the way of Ella's visit to the doctor, but neither would she facilitate it, staying home to pray.

FIGURE 1.2. Annabelle Jenkins, Ella's mother, ca. 1930s.
Personal collection of Ella Jenkins.

When her mother was hospitalized with cancer, Ella might have prayed to God to make her better. But as a Christian Scientist, she learned to focus her mental and spiritual attention on God's goodness in and of itself. The notion that Divine love would rise to "meet every human need" provided Ella with spiritual armor against sticks and stones, both real and metaphorical. "Christian séance," Ella's classmates would taunt her, seizing on the popular perception of Eddy's religion as a spiritualist cult. Sometimes she bemoaned her mother's conversion, particularly Annabelle's decision to banish birthday celebrations. (The Bible said your "days shall be numbered," and Annabelle took this as a sign that celebrating birthdays was a way of "counting your days," usurping God's role.) But rather than feel embarrassed or excluded, mostly Ella and Tom felt a sense of specialness in being Christian Scientists. During the Depression, Ella remembered, "people had very little, and almost everyone on our block was on welfare, including us. But our attitudes were a little different. We strongly believed in God and felt that God's supply was unlimited. That kept us going and kept us with a positive state of mind."[14]

Eddy's theology also equipped Ella to confront racism as a *spiritual* illness. While Christian Science texts never addressed race overtly, their distrust of the mortal body and the physical world rendered race a fallacy of materialism, or what Eddy called "mortal mind." As her consciousness of racism developed, a teenaged Ella took comfort in the notion that God's love would prevail over "discordant conditions."[15] Assurances of God's protective care taught Ella a "state of mind" that equipped her to confront adversity and oppression. To outsiders, the Christian Science discipline of resisting the fallacies of the material world could seem idealist to the point of escapist, but to Ella it was "a useful tool in my pocket." "I was trained to look at life as life is," she once explained. "Life is not all beautiful but mostly beautiful. You can take the beautiful part of life and apply it."

Yet Christian Science beliefs could not shield Ella from her mother's use of corporal punishment in the service of her spiritual health. Once, when Ella wet the bed, Annabelle used a whip that left welts on her arms and legs. Ella was an alert and curious child, sensitive to the moral contradictions of hurting children as a means of displaying love. She shed tears for herself, but she also wept when she overheard the cries of neighboring children as they were spanked or whipped. The cries nagged at her at night. Why, she wondered, did parents hit their children?

And why did her mother seem to be angrier with her than with her big brother? Ella loved Tom and looked up to him, shaping herself through his example. If Tom liked a game, then Ella would play it, too.

FIGURE 1.3. Ella and her brother Tom, ca. 1934.
Personal collection of Ella Jenkins.

If he learned a song, then Ella would learn it, too. But Ella saw Annabelle punishing her more harshly and for more minor offenses than she
punished Tom. When Tom did something that merited punishment, he

would be instructed to go outside and find a "switch." But when Ella did something that likewise merited punishment, she would be directed to find a bigger switch and would be whipped longer and harder.

The special ire that Annabelle reserved for Ella may have responded to social anxieties about the welfare of South Side girls. The relative anonymity of city life, and the multiplication of opportunities for urban "vice" in the form of gambling, prostitution, and speakeasies, provoked special concerns about the vulnerability of Black girlhood, among both established middle-class Black Chicagoans and recent migrants themselves.[16] Migrants like Annabelle were also drawn to the "politics of respectability," scholar Evelyn Brooks Higginbotham's term describing how Black women challenged racist depictions of them as "immoral, childlike, and unworthy of respect or protection."[17] Ella recalled that her mother would occasionally point to a stranger's swollen belly and warn Ella of the "fate" that could befall her if she were not "careful." Although they did not talk about sex, Ella came to understand that a pregnancy outside of marriage was a mark of shame and a sure path to economic hardship.

Maternal love and maternal control around gender also dovetailed in Annabelle's tendency to find fault with her daughter's facility in the "feminine" arts of housekeeping. Where Annabelle maintained a spotless home and an immaculate appearance, Ella, in her eyes, was careless and bungling. Ella internalized her mother's criticism, imagining Annabelle as a beacon of piety and domestic rectitude and herself as a girl who failed at the simplest tasks. A particular story emblematized Ella's inadequacies. Once, Annabelle left Ella with instructions to take some biscuits out of the oven at a set time. But Ella was too busy playing football with a group of neighborhood boys to remember. By the time she saw black smoke coming from their apartment window, it was too late—for the oven as well as the biscuits. The smoke was so thick that the fire department had to be summoned, making it impossible for her to make up an excuse to save face.

While Ella later relayed the biscuit story in humorous fashion, savoring the memory of the chaos she had unleashed, its subtext was her unconventional gender expression. From an early age, she was uninterested in typically feminine concerns. For example, she allowed her mother to take her to get her fine coiled hair pressed exactly once, in her early teenage years, and vowed that she would never again endure a burning scalp just for a "smooth" style.

Ella was also reprimanded by her mother for being drawn to the pastimes of boys. She retained a sharp memory of angering Annabelle by muddying the hem of her dress while squatting down to play marbles. And when Ella would imitate Tom and practice whistling, Annabelle would correct her, noting, "A whistling girl and a crowing hen will always come to some bad end." Ella felt keenly the inherent injustice of her brother's gendered advantages: his getting to deliver the *Chicago Bee*, and therefore earn pocket money for movies, or attend Boy Scout Camp, where they taught campfire songs and learned about nature. Ella's natural gravitation toward such "boys'" activities and the general freedom they represented elicited the label "tomboy" from some of the adults around her. She seems not to have objected to the word, imagining herself good-naturedly as "roughy-toughy." But as Ella matured into adolescence her lack of concern for conventional femininity increasingly pressed against her mother's more orthodox ideals, including marriage.

Already tense, Ella and Annabelle's relationship grew more strained after Annabelle wed Charles William McKinley, a Kentucky migrant, in 1937, when Ella was just shy of thirteen. The marriage was an economic boon, allowing them to move to East Fifty-Sixth Street, a "high" address near Washington Park. But from the start Ella disliked and distrusted Charles. Worse, Annabelle sometimes took her husband's side in disputes. The stress peaked when Charles acted violently toward Ella in an incident that ultimately involved the police. Ella never forgave her mother for demanding that she visit her stepfather while he was briefly jailed to offer *him* an apology, when *she* was the victim of his transgressions. As an adult, Ella was loath to discuss the incident in detail. But it is clear that it left a significantly deeper wound than the one caused by glass. "For months and months I had to pray that I would stop hating that man and wishing awful things on him," she said. If other men were like Charles McKinley, she decided, then she would never marry.

In an unpublished memoir, Ella wrote dispassionately of Annabelle: "Mother was an authority figure in the home. She was a strong woman, kind of stern, a neat housekeeper, a good budgeter and a very religious member of the Christian Science faith. However, she wasn't a very affectionate woman."[18] Ella's "however" expressed the rift between mother and daughter, which remained a constant throughout Ella's life. But it was also a reflection of Ella's understanding of the price Annabelle had paid to "maintain" her and her brother. For as long as Annabelle lived, Ella wrestled with the ambiguity of love mixed with resentment, admiration laced with hurt.

Notwithstanding her mother's stringency around respectability, Ella was a gregarious and curious child. And while Annabelle was a disciplined steward of their household, Ella found relief in the household of her aunt, Annabelle's sister "Big Mama" Willie Mae Johnson and her husband, Floyd "Uncle Flood" Johnson, who had no children of their own. A large woman with dimples she liked to call "angel's kisses," Big Mama was outgoing and had a wide circle of friends. It impressed and thrilled Ella to hear Big Mama express her disdain for white people in colorful language her mother avoided; she particularly never forgot how her aunt referred to one of her schoolteachers as a "white heifer." Neither did Big Mama's religion prohibit her from pastimes like playing cards. Uncle Flood, meanwhile, was hardworking and reserved. He was born in 1895 in the northern Louisiana town of Monroe, and by the age of fifteen, was working full-time to help his mother support a family of five children, including a baby sister Eadie, whose father was white. To get to Chicago, he traveled the same Illinois Central line that had carried Big Mama and Annabelle there from Mississippi.

On weekends Big Mama and Uncle Flood would have parties where they would play cards and dance. The music was courtesy of a giant jukebox that Uncle Flood had somehow managed to acquire; a man would come to change the records every month. Over the years, the jukebox played discs by everyone from Billie Holiday to Bing Crosby to Bessie Smith, whose posthumous release "At the Christmas Ball" was a perennial hit beginning in 1940. Later, Ella would hear recordings by influential Chicago-based musicians including Memphis Slim, Little Brother Montgomery, and T-Bone Walker.[19]

Ella was still in grade school when she began listening to Uncle Flood play an instrument he called his "mouth harp." It was nothing more than a small metallic rectangle with holes on one side, but by cupping his hands and blowing into it, he could make all kinds of interesting sounds. Uncle Flood usually played in the evenings after working his shift at a Gary, Indiana, steel mill within daily commuting distance of Chicago. The job was physically taxing and dirty—so dirty, Ella recalled, that when he peeled off his overalls, "they would stand up by themselves." Ella enjoyed observing her uncle's evening routine, which consisted of a bath and shave, dinner, and a change into fresh clothes. He liked to wear a crisp white shirt and a gray pinstriped vest with several pockets; some held harmonicas, others contained slips of paper with notes about songs scribbled on them. Choosing a harmonica, he would warm up on the low notes, then move to the high notes, then start blowing on chords. Uncle Flood explained to Ella that different harmonicas were tuned to different keys, blowing a few notes from each so she could hear what that meant.

If Christian Science gave Ella a mental and spiritual framework for navigating a perilous world, Uncle Flood gave her a musical language for communicating her experiences in it. He was what Ella called her "great inspirer."[20] Much like the music she had heard as a young child in Mississippi, the blues songs he played, sometimes for hours at a time, conveyed knowledge that she could not then have picked up in history books. Some songs expressed feelings of romantic or carnal love she could not yet understand. Others were rooted in experiences of forced labor, white supremacist violence, and natural disaster—the sort of conditions that had sent Black people packing their belongings and heading north. Some conveyed hopeful expectation, such as the one where Uncle Flood imitated the sound of a freight train "coming on down the line."

Uncle Flood never gave Ella formal lessons in blues harmonica. Rather, he allowed her to play one of his instruments and facilitated her own exploration. Once she had gone as far as she could on her own in pursuing a certain sound, he would step in, perhaps showing her the three notes that made up a C chord. Ethnomusicologists would call this form of teaching "folk tradition" or "oral transmission," but for Ella and her Uncle Flood it was simply how Ella learned how to play "Red River Valley," the western folk lament that was her first song. By listening to and observing her uncle, Ella acquired technical knowledge: the differences between major and minor chords; the significance and sounds of blue notes; the importance of tonality; the feel for rhythm; the use of syncopation to produce a "swinging" effect.

When she was at home with her mother and could not borrow one of her uncle's harmonicas, Ella fashioned makeshift instruments by placing a thin piece of paper on a wooden comb. "If you blew on it just right," she recalled, "you could get it to make a pleasant buzzing sound." Annabelle recognized her daughter's interest. One Christmas day when Ella was eleven or twelve, she presented Ella with her own mouth harp—the "fancy and expensive" chromatic instrument she wanted. Ella was excited to show it to Big Mama and Uncle Flood. But later that day, Ella, unused to riding in cars, left the harmonica in a taxi they had splurged on to get there. Ella recalled, "I cried for it for days, weeks, months."[21]

Annabelle's sensitivity to Ella's attraction to the harmonica, together with her empathetic reaction to Ella's loss of it, revealed a mother who, if not outwardly affectionate, was nonetheless capable of expressing a powerful love for her daughter. This explains why the harmonica incident left a particularly traumatic imprint on Ella's memory. The tears she shed were simultaneously for the instrument, for her mother's lost labor (Annabelle had put in an extra day to buy it), and for her carelessness with Annabelle's "gift" of recognizing her daughter's distinct dreams and desires. Through the harmonica, Annabelle had demonstrated that she *saw* Ella for who Ella was. Perhaps this is why Annabelle, drawing on Christian Science wisdom, could assure her daughter that when the taxi drove away with the harmonica, "nothing was really lost." But to Ella the incident revealed a fault in herself, rather than a faulty attachment to the material world. That day she vowed "later to really learn to play the harmonica" so that her mother's efforts would not be in vain.[22]

Outside of Ella's aunt and uncle's home, Bronzeville pulsated with rhythms: rhythms Ella could feel and wanted to emulate. They emanated from radios and the loudspeakers at record stores, from street buskers and singing evangelists, and from a bustling nightlife she glimpsed on after-church visits to the cavernous Regal Theatre, where she, Tom, and their mother would take in vaudeville-style entertainment, featured movies, and musical performers, including Ella Fitzgerald, Cab Calloway, Erskine Hawkins, Billy Eckstine, Dinah Washington, Sarah Vaughn, and the tap-dancing Nicholas Brothers.[23]

On the playground at Herman Felsenthal Elementary School, Ella learned songs and chants: "One potato, two potato," "Miss Mary Mack," "Little Sally Walker," and "Head and shoulder, baby, one two three." She played hopscotch, marbles, jacks, and double-dutch, all games with distinct rhythms. She heard Bronzeville children revise the familiar counting game "Eeny Meenie Miny Moe," which white children recited using a racial epithet. "Eeny meenie miny moe," they would instead sing,

Catch a white man by the toe
If he hollers make him pay
Twenty dollars every day!

In the Black Metropolis of Ella's girlhood, the "down home" music of diverse Southern migrants, carried north via memory or shellac, mingled and mixed with other sounds. At Pilgrim Baptist Church, just a few blocks from the East Thirty-Fifth Street apartment of Big Mama and Uncle Flood, Thomas Dorsey, the Georgia-born former sideman for Ma Rainey, was busy popularizing the gospel blues, a glorious mash-up of secular and sacred music that especially appealed to migrants. In Bronzeville, Ella later observed, "you couldn't help hearing a variety of church music—organ and piano playing, rhythmic foot-stomping, intricate hand-clapping, versatile tambourine beating and tambourine-shaking, some singing, some shouting—on a Sunday morning or afternoon because many churches—large ones or small storefronts—used to amplify their services to the outside so that anyone passing by could 'catch a little goodness.'"[24]

In later life, Ella would carry forward in her memory the songs and chants of Bronzeville playgrounds, the sounds of her Uncle Flood's harmonica blues, the rhythmic pop, blues, and swing music of his beloved jukebox, and the camp-song repertoire that she learned from her brother Tom. These disparate sounds, combined with the work and church songs of her Southern kinfolk, called out to her. She wanted to understand them. The busy city-within-a-city, alive with hustle and hum, laid the sonic foundation of Ella's later musical ventures. For the rest of her life, she would play on its themes.

Dear Miss Jenkins,

Thank you for letting us here you Sing your
nice Songs. It Was nice to get cheered uP in
The Morning. Thank you agen.

your friend
Timmy

(WINNETKA, ILINOIS, 1971)

2
REBEL DAYS
1938–1948

Ella enrolled at DuSable High School, an enormous Art Deco–style building on South Wabash Avenue, in the fall of 1938. Upon its opening in 1935, the school—the first built to educate Black South Side students—had become a tangible symbol of migrants' aspirations for education. Future Chicago mayor Harold Washington, who was a few years ahead of Ella, called DuSable "the fulfillment of a dream."[1] In those days of both de facto and de jure segregation, DuSable, which drew distinguished Black teachers, was seen as a community institution. Migrant yearnings were implicit in the school's namesake, Jean Baptiste Point du Sable, a West Indian–born man of African descent who was Chicago's first non-Indigenous settler. And they were given voice in its motto, "Peace, if possible, but justice at any rate," a phrase attributed to nineteenth-century abolitionist Wendell Phillips, but resonant with more modern struggles for freedom.[2]

During Ella's high school years, DuSable established a reputation as an incubator of Chicago's young music talent. Under the direction of music teacher "Captain" Walter H. Dyett, the school nurtured the fledgling careers of artists including pianist Dorothy Donegan and Ruth Lee Jones, the vocalist better known by her stage name Dinah Washington. Other DuSable graduates of the 1940s—most notably, historian Sterling Stuckey, whose mother, poet Elma Stuckey, Ella came to know quite well—retained vivid recollections of school dances that ended with "a hundred or more" students "moving around the gym in a slow, counterclockwise Jazz 'walk'" that resembled the Ring Shout of enslaved Africans.[3] Yet although Ella was aware of such rituals and of DuSable's annual "Hi-Jinks" shows, musical revues that were a highlight of the student calendar, she never sought to join one of Captain Dyett's many musical ensembles.[4] Perhaps because of her mother's respectability politics, in combination with the conservative musical culture of Christian Science—which exalted the classic hymn tradition of German composers—in her teenage years Ella associated music with middle-class children who could afford piano or violin lessons. Once Ella convinced Annabelle to let her take piano lessons, but the man who had offered to teach her absconded with her mother's money. In her disappointment, Ella took the theft as providential, concluding that "formal" musical instruction was not for her.

But there was a more important, more idiosyncratic, reason for Ella's remove from DuSable's music programs: during her freshman year, she discovered an unexpected talent. One afternoon, she accompanied Tom to the table-tennis pavilion at Washington Park, where he had been learning to play. The two young Black men who oversaw competition were not particularly keen in letting a girl participate. But Ella persisted. Soon, she could outplay not merely Tom, but most boys who cared to challenge her.

At the time, table tennis—or "ping-pong"—was enjoying a surge in popularity, as both indoor pastime and a competitive sport. Under the aegis of the US Table Tennis Association, founded in 1933, US players had quickly risen to the level of European players, taking titles in both the men's and women's divisions at the 1937 world championships in Prague. Boosters of the game assured skeptics that it required levels of fitness and endurance comparable to lawn tennis. The sports sections of newspapers informed readers that table tennis "takes so much speed and co-ordination that top-notchers fade out when they reach 22 or 23 years of age"; that Montana police and firefighters played table tennis for their daily "workout"; and that Texans regarded table tennis as a "He-Man's Game." "Girls who play it need never diet to reduce," assured one top-ranked female player.[5]

More significantly for Ella, table tennis had found its way into the physical education curricula of American high schools, including DuSable, where Ella quickly rose to become its top female player. "It was wonderful to be the best at something," she said. Sport gave Ella her first taste of "performing" for an audience (she discovered that she liked it). Her minor celebrity might also have eased the loneliness of high school, where Ella felt her poverty acutely and may also have suffered from the realization that she was attracted to girls, not boys. In later years she would not reminisce about her friends from DuSable. But she relished the memory of winning the school title in table tennis, before several hundred cheering students, in her senior year.

Upon her graduation, Ella was recruited by representatives of the US Table Tennis Association, and although she could not afford to play professionally, she became one of a handful of Black women to compete at a national level in the 1940s. Newspapers preserve the record of Ella's participation in only one out-of-town competition: the 1944 Nationals, held in St. Louis, where she would have stayed with her father or paternal relatives while competing both in singles and doubles divisions. After that, she seems to have competed at the highest levels only in Chicago or within easy driving distance. For example, in 1947 she played for the women's national title at Chicago's Rainbo Arena, where she was handily defeated by Leah Thall, a star white competitor from Columbus, Ohio.[6] But a significant March 1948 victory made the pages of the *Defender*, in an article headlined "Ella Jenkins Is Chicagoland's Table Net Champ." "Miss Ella Jenkins of the Washington Park table-tennis club won the women's championship in the Chicagoland table tennis championships at the Navy Pier," the paper reported. "In the finals Miss Jenkins defeated Miss Lucille Gorka, white, of Whittier playground, 21–10, 21–10."[7]

Sisters Amy Billingsley and Eileen Tate Cline, who also grew up in the Eighth Church of Christ, Scientist, fondly remembered Ella in this period as "the Joe Louis of table tennis."[8] Of course, a game played with rubber-coated paddles and weightless cellulose balls carried none of the physical symbolism of boxing. But just as Louis proved his superiority to white opponents, in a quiet corner of the sporting world, so had Ella.

Table tennis served Ella's development in other important ways. In retrospect, it was a rehearsal for her future vocation as a "rhythm specialist" who created meaning through subtle variations in the way she struck a conga drum. To play table tennis well requires a related rhythmic agility. As in lawn tennis, it means anticipating a ball's trajectory, placing one's body in the right position to return the ball, and hitting it with calculated restraint as well as power. The rapid-fire nature of the game imbues it with a distinct sonic component, as players listen to the ball bouncing and its contact with the opponent's paddle. Ella's match with Leah Thall was refereed by a young blind man, who discerned the various "cracks" and "clicks" of the ball, and whose acumen in detecting "edge" shots (on the tip of the table) was said to be "more accurate than the eyes of the players."[9]

As well, the confidence Ella derived from being good at table tennis emboldened her to live up to the DuSable motto of pursuing justice. While some white players, like Thall and her twin sister Thelma, were cordial competitors, others openly expressed their displeasure at being asked to compete with Black women. In one instance Ella was playing in a Chicago tournament when a white woman player caused an ugly scene by refusing to play her Black female opponent (not Ella). In an act of solidarity, Ella threatened to pull out of her own match. Ultimately, the white woman agreed to play.

Ella's development as a player paralleled and supported her growing consciousness of her identity as an African-descended American woman. Ella graduated from DuSable in 1942, a few years before

FIGURE 2.1. Ella with her table-tennis racket, ca. 1948.
Photo by Tom Jenkins.

artist-activist Margaret Burroughs joined its faculty and introduced
formal instruction in "Negro" history, the field pioneered by Carter
G. Woodson, a University of Chicago–trained historian. But the South
Side's many vibrant cultural institutions offered plenty of informal

ways to learn about her culture, beyond such familiar figures as Frederick Douglass, Harriet Tubman, and poet Paul Laurence Dunbar. During her last years of high school, she enrolled in classes at the South Side Community Arts Center, where Burroughs and writer Gwendolyn Brooks taught, and where Woodson's ideas about Black history were energetically embraced. She found further refuge in the George Cleveland Hall Branch of the Chicago Public Library, an intellectual center of Bronzeville life named after one of Woodson's collaborators and helmed by pioneering Black librarians Vivian G. Harsh and Charlemae Hill Rollins.[10]

Such Black female community organizers and intellectuals were some of Ella's earliest female role models, demonstrating that activism was not separate from culture but could extend to creative expression. Associated with the mid-century revitalization of Black arts known as the Chicago Black Renaissance, they fused pan-African political consciousness with cultural institution-building and grassroots racial uplift. Through their example, Ella learned that it was possible to have a powerful impact despite meager resources. They showed, too, that while they might be disempowered within male-dominated spheres of politics, commerce, and religion, Black women were leaders within Black communities.[11]

Ella was open to the examples of these eminent South Side women because of the fortitude and determination of her own mother. Annabelle lacked their educational advantages but she, too, was a "modern" woman: modern in her strivings and mobility; in her openness to the new religion of Christian Science; and in her aspirations for her children. Had she herself enjoyed more opportunities, she might have urged Ella to continue her education after DuSable so that she, too, could join the ranks of such leading Chicago women. Yet while she encouraged Tom to enroll in classes at Wilson Junior College, there was no talk of more school for Ella. Rather, she was expected find a job to help support the household.

After that, she might find a husband and busy herself with marriage and motherhood.

Growing national and familial turbulence accelerated Ella's passage into adulthood. Drafted in early 1942 after the United States declared war on the Axis powers, Tom was awaiting his deployment. Meanwhile, Annabelle had finally decided to separate from Charles McKinley. Ella felt relief that she would no longer need to tolerate his presence. But the split brought new pressures. Unable to stay at their old apartment, Ella, Tom, and Annabelle squeezed temporarily into Big Mama and Uncle Flood's place on East Thirty-Fifth Street. With a keen sense of wanting to contribute, Ella looked for work.

At the time, Chicagoans were rallying around labor leader A. Phillip Randolph's March on Washington Movement, which sought to pressure Franklin Roosevelt's administration to ban discrimination and segregation in the defense industries and the US military.[12] Ella encountered such discrimination firsthand, finding that even amid the wartime uptick in jobs for women, she was locked out of employment beyond child care and domestic service. The Help Wanted pages of local newspapers carried advertisements promising factory work for "girls" aged seventeen to thirty-five, but "girls" was code for white women. Ella's patriotism had been stirred by the Japanese attack on Pearl Harbor. With Tom, she had bought war savings stamps at the *Defender* office. But the disjuncture between her support of her country and the hostility of white employers was sometimes too much to bear. At those times, Ella would use the money Annabelle gave her for streetcar fare to see a movie; at least in the darkened theater she could find a momentary respite from the tension of holding it together for another day. Table tennis also offered an outlet for her frustration. It was satisfying to watch a white competitor trip over herself trying to return a ball on which Ella had put a wicked spin.

After several months of searching, Ella finally landed a job at the Wrigley Gum factory at 3535 South Ashland Avenue. Wartime need had transformed Wrigley from a maker of chewing gum to a producer of K rations for US soldiers, and Ella's job was to apply wax sealant to paper boxes filled with biscuits, chocolate, powdered eggs, Spam, cigarettes, and Doublemint gum. But as the only Black woman on the line, she dreaded lunch, where she was shunned and forced to eat alone. One day, a Polish American woman named Marilyn Alleva asked Ella to join her while they ate. Soon after they were joined by Margarita Hernandez, who was Mexican American. To Ella, the women's kindness was more than personal; it embodied noble pluralist ideals of the sort that the United States gave lip service to even as it painted itself as a global defender of democracy. She also saw their friendship as an opportunity to learn about their cultures and thereby cultivate her own understanding and sympathy.

By the time Ella got the Wrigley job, Tom had been inducted into the US Navy. During an initial deployment to France, he sent Ella postcards that made national service seem like a grand adventure. They bore images of Napoleon's Tomb at Les Invalides, the Eiffel Tower, and the quays of the Seine. To hear about such things from Tom was exciting for Ella; so was imagining that through her job at Wrigley she was contributing in some small way to sustaining him and the soldier-pals he wrote about. But Ella did not stay long at the gum factory. After briefly working at a publishing company, around 1944 she landed a job delivering mail at the University of Chicago metallurgical laboratory, located in conjoined Gothic buildings in Hyde Park. The leafy campus was geographically part of the South Side, across Washington Park from Ella's former East Fifty-Sixth Street address, and yet segregation rendered it socially and culturally distinct from the surrounding, majority-Black South Side environs. When Ella worked there, the university enrolled very few Black students. Those who did attend were mostly pursuing advanced degrees.

Ella delivered mail to J. Ernest Wilkins Jr., an African American prodigy who obtained his PhD in mathematics from the university at age nineteen. Others on her route included physicists Enrico Fermi and Samuel K. Allison. Ella knew that they were conducting research related to the war. She had no idea, however, that the "Met Lab," as everyone called it, was a wartime cover for the Manhattan Project, the top-secret program to develop nuclear weapons. Not until the US government dropped its first atomic bomb on Hiroshima, Japan, on August 6, 1945, Ella's twenty-first birthday, did she begin to realize what she had unknowingly been a party to. The revelation of the bomb's terrible destructiveness permanently altered her perception of US militarism, tempering the reflexive pride she had always felt when she saw men like her brother in uniform. It brought home the gravity of the killing of people and the poisoning of the earth, sparking her interests in environmentalism and peace activism.

In 1944, though, the University of Chicago scientists were remote figures. She mostly spent her time at the Met Lab with four young Jewish women who had applied for jobs the same day she did. They were assigned secretarial positions, while Ella was tasked to the mailroom. One of them, Lillian Osran, knew it was because Ella was Black; perhaps out of shame, she continually encouraged Ella to go to college to improve her prospects. Ella said she needed to support her family, but Lillian persisted: "Is this what you're gonna do all your life?"[13]

Ella was initially self-conscious around her, Lillian remembered, but once Ella got to know her and the other women she revealed herself to be something of a cut-up.[14] On warm days, the five women would take their lunch breaks on the verdant green outside of their offices. Sometimes they would playfully pose for photographs. Once, when they were joined by a male friend in his military uniform, they decided to it would be funny if they knelt before him in mock-worship. Ella gamely joined in role-playing the admiring female supplicant.

Ella displayed the sharp edges of her humor more overtly in a postcard she sent to Lillian that year. The front of the card featured an image of Indiana Dunes National Park, about fifteen miles east of Gary, Indiana, on Lake Michigan. Ella had probably purchased the postcard without visiting the dunes, which were near a "sundown" town hostile to Black visitors. But that only made her satire more cutting. "Hello, Honey Child," she began, using her nickname for Lillian. "I'm having a gorgeous time. And living the life of Riley. Too bad you kids can't be here. The people are just grand. And the food is

FIGURE 2.2. Ella and her Met Lab friends at the University of Chicago, ca. 1944. Personal collection of Ella Jenkins.

marvelous. Hope I don't become too corpulent. So long for a while, Ella." The snooty diction, conjuring a world of carefree luxury and abundance, made for a sharp satire of race and class. Lillian, in on the joke, never threw the postcard away.[15]

Ella increasingly wanted to follow up on Lillian's counsel regarding college, but her plans were postponed when she received news that spring that her father Obadiah was gravely ill with cancer. In late May of 1944, Obadiah was transferred from a Veterans Administration hospital in St. Louis to one in Hines, Illinois, about twelve miles west of Chicago. Ella never knew whether he ended up there by chance or requested the move to be closer both to his children and his Chicago-based siblings, but by the time she and other family members were able to visit with Obadiah, he was breathing with difficulty through an oxygen mask.

The exact nature of Ella's relationship with her father is hard to assess. When she saw him, Obadiah could be playful, calling her by her childhood nickname "Cat Eyes"—a nod to their unusual olive color. On one occasion he sent her a Bible bearing a ceremonious inscription in a carefully looped script: "From your Father Obadiah Jenkins to my Daughter Ella L. Jenkins." When she was in high school and he was working in a factory that molded metal, he gifted her a ring of his own design, which she wore proudly. But these tokens of his affection co-existed with Ella's sense of estrangement from Obadiah. The shiny ring made her feel special and important, but it also reminded her of her father's absence.

With Tom serving in the Pacific and Annabelle recently remarried, this time to a Mississippi-born man named Odell Smith, the burden of caring for Obadiah fell on Ella. In 1942 Obadiah had filled out a draft card, although at forty-seven he was too old to serve. Now, just two years later, he prepared his will. It took the form of a handwritten note to Ella, directing her to distribute his money (one hundred dollars to his mother in Alabama and fifty dollars to his "lady friend" back in St. Louis), his clothes, and the trunks he used to store and transport his possessions. He expressed a wish to be buried at Jefferson Barracks National Cemetery in St. Louis and to have "My Soul Is a Witness" sung at his interment. "Be sure to equal divide the remainints with your Bro. Thomas Jenkins," he wrote. "Please that this go like I am asking. May god bless you. Good by. Your Dady, Obadiah." He passed away six weeks later, on October 18, 1944.

Ella saved Obadiah's handwritten note and mounted it in a scrapbook she assembled in the early 1950s. Underneath it, in block print, she wrote, "A Poor Man's Will; A Brave Man's Courage."[16] Next to the will, she copied out in longhand a brief memorial of Obadiah she would later compose for a creative writing class at San Francisco State College. Titled "A Father Is Dying," Ella's visceral essay is written in the third person and bespeaks both tenderness and alienation.

The memorial features two characters: the "dying father," a "nearly deceased man who no longer communicates with things present or past," and "the daughter," who is "sitting crouched in a straight-backed chair" and weeping quietly as her father takes his last belabored breaths. The daughter's heartbeats match the rapid pace of the father's strained respirations, suggesting an emotional synchrony between the two figures. Yet the essay ends on a note of estrangement, as the daughter "shuffles away slowly" from the dead father's bedside, "thinking quietly, 'He will look well in blue.'" For all of the shared anguish the essay portrays, it is distinctly unsentimental in its depiction of a father and daughter who never actually communicate.[17]

When Obadiah passed away, Ella set out to fulfill his dying wish to be interred in a military cemetery. Through the hospital, she arranged for a permit to transport his body by train to St. Louis. "That was a lonely ride," she recalled, "because my brother was still in [the] service and I was on there and I knew my dad was somewhere in the train in a casket."[18] During the trip she was able to review various official papers, including a document that enumerated the dismal inventory of his possessions: two bathrobes, a pair each of slippers and shoes, three pairs of socks, one pair of garters, one shaving brush, and seven packs of cigarettes. Along with these, Ella had one photograph of herself with her father, taken at a studio a few years before he died. It showed Obadiah in a three-piece suit and a fedora, Ella in a flowered dress with a trim jacket, her hair styled in a fashionable pompadour. Despite the suggestion of a special occasion, it is a curiously strained image, in which father and daughter stand at an angle from each other. Obadiah looks away from his daughter. Neither appears very happy.

When she arrived in St. Louis, Ella asked around for the nearest Christian Science church, hoping for a quiet space where she could pray. But when she found the church, the white man who met her at the door coldly asked how he could help and, when she told him she wished to pray, pointed her to a staircase that led to a separate balcony. It was a stingingly cruel act, made all the more devastating because Ella, as a co-religionist, had genuinely not anticipated it. At a crucial

FIGURE 2.3. Ella with her father, Obadiah Jenkins, ca. 1940s.
Unknown photographer.

moment, the Church provided no refuge from her loss; if anything, it
only exacerbated her sense of loneliness.

The shock of her humiliation that day opened a rift between Ella
and the Christian Science Church. After burying her father, Ella would
still count herself a Christian Scientist, periodically returning to her
underlined copies of Mrs. Eddy's writings, and dutifully reading the
Christian Science Monitor clippings Annabelle regularly shared with
her. But she would never find a way to reconcile Christian Science

as an institution with the way she had been treated at a supremely vulnerable moment. Thinking about Obadiah several years later, she added her own inscription to the Bible he had given her. "Dear Father," it said, "I shall read at least one chapter a day in memory of you. Your devoted daughter, Ella. 8-10-51." But she subsequently amended this vow, inserting the words "try to" with a caret. "I shall *try to* read," it now said: a statement of intention, but not a promise.

In February of 1945 Ella followed the advice of Lillian Osran and enrolled at Wilson Junior College. For the next two years, while she lived with her mother and Odell at their Woodlawn apartment at 6031 S. Prairie Avenue, Ella worked part-time while taking a full load of college classes, with an emphasis on social sciences. She barely passed some of her comprehensive exams, but as her friend Annette Haase quipped, at the time she was also "majoring in table tennis."[19]

Ella transferred to Roosevelt College in the fall of 1947, which is where she met Annette and got to know her family. Founded in 1945 in the wake of a faculty and student uprising over the use of quotas in student admissions at Central YMCA College, Roosevelt was the first integrated private college in the city and a bastion of political leftism in the early Cold War years. Its progressive mission to educate students regardless of race, creed, or national origin drew a distinguished faculty, including sociologist St. Clair Drake and Lorenzo Dow Turner, a renowned linguist who would go on to chair its African Studies program.[20] Eminent historian John Hope Franklin also taught there, and although it is unclear whether Ella ever took a course with him, she recalled their informal chats. The college had recently come to occupy the Auditorium Building, a grand edifice fronting Michigan Avenue. From its domed tenth floor, Ella could take in an impressive vista that included Buckingham Fountain and Grant Park, leading out to Lake Michigan.

While Ella only took classes at Roosevelt for two semesters, in fall 1947 and spring 1948, she was there long enough to absorb its atmosphere of earnest radicalism. "They used to call it the communist college," she remembered. "It was nice to hear people talk about revolution." For their politics, the students drew variously from the Black protest tradition, Japanese American denunciations of anti-Asian US

FIGURE 2.4. Ella posing at Roosevelt College, ca. 1948.
Personal collection of Ella Jenkins.

nationalism, and the left-wing Zionism and antiracism of Jewish students still processing the horrors of the Nazi genocide. Their shared opposition to fascism and capitalism united Roosevelt students as "brothers under the skin."[21] Many—including Annette, the granddaughter of German Jewish socialist Hugo Haase—identified as political radicals: not only communists, but also socialists, anarchists, or Trotskyites. With the exception of New York's City College, no other college in the country offered such a progressive environment.

Ella flourished in this vibrant political and intellectual climate. In addition to Annette, she befriended Harold Washington, then active in the college's student government. She joined Students for Wallace, the largest club on campus, supporting the 1948 candidacy of Progressive Party presidential candidate Henry Wallace. And she signed up for a group called American Youth for Democracy (AYD), an offshoot of the US Communist Party. On other college campuses, AYD was banned for "un-Americanism," its members accused of trying "to stir up race antagonism, create dissention, and revile every good influence in this land."[22] Although the Hitler-Stalin pact of 1939 had soured many African Americans' views of communism, Ella joined the AYD while developing her own political consciousness, free of her mother's influence. She knew that Annabelle would have had a fit had she discovered her daughter was flirting with the political left.[23]

But while Ella's affiliation with the AYD was short-lived, communism would have had a "commonsense appeal" to her as Black girl who had grown up poor on the South Side.[24] Even as a young child, Ella once wrote, "I was conscious of the fact that I was colored because all of the stores in my neighborhood were owned by whites. This included the grocery stores, clothing stores and drug stores. The Blacks didn't own anything and I knew what prejudice and injustice existed."[25] She saw how her mother and aunt, despite working fifty hours a week for years, remained ineligible for Social Security benefits, how white trade unionists preached brotherhood but refused to include men like her Uncle Flood; and how Black families were subjected to high rents in run-down kitchenettes.

Ella referred to the period between 1942 and 1948 as her "rebel days," finding in civil rights activism a particular outlet for her developing political consciousness. At Wilson Junior College she had joined a group called Youth on Minority Problems, an affiliate of the Chicago Council against Racial and Religious Discrimination, and become involved in Funference, an interracial group that organized social outings and performed community service. Through Tom's connections at the University of Chicago, where he enrolled after being discharged from the Navy in the summer of 1946, she also became "very active" in the Chicago branch of the Congress of Racial Equality (CORE), a group pioneering the use of nonviolent direct action in civil rights protest. CORE's methods of challenging discrimination "directly, without violence or hatred, yet without compromise"—an outgrowth of its rootedness in Christian pacifism rather than socialist or communist traditions—fit well with Ella's aversion to confrontation and her belief, instilled through years of Christian Science Sunday School, in the reality of good and the unreality of evil. Ella attended CORE meetings in members' Hyde Park apartments, rubbing shoulders with Homer Jack, a white divinity student who was a CORE co-founder, and meeting Black civil rights activists James Farmer and Bayard Rustin, who at one point headed the Chicago chapter.[26]

Later, at Roosevelt, Ella participated in pickets of local restaurants that refused to serve Black students. She also received training in how "not to react" when conducting "tests" of such venues. A small group of white students would find a table, where they would eventually be joined by one or two Black members. If the waiter or manager asked the Black students to leave, they would sit quietly. If things got heated, the group would file out. Several times Ella heeded a call for volunteers for CORE actions downstate, including at the University of Illinois in Champaign. At one point she joined Cordy Tindall Vivian, later a close ally of Martin Luther King Jr., in sitting in to protest discrimination at a Peoria Steak 'n' Shake. Ella disliked Peoria, considering it "Southern" in its attitudes toward African Americans. Once she had played a table-tennis tournament there and had had to work to retain her composure in the face of white spectators' stares.

Ella took the ideals of the nonviolent civil rights movement with her to a summer 1948 job as a counselor at Camp Reinberg, in the Deer Grove forest preserve in the Chicago suburb of Palatine. Touted by the *Defender* as a camp "where real democracy works," Camp Reinberg was established to give low-income Cook County children an experience of "fresh air."[27] It brought in cohorts of eight- to fourteen-year-olds through three social service agencies: the Marcy Center, serving Jewish children; the Newbury Center, serving Black children; and the county's Aid to Dependent Children, serving white children. Over twelve-day sessions the children lived with their agency groups but otherwise interacted with children from other groups. They enjoyed a range of camp activities, including nature hikes, arts and crafts, square dancing, campfires, cookouts, and donkey rides.

Ella was part of the staff for the Aid to Dependent Children group, joining a team that included two men of Asian descent and a white woman, all college students. She arrived with as little experience of "camp" as some of the children. Donkey rides were new—"I thought I was going to break my neck," she said—but so were more pedestrian camp activities, including swimming and climbing trees, the latter a "boy" activity she had been discouraged from trying as a child. When she took the children on hikes, she would sometimes get so distracted by the landscape and forest animals that she would have to rely on them to find the way back.

Camp Reinberg gave Ella her first extended taste of living outside of her mother's watchful orbit. "It was a good chance to be away from home and to live without being told what to do," she said. It also gave her an opportunity to test her vocational interest in "group work," the subset of social work that she had by then decided would be her field of study in college. That meant learning how to interact with children like Bill Pulumbo, a white boy who had been labeled a "problem kid" by "inexperienced group workers." But "a professional worker understands him as a 'kid with problems,'" she wrote in a journal from the summer, flexing her expertise.[28]

That summer Ella made an important discovery. When she was out with the children, she noticed that they responded well to group singing. At some point, she hit upon what she would later term "call and response." As the leader she would call out a chanted phrase and the children would repeat it. As a high school babysitter and mother's helper, Ella had learned to settle unruly toddlers with a melody. Call and response similarly used music as a game to focus the campers' attention and interest. At first, Ella used songs she knew, but gradually she experimented with improvised phrases and made-up words that sounded good. "Tah-boo," she would call. "Tah-boo," the kids would respond. The game modeled the serious work of integration by requiring everyone's participation and excluding no one. Years later, Ella titled the first song on her first album "Tah-boo," and credited its composition to her time at Camp Reinberg, a place where she felt she was really *living* "brotherhood," not just aspiring to it.

Nineteen forty-eight, Ella later wrote, "shall always be a memorable year, for it was there that I so easily came upon a very pleasant path to Independence." She was referring to her work at Camp Reinberg and to her independence from Annabelle, but her words anticipated other, "larger steps down that path."[29] Ella had enrolled in fall classes at Roosevelt, but late that summer she moved to Berkeley, California, planning to complete her degree on the West Coast. Her choice to depart was so sudden that it resulted in *Ls* (for "Left") on her Roosevelt transcript, indicating that she missed the deadline for withdrawal.

Over the years, Ella's narrations of this period tended to be perfunctory, depicting the move to California as merely another chapter in the story of her education. As she wrote, "So I went to Wilson Junior College and then studied a year at Roosevelt University and finally went to the West Coast to San Francisco State College where I graduated." When pressed in a 2006 interview about the abruptness of her move, at an age when other women were getting married, Ella explained, "I wasn't doing what I wanted to do in Chicago so when I heard about California, California always sounded—besides the movie stars and whatnot, sounded like it was another nice warm climate and whatnot, so why not try it?"[30]

Ella later admitted that she had never entertained relocation to the West Coast until she met Nicky Miltenberger and her friend Mary Sherwood, in 1947. The two Berkeley residents had moved to Chicago to take summer classes at Roosevelt, drawn by the school's left-of-center reputation.[31] Nicky and Mary were both white, and were both what people called "political," suggesting an affiliation with the communist left. It is not clear whether they were a couple, or just a couple of free spirits. But Ella—who recalled them as "very independent women"—must have been deeply captivated to join them in California.

Perhaps Ella was lovestruck, or perhaps the two women's descriptions of their lives in the Bay Area awakened a desire for sexual self-exploration better pursued outside of the South Side of Chicago. Although she attended her DuSable prom with one of Tom's friends, Ella had never had a "beau." Later, over lunches at the Met Lab, she would stay silent while Lillian and the other women chatted about their dates.[32] As "Honey Child," her nickname for Lillian, suggests, she may have harbored crushes on straight women. But at that point she did not have any romantic relationships, although she was firmly aware of her desires: "I didn't like guys. I liked girls," she said. "My heart, my feelings, my actions just went that way."

Ella "knew" from an early age, but she was reticent to put a label on herself. As she disliked the ways that racial labels divided people, subscribing wholeheartedly to the Roosevelt ideal of "brothers under the skin," so she was averse to the idea of categorizing people according to whom they wished to be with. At Roosevelt Ella had begun to experiment with "mannish" forms of dress—donning "a sporty cap with three or four points" or neckties, although it is unclear whether she overtly identified as a lesbian. Ella's reticence to discuss the fact that she "liked girls" was also pragmatic and protective, a means of ensuring no one would have the chance to pathologize, fire, exclude, or further ostracize her. It was emphatically not, however, a sign that she was "repressed" or fundamentally shamed by her desire.

She also regarded her romantic inclinations as no one's business, just as she assumed that the sexual lives of others were beyond discussion. Like everyone else in Bronzeville, she knew male homosexuals, including Bayard Rustin, from CORE, and Theodore Stone, the opera singer and music critic who attended the Eighth Church. Rudy Richardson, a queer performer who performed torch songs in South Side clubs, graduated in her class at DuSable. In her neighborhood it was broadly understood that you gave such "bachelors" their space to be. In Bronzeville in the 1930s and '40s, homosexuality was accommodated and tolerated as long as Black gay men, lesbians, and other sexually nonconforming people made no attempt to "flaunt" it.[33] In the mid-1940s there were not yet Cold Warriors seeking to tar homosexuals as a threat to the nation, but neither were there organized spaces in which Black lesbians might create a socially affirming "culture." The Bronzeville clubs that offered opportunities for meeting other Black women who "liked women" were far outside of Ella's comfort zone.

Yet even if homosexuality was not discussed, and even if Ella was not the type to venture into queer nightlife, she would still have known about the lives of "sissy" men and "bulldagger" women from the music she had grown up with. There was Ma Rainey, the Georgia-born "Mother of the Blues," who sang provocative songs of sexual braggadocio even while asserting a right to be left alone, particularly by prying vice officers. "They said I do it, ain't nobody caught me," she sang. "Sure got to prove it on me." In her 1923 version of "Tain't Nobody's Biz-ness if I Do," Rainey's acolyte Bessie Smith expressed a similar disdain for "nosey" people looking for a reason to talk, even as she portrayed herself as fearless in her own pursuit of pleasure. Ella may have also felt her desires were "nobody's business," but she was interested in understanding them better, and perhaps even acting on them, in a new environment.

Ella departed for California on the City of San Francisco train in October or November of 1948. She was twenty-four and had worked full-time while completing half of the credits toward a bachelor's degree in sociology. She had racked up trophies and ribbons as a competitive table-tennis player. She had joined in civil rights sit-ins and protests, affiliating herself with CORE and a variety of leftist organizations. She had buried her father and been treated as a second-class member of her church. She had befriended white women and visited the houses of Jewish and Mexican American friends, tasting their food, observing their customs, and listening to members of their families speak in accented English, or in foreign languages.

But she had never lived on her own or had a romantic partner. Nicky and Mary's offer held out possibilities of freedom that she could not turn down. "I'm looking for something, I'm not sure what I'm looking for," Ella told her mother. Annabelle may not have approved, but neither did she stand in her daughter's way.[34] It was surely becoming clearer to her that Ella would not be fulfilling her expectations of marriage and motherhood. Ella herself was unsure whether California would reveal the "something" she yearned for, but she knew that whatever it was, she had not found it in Chicago. She would have to leave the city that defined her to find herself.

Dear Ella Jenkins

I appreciate you coming all the way from
were you live up to Alaska.
    I like your songs because they are in a
different language.
    I think you could visit every place in the
world and you could meet new people and see
new things.

Your friend,
Jenifer

(FT. WAINWRIGHT, ALASKA, 1992)

3

WEST COAST

1948–1952

Ella cried all the way to California, hunkered down in a coach seat next to a uniformed serviceman. Through tears, she watched as the landscape outside her window slowly transformed from flat Midwestern fields to jagged peaks. Her first sight of real mountains lifted her spirits. But then she remembered that beyond the two friends she had made that summer, she had no roadmap, no safety net, and no guarantee that she would eat.

At first Ella slept on a couch at Nicky Miltenberger's place in Berkeley. Nicky had two roomers, a mother and son from Lake Charles, Louisiana, part of an influx of Black migrants to the East Bay area during the War. Their housing arrangement was atypical. Most of the Black residents of the city—and a small population of Asian Americans of Japanese, Chinese, and Indian descent—lived in the South and West Berkeley neighborhoods.

In those first weeks, Ella tagged along with Nicky and her activist friends to various protests and pickets. They attended pro-labor actions as well as demonstrations against racial discrimination in employment and housing, both of which were on the uptick after the end of wartime federal protections. On one of these outings Ella met a man who worked at the recreation center of Codornices Village, a massive public housing project that straddled Berkeley and the adjacent town of Albany. The majority of its residents were Black migrants from Texas, Georgia, and Louisiana, but there were also white migrants from Oklahoma, Mexican and Japanese Americans, and married University of California or San Francisco State students. Ella asked the man whether the center had table tennis. She had been in search of a place to play, but she also needed a job.

When she visited the "Rec," she found it filled with teenagers. Heading over to the table-tennis area, she saw a group of boys messing around with the paddles and began offering them some pointers. "If you handle your paddle this way, you could probably strike the ball more successfully," she said, choosing her words carefully to avoid embarrassing them. Her impromptu lesson produced the attention

FIGURE 3.1. Ella working with children at Codornices Village, Albany, California, 1949. Photo by Tom Jenkins.

she sought. The white head of the center approached, complimented her on her skills with the teens, and offered her a job on the spot. Her pay as part-time recreation director would be only seventy-five cents an hour, but Ella lived frugally.

Because tuition was cheaper for her than at Cal (as the University of California at Berkeley was known), Ella signed up for classes at San Francisco State College, adding to her major in sociology a minor in recreation, an innovative program that included courses in guidance and counseling. She also began scouting out a place of her own. Most of the real estate on or near the Berkeley campus was segregated, but she ended up finding a room at Stebbins Hall, a women's co-op in a three-story building at 2527 Ridge Road. The idea of cooperative living, in which each resident contributed to the general good, appealed to her sense of social justice. Her rent of forty-one dollars a month included a small room and three meals a day, the food prepared off-site and served in a central kitchen.[1]

Like other Cal co-ops, Stebbins was attractive to students and young adults on the political left at a time of mounting Cold War repression. One of these students, Stebbins president Zoe Borkowski, recalled getting trailed by FBI agents for handing out "subversive" leaflets on Shattuck Avenue, a main Berkeley thoroughfare. Unlike in her "rebel days" in Chicago, in the Bay Area Ella seems to have shied away from overt identification with leftist (i.e., socialist- or communist-leaning) organizations. She would later explain that she was not a "joiner" but, as she knew from her work with CORE, even membership in civil rights or pacifist organizations could be used as a pretext for government harassment.

So could being seen in gay or lesbian bars in the midst of the Cold War "Lavender Scare," which portrayed gay men and lesbians as sexual deviants and national security risks. The emergence of lesbian and gay nightlife subculture in San Francisco in the late 1940s and early 1950s was accompanied by a parallel increase in the policing of such venues. Even in liberal Berkeley in the late 1940s, Borkowski recalled, "for the most part you were scared" to be known as gay. "If you went to a gay bar, you always knew where the back door was. You were scared to be known professionally, because if people knew you were gay you wouldn't be hired." Discovering other young gay women required skills of discernment. "You just noticed that there were some girls that got together and you got to know them," she remembered. "It was all sort of intuitive and very gentle."[2]

Borkowski and Ella, who knew each other superficially, never talked about such matters. But it is likely that Ella, too, did a similar sort of "noticing." Watching Borkowski and other women at Stebbins, she would have noticed how they communicated through their dress or hairstyles, body language and cultural references. The key was to avoid attracting unintended attention. Even being seen with copy of *The Well of Loneliness*, Radclyffe Hall's popular novel about upper-class British lesbians, could draw stares.

Ella learned and practiced discretion. In time, she came to own a copy of Hall's volume, as well as volumes by such sexually noncon-forming authors as Oscar Wilde, Emily Dickinson, Walt Whitman, and Edna St. Vincent Millay.

Like other politically minded residents of the Berkeley co-ops, the Stebbins students were drawn to the progressive world of folk music. In the evenings they would listen to records by Pete Seeger, the Weav-ers, and Josh White, or stage their own informal jam sessions. The vibe of these sessions was distinctly populist, following the example set by People's Songs, which propagated folk song as a vehicle of left-ist organizing. "It was felt that anybody could sing," said Borkowski, remembering participants who were long on enthusiasm but short on talent. Because she was busy with school and work, Ella never had a chance to join these informal musical gatherings. Not counting her summer at Camp Reinberg, to that point she had not sung or played an instrument publicly.

Ella's situation would change in the fall of 1950, nearly two years into her time in the Bay Area, when she stumbled upon an unlikely source of housing near the San Francisco State campus. One day she noticed female students heading for an attractive brick edifice just a couple of blocks away at 300 Page Street. A polite inquiry revealed it to be the Emanu-El Residence Club, offering affordable housing for unmarried Jewish "working girls" in their late teens and twenties. Run by the Sisterhood, or women's group, of its namesake of Temple Emanu-El, San Francisco's oldest Reform Jewish congregation, it primarily served local women, but 20 percent of its residents were immigrants and refugees, giving the club an international flavor. Like the Berkeley co-ops, the Emanu-El club provided meals. But it was a step up from Stebbins, boasting a tastefully decorated TV room, a grand piano, and circulating libraries for musical recordings as well as books. Residents enjoyed regular presentations by an impressive roster of local actors, artists, dancers, scholars, and musicians. They also participated in fundraisers for Jewish social welfare groups and observed Shabbat, as well as Jewish holidays and festivals, according to Reform Jewish conventions.

During her "rebel years" in Chicago, Ella had come to regard the pursuit of interracialism and interculturalism as a powerful means of turning civil rights ideals into practice. On a more personal level, she had learned from Christian Science to bravely pursue her desires, trusting in God's goodness. The Emanu-El residence was reasonably priced, well appointed, and close to her classes—a "nice place to live." Why should she not seek to live in such an attractive place? Besides, the "roughy-toughy" girl who had defied familial and social expectation in traveling alone to the West Coast was not about to be told whom she could live or eat with.

As with her attraction to table tennis, in deciding to live at the Emanu-El residence Ella may also have been following an example first set by her brother. In 1946, when Tom enrolled at the University of Chicago, he shared a room in a Hyde Park co-op with a Jewish graduate student named Leonard. Eventually, he and Leonard left the co-op for a "regular" apartment in the Kenwood neighborhood, which Leonard found for them, knowing that the white landlord would balk at renting to a "Negro." In the course of their friendship, Tom learned about Jewish ritual and tradition and had his first taste of matzo-ball soup.[3] Through her friendship with Annette Haase in Chicago, Ella too had been welcomed into a Jewish home.

Before she could get into Emanu-El residence, however, Ella would have to overcome the resistance of Mary Michaels, the formidable woman who oversaw it. She treated their phone call a bit like a table-tennis volley, looking for a place to deliver the winning shot. First, she asked Mrs. Michaels about the rent. At $54.50, it was a substantial step up from Stebbins, but by then Ella had received a raise and could afford it. She then asked whether the club was "restricted."

"What do you mean?" Mrs. Michaels asked.

"Well," Ella replied, "I'm colored."

In response, Mrs. Michaels noted that while the Emanu-El residence placed no restrictions on who could live there, "it just would be more comfortable for a Jewish girl."

"Well, I like Jewish music," replied Ella, without missing a beat.

When Mrs. Michaels noted that Emanu-El residents observed Jewish religious rituals and consumed kosher food, Ella assured her that she "loved" kosher food. And when, after meeting Ella, Mrs. Michaels offered her a room in the basement, next to the laundry room, explaining that it was the only space available, Ella readily agreed. "She couldn't discourage me," Ella said.

Ella quickly acclimated to the rhythms of Jewish life at Emanu-El. By the end of her first month she had celebrated Sukkot, a harvest festival, for which residents festooned a courtyard with gourds, branches, and other symbols of autumn. By December she had lit the Chanukah candles and attended a reading of works by Sholem Aleichem, whose writings formed the basis of *Fiddler on the Roof*. Surviving records indicate that Ella eventually moved to a higher floor and participated fully in Emanu-El activities. At an April 1951 "Monte Carlo night" fundraiser for a Jewish social service agency she volunteered her skills as a "masseuse." In April 1952 she participated in a staged reading of the Clare Boothe Luce play *The Women*. And at Passover that same year she served on the program committee, helping to choose records for the dancing that followed the Seder.[4]

At Stebbins singing was a form of recreation. But at the Emanu-El residence, music was part of everyday life. Every ritual observance had its own chants and songs, some sacred, like the Sabbath blessings over the wine and challah, and some secular, like "Hatikvah," the folk song-turned-new Israeli national anthem. Living there for a year and eight months, Ella learned this material by ear, in the manner of American Reform Jewish women who had received no formal Hebrew instruction.

It was at the Emanu-El residence that Ella began formulating ideas about musical "cultures" and "traditions," in both their distinctiveness and their universality. She observed practices of call and response in Jewish prayer. She heard similarities between the minor-key sounds of Ashkenazi Jewish music and blues. She listened to the lilting melodies and insistent rhythms of Sephardic and Mizrahi Jewish songs, thinking about the ways they contrasted with the Euro-American hymns she knew from the Eighth Church of Christ, Scientist. Ella's sonic investigations were informed by 1940s ideas of cultural pluralism, which held that the nation was enhanced when immigrant groups retained aspects of their national or ethnic "heritage," including language and culture. And while cultural pluralism largely centered on the European immigrants favored by US law after the restrictive 1924 Immigration Act, Ella would have meshed it with the principles of the Negro History Movement, which emphasized the importance of Black people's knowledge of Black contributions to American social and cultural life.

Diane Jacob, Ella's friend from his period, remembered how interested Ella was in learning songs from her. The Burma (now Myanmar)–born daughter of Baghdad-born parents, Diane had briefly lived in India before immigrating to the United States from England. As a result of this background, she spoke several languages, including Arabic and Hebrew. Ella only had high school Spanish, but "she would pick it up so fast," Diane said, remembering how Ella absorbed the new words and sounds. "She was so good at it."[5]

Diane first heard Ella sing at an Emanu-El fundraiser for Israel, sharing a stage with the acclaimed modern dancer Anna Halprin. Ella had a warm timbre and sang in an alto register. She enunciated clearly and used vibrato sparingly. Hers was not a "trained" sound—she possessed neither a "church" nor an operatic voice—but she had a fine sense of timing and pitch and sensitivity to lyrics. When the other women at the Emanu-El residence "found that I could sing," Ella said, then "they all wanted [me] to sing in our programs." Ella not only performed Jewish and Israeli folk music, but also shared spirituals and Black folk songs, which her Jewish housemates knew from the popular recordings of artists like Paul Robeson.

Ella first began "bartering" songs at 300 Page Street. *You teach me one of your songs*, she would say to a housemate, *and I'll teach you one of mine.* The inherent reciprocity of this method of building her repertoire diverged sharply from the "ballad hunting" of the white male folklorists and collectors who were most responsible for creating a mid-twentieth-century canon of American folksong.[6] The folklorist's emphasis was his discovery of "unheard" material: song was bounty. Ella's bartering method put the accent on the social intimacies of cultural exchange: song was relationship, a means of recognizing the other.

Ella carried these relationships from Emanu-El with her, remaining friendly with Diane and developing a "very close" relationship with Mary Michaels, who became something of a mother figure. It is likely that Ella turned to Mrs. Michaels when she found out she would have to have a partial hysterectomy to treat symptoms that developed during her time in California. (Her mother may not have supported her decision to have surgery.) In 1957, when Ella released her first album, she sent Mrs. Michaels a copy, which the older woman tucked away for safe-keeping.

FIGURE 3.2. Ella with Mary Michaels at the Emanu-El residence,
San Francisco, ca. early 1950s. Unknown photographer.

The Emanu-El residence was only one site of Ella's musical adventures in San Francisco. In the early postwar era, the increasingly multicultural city pulsed with diverse rhythms. Ella was particularly drawn to the North Beach neighborhood, a vibrant urban space where different groups mingled and overlapped. "North Beach bubbled as noisily and colorfully as the main street in a boom town," recalled Maya Angelou, who appeared as a calypso singer-dancer in its clubs before she became better known as a writer.[7] In addition to Italian establishments, the neighborhood featured Chinese restaurants, clubs featuring a variety of Latin music or jazz, and gay and lesbian nightspots.

North Beach was also ground zero of the city's burgeoning folk-music scene. It is unclear how Ella came to know many of the major folk performers. It was perhaps through San Francisco State's small Folk Music Club, a mostly white but interracial group that reflected the demographics of the larger folk milieu.[8] Whatever her exact path, within a year of moving to San Francisco Ella had befriended banjoist Billy Faier, singer-guitarist Stan Wilson, and singer Jo Mapes. (She also came into contact with Barbara Dane, another singer.) Over time, Ella developed particularly close relationships with Mapes and Faier, even if she did not quite aspire to their bohemianism—whether because of her mother's respectability politics or her own sense of the risks inherent to Black woman's social, cultural, and sexual experimentation. Since discovering the Greenwich Village folk scene in 1947, the mercurial Faier had been devoted to the five-string banjo. In 1951, to evade the draft, he moved out west, eventually making his way to San Francisco. A streetcar worker, he offered Ella free rides, but she demurred, fearful of getting him fired. Mapes was a Chicago native who had grown up in Los Angeles, attending high school with Odetta Felious, then an aspiring singer-actor not yet known as the folk singer Odetta. A free spirit, Mapes had married her husband Paul, a merchant seaman, only a few weeks after meeting him; at the time, they lived in a garret apartment that doubled as space for candlelit after-hours jam sessions.

In her free time Ella would meet up with Mapes in North Beach to hear music. She particularly liked Vesuvio, a café on Columbus Avenue, where poets and musicians played into the early morning hours. The folk performance ethic of group singing called to mind Ella's earliest musical experiences in the Baptist churches of her maternal relatives and in the cotton fields where her kinfolk worked. But at Vesuvio such familiar practices took on a countercultural air as music "of the people." Founded as an artist's haven, the café featured walls covered with paintings and drawings, including nudes. It had a community bulletin board, graffitied bathroom stalls, and matchbooks with clever quips ("The customers in this bar are entirely fictitious. Any resemblance to actual, living persons in purely accidental"). It is likely that Ella knew of North Beach's vibrant gay and lesbian nightlife, which included bars like the Black Cat, Mona's Candlelight, Club 440, Finocchio's, and the Beige Room.[9] But she preferred the gentler, caffeine-driven energy of the folk venues to the alcohol-fueled pick-up scene at the bars.

Ella's writings from the time reveal hints of romantic attachments, perhaps even relationships with other women. On the inside cover of a collection of Emily Dickinson poems, she inscribed a short poem titled "Enlightenment," about a woman (ostensibly Dickinson) anticipating a clandestine visit from her lover. On the inside front cover of her copy of *The Poems and Fairy Tales of Oscar Wilde*, she scribbled a cryptic question: "Must new knowledge of LIFE always be accompanied by a painful experience?"[10]

In other writings Ella gave voice to complex feelings about being a Black woman in white spaces. In a paper written for a sociology course, she referred knowingly to the experience of being patronized by white people who "feel as part of their philosophy that they are more or less obligated to mix with peoples of various nationalities and racial groups."[11] On the other hand, in an autobiographical piece titled "My Sensitive Soul," composed for a creative writing class in the fall of 1951, she explored the harm that could arise from a white friend's obliviousness to her experience. In the story the Black narrator joins such a friend at a "rather exclusive restaurant" that the friend has recommended. After they are seated, the friend scans the menu, unconcerned by its steep prices and unaware that the narrator is the only "Negro" in the venue.

As the narrator ignores the questioning looks of white patrons and sits in dread of being denied service, she grows increasingly angry at the friend who has put her "in such an insecure position."

The story ends on an upbeat note—with the narrator's relief as the "blue-eyed waiter" graciously takes her order. Yet the alleviation of her dread does not mitigate the themes of "My Sensitive Soul," which include the narrator's management, alone, of the anticipation of racial rejection and her complex feelings for the white friend who has thoughtlessly, if unwittingly, caused her pain. "I could also feel the eyes of the seemingly millions of white faces anxiously waiting to see me refused [service]," the narrator says. "How they would revel in my embarrassment!"[12]

If Ella was in search of spaces where she could discover herself more fully, her quest was rewarded one afternoon in 1951 when she was walking in North Beach and noticed a young Black man toting a large conga drum. She walked up to him and asked him whether he played; he told her, in Spanish-accented English, that with his band the Afro-Cubans he was about to begin a gig at the Cable Car Village, a nightspot at 1390 California Street, in Nob Hill. He urged her to stop by, and she promised she would.[13]

Ella's receptivity to the man's offer opened the door to a Black musical world that would alter the course of her life and, in time, shape the course of children's music. The man was Armando Peraza, one of the most important Cuban percussionists then working in the United States. Ella had been fascinated by Latin rhythms since seeing *Pan-Americana*, a forgettable 1945 movie that nevertheless contained transcendent musical numbers. She particularly loved Miguelito Valdés's cameo performance of "Babalú," set in a swanky Havana dinner club. Appearing barefoot and in folkloric costuming that emphasized his prizefighter's physique, the powerhouse baritone passionately invoked "Babalú-Ayé," deity of disease and healing in the Afro-Cuban religion of Santería, to the accompaniment of a thunderous chorus of six conga drums. Valdés's performance delighted and excited Ella, who felt the passion of "Babalú" even if she did not then fully understand the song's cultural references.

Since the movie's release, Cuban polyrhythms had increasingly punctuated the sounds of US popular music. Ella had observed the national dance craze launched by the 1949 release of Perez Prádo's "Mambo No. 5."[14] By the time she spotted Peraza, clubs and ballrooms from Fresno to Oakland were cashing in on the popularity of mambo with regular Latin music nights, some featuring hired dancers. The Arthur Murray Dance Studio, which boasted numerous Bay Area outposts, promised to have students "swaying to the Rumba rhythms or dancing the latest Mambo" with a few hours of instruction. Afro-Cuban percussion had even begun to influence the habitués of North Beach cafés—the future Beats—who embraced bongo drums as a symbol of their social and political rebellion.[15]

Like Ella, Peraza was a relative newcomer to San Francisco, having landed there after an acrimonious split from bandleader and vocalist Slim Gaillard. Since then, he had struggled to support himself as a freelancer. Outside of the lively jazz scene of the predominantly African American Fillmore District, Black musicians were generally not welcome in San Francisco clubs, with the most profitable gigs reserved for white—or white-appearing—players. Peraza himself had been denied entrance to the prestigious Palomar Ballroom because "black people weren't allowed." So intense was pressure from the white musicians' union in enforcing segregated venues that Merced Gallegos, one of the area's first Latin bandleaders, had initially hesitated to allow Peraza to sit in with his band, fearing a backlash. "You cannot imagine the discrimination I went through in those early years," Peraza later remembered.[16]

For both Ella and Peraza, the Cable Car Village offered an alternative to such racially policed spaces. Whether or not it was also then a gay bar, as it was by the late 1950s, its ambiance was such that Ella felt comfortable showing up alone, either to dance or simply to listen.[17] As their name suggested, the Afro-Cubans primarily played a Cuban repertoire, but because their diverse personnel—which included Italian American pianist Phil Longo, Cuba-born singers Israel del Pino and Juanita Silva, Mexican American brothers Manuel and Carlos Durán, and Allan Smith, an African American trumpeter who had studied at San Francisco State—they also incorporated Mexican and African American styles. The affable Peraza cut a flamboyant figure on the club's small stage. To accentuate the velocity of his playing, he would decorate his fingers with fluorescent paints and put fluorescent lights on his congas. Silva, billed as "Juanita la Chiquita," was a rare female percussionist, playing maracas. Ella was not alone in her appreciation for the group. A year into their Cable Car Village residency, the *San Francisco Examiner* would still be touting the Afro-Cubans as "the most talked about [Latin] musical group" in the Bay Area.[18]

Ella was viscerally moved by the sounds of the Afro-Cubans. "Their music was *so great*," she recalled in a 1978 interview. "This was different from the Mexican music that I had been inspired to listen to" back in Chicago. "This Cuban music's what I *really* liked, cause it was pulsating. It did something to me that no other music did. It just caught hold of me."[19]

What did Ella hear in the Afro-Cuban music? Sounds that were intoxicating and sensual, causing her to sway and rock her shoulders and hips. But also sounds that led her out of her body, into realms of fantasy and even spiritual epiphany. When the Afro-Cubans played "some of the secret-society type of music that came from Cuba," Ella said, she would get so "carried away" by the rhythms that she would forget she was in a club. Her experiences recalled those of writer and anthropologist Zora Neale Hurston, who wrote about being transported by the sounds of a jazz orchestra and feeling "great blobs of purple and red emotion." As the musicians played, Hurston danced "wildly" within herself, expressing emotion that had few sanctioned public outlets for a Black female intellectual.[20]

Ella was similarly affected by Afro-Cuban music. A novice listener, she was less attuned to the music's technical elements than to its sonic qualities and the sensations they produced. It was only later that she would come to understand how the players' masterful control of poly-rhythm—a hallmark element of both 1950s Latin jazz and Afro-Cuban styles—gave the sounds their "pulsating" quality. Likewise, when she first heard Armando play she did not know the history of the modern conga drum, a "creolized" version of the African instruments that enslaved workers smuggled onto Cuban plantations to practice their religions.[21]

But Ella immediately sensed the importance of these rhythms to her self-understanding as an American woman of African descent. In particular, she seems to have intuitively recognized a common "Afri-can" ancestor in the Cuban music and the Black music she knew. Later, she would come to embrace this resilience of African rhythms and to regard Black music in light of the strength and elasticity of sonic prac-tices that survived the Middle Passage and more than four centuries of chattel slavery.[22]

Ella's emotional connection to the music explains why she sought to understand it through her own music-making. She took to drumming—initially on makeshift instruments: tin cans, water pails, and wastebaskets. At the Cable Car Village she drummed on the table with a fork while the band played. Eventually she acquired a Chinese tom-tom, before saving up money to buy a small conga drum.

During this period of listening and experimentation, Ella never took a lesson; she simply followed along, after the model of sitting at Uncle Flood's feet as he played the harmonica. Peraza and his musician-friends supported her with occasional tips, but it was assumed that Ella would learn through her own trial and error. Ella never seems to have been intimidated by the complexity of Cuban polyrhythms or to wonder whether a woman could play conga, although all of the players she knew of were men. Instead, she pursued hand percussion as she had other "boy'" pursuits: resistant to others' expectations and focused on making the sounds she desired.

When teaching herself to play hand percussion, Ella's goal was profi-ciency, not virtuosity. As her partner Bernadelle would later explain, "Ella has always used an instrument to get a point across. It was never about being able to play really well. She used it as a means. Like writing—you use a pencil. You want to get it out there." At the Cable Car Village Ella had noticed that when Peraza started playing, audiences snapped to attention. In Afro-Cuban religious practice the rhythms of the conga summoned the orishas, or spirits. Ella recognized and wanted to harness this latent communicative power of the conga, even as she was still working out the details of what, exactly, she wanted to use the instrument to say.

As she had with table tennis, Ella persisted in her drumming, despite a lack of role models, formal support, or even a clear destination. In the year or so after meeting Peraza, she became a devoted acolyte of Latin, and particularly Cuban, styles. She taught herself some of the core patterns played on conga and bongo drums, claves and maracas. Ella tended to play without bluster or excessive "showmanship." As much as she admired Peraza, she did not dream of dazzling audiences. She played first and foremost for herself.

Through her studies of percussion, Ella came to perceive how Peraza and his bandmates created a pulsating effect through a mix of timbres, pulses, and meters. To produce the sound that had touched her so deeply, each player had to listen to the others' patterns without losing the rhythms of his own. Through such collective listening, the ensemble produced a base from which individual expression could take flight.

Polyrhythm, Ella was realizing, was about relationships. The intoxicating, swinging sound of the music arose from musicians who were confident in their own rhythms, and yet simultaneously alert to the rhythms of others. All rhythms, not just Afro-Cuban ones, expressed this fundamentally social principle through sound. The realization helped Ella understand why she was so captivated by the songs and chants of Bronzeville playgrounds. Through Peraza's band, she had discovered the secret and yet very obvious fact that rhythm was everywhere. Life was rhythm, rhythm was life.

Ella first performed music publicly in San Francisco, playing her tom-tom and singing in Spanish in a restaurant whose name, like the name of her song, is lost to memory. Yet the fact that Ella realized a *desire* to perform is more significant than any details of the gig. Ella had always been an extrovert. But at the Emanu-El residence she had discovered not only that people liked to hear her singing, but that she liked the feeling of singing for an audience. Music afforded her a means of communicating that felt both authentic and validating. Even before the audience of Jewish women, most of whom would be considered white, she felt confident and unselfconscious, quite unlike the young woman depicted in "My Sensitive Soul." At the time of these first performances, she had not yet figured out "what I was going to do, who I was going to be."[23] But in retrospect it is clear that in that unnamed restaurant, she crossed an important threshold.

When Ella finished the coursework for her BA in the summer of 1951, her boss at Codornices Village offered her a full-time job, but she turned the offer down. In his letters Tom had begun to tease her, warning her that if she didn't come back soon her South Side friends would forget her. Notwithstanding their history of conflict, Ella also felt the tug of filial responsibility to her mother and missed her aunt and uncle. She informed Mrs. Michaels that she would be returning to Chicago.

Contrary to her experience on the way to California, Ella did not cry on her train ride east in 1952. A couple of months before she left, she inscribed a short poem on the flyleaf of her copy of *The Rubáiyát of Omar Khayyám*:

The grape burst open
And its juice was sweet to my tongue
I thought to myself,
"What a passionate fruit,
And how good it is to be young."[24]

She may have been expressing delight in a love affair. Or perhaps the "passionate fruit" was something she had tasted in the rhythms of Peraza's band, or absorbed in bohemian North Beach folk soirees. The poem conveyed the pleasurable jolt of new knowledge and the heady sense of possibility. By the standards of the 1950s Ella, at twenty-eight, was approaching old-maidhood. Most of the girls in her graduating class at DuSable were married with children. But Ella, having chosen a different path, felt youthful. She had gone away and tasted the fruit, and was now returning home, her life spreading out before her.

I like the whole thing but I liked the drum
the most when you made it talk. I wish I
could do it that well.

Thad

(PULLMAN, WASHINGTON, 1959)

4
FOUR YEARS AT THE YWCA
1952–1956

Ella's first address when she returned to Chicago was at the Harriet Hammond McCormick YWCA, on the North Side. The handsome brick high-rise—which had only begun admitting Black women after 1946—was considered a desirable, even "luxurious," destination for "working girls." Its motto, "A Home of Charm for a year or a day," appeared on postcards that touted its "ideal location" in the vicinity of Michigan Avenue, the Newberry Library, and the Tribune Tower. The McCormick Y cost more than other boarding houses, its features including a pleasant courtyard and dining room and its own laundry facilities.

In many ways, the Y was comparable to the Emanu-El residence. Yet its music was different. As she passed through the hallways, Ella heard the soulful humming of one of its Black maids, whose voice evoked the sounds of her own Southern kin. "It was a hum that you can't duplicate . . . like certain blues," she said.[1] Most of the Black people Ella encountered in the Bay Area had migrated from places unfamiliar to her—Louisiana or Texas. Their songs bore the history of those specific places. But she had come to appreciate their resonant similarities with the hums she heard during visits to grandparents and cousins in Mississippi and Alabama.

Ella's fledgling identity as a percussionist led her to be newly attuned to the rhythms of Chicago. As she ventured through its neighborhoods, she paid fresh attention to their cadences, textures, and pulses. She listened in the manner of someone learning a language and latching on to familiar words. Most of what Ella had been taught about "Negro" history as a teenager had been smuggled into classrooms by enterprising teachers or discovered outside of school, from women like artist-activist Margaret Burroughs at the South Side Community Art Center or librarian Charlemae Rollins at the Hall Branch of the Chicago Public Library. But her serendipitous discovery of the Afro-Cubans made Ella want to understand more about the histories that were carried, preserved, and interpreted through music.

It took Ella several weeks to find a job befitting her new college degree. At one point she contemplated taking a live-in childcare position in the suburbs. But Tom, then working on his master's in sociology at the University of Chicago and living in Hyde Park, advised her to hold out for something better.

The job she ultimately landed, of Teenage Program Director of the South Parkway YWCA, in the heart of Bronzeville, warranted her patience. It initiated an intellectually and creatively fertile period of her life she would dub "Four years at the YWCA." Between 1952 and 1956 she translated the polyrhythms of San Francisco life to her new routines in Chicago. Work at the Y was like the conga drum, laying down a steady foundation for her waking hours as she conducted programs teaching Afro-Latin rhythms to teenagers and young adults. Performing Afro-Latin music—first in restaurants and coffee houses, but eventually on more formal stages—was like the bongos, allowing her to work ideas out via improvisations. And her adventures in listening—to a wide range of Latin, jazz, pop, folk, and blues music—were like the cowbell, maracas, and claves: complements and counterpoints that made the whole thing swing.

In joining the South Parkway Y—first at 4559 South Parkway and later in the community center of the Ida B. Wells Homes, a large public housing development at 436 East Thirty-Ninth Street—Ella joined a Bronzeville institution headed by politically and culturally active Chicago "race women." Like their sisters at YWCAs in New York and Washington, DC, these women were community leaders, stewarding institutions that offered social services, education, and job training, in addition to recreation. Black women had also been at the forefront of combating racism and segregation both at local YWCA branches and within the national organization. In 1946 their activism resulted in the passage of a national "interracial charter," which declared: "wherever there is injustice on the basis of race, whether in the community, the nation, or the world, our protest must be clear and our labor for its removal, vigorous, and steady."[2]

When Ella joined the staff of the South Parkway Y, much of its programming reflected a Black middle-class politics of respectability that would have been familiar to her. But the girls and women she worked with were also pressured by reactionary Cold War gender politics, which idealized marriage and domestic motherhood and demonized deviations from heterosexual norms. By 1952 leaders of Metropolitan Chicago YWCA, as well as the South Parkway branch, had begun to fret over "rising delinquency"—another 1950s bugaboo. At the Wells Homes, which overwhelmingly housed Black lower-middle-class families, young women bore the stigma of delinquency in gendered terms; as one report referring to out-of-wedlock pregnancy put it, "the girl problem is major."[3] Like other South Side service organizations, the South Parkway Y offered after-school and early evening programming that sought to keep teens occupied and help them become responsible citizen-adults. Both boys and girls were encouraged to complete high school and set their sights on respectable employment or college. But girls were also coached in habits of "good grooming" and to taught to prepare for marriage by learning domestic skills.

Ella negotiated these wider concerns about Black girlhood while juggling roles as a teacher, a social worker, a community organizer, and a manager. She oversaw a half-dozen or so girls' social clubs bearing names that sounded a bit like the era's popular doo-wop groups: the Cloverettes, Las Amigas, Las Palomas, the Typical Teens, and the Sophisticated Imps. She presided over a popular Y-Teen Club, a co-educational group that sponsored an Interclub Council and produced the *Y-Teener*, a newsletter staffed by budding journalists and artists. She facilitated a Record Session group that organized weekly dances. She made do with scant resources, fickle volunteers, and low expectations born of histories of neglect. "Well, how long are you gonna be here?" the Wells Homes teenagers, inured to staff turnover, asked when they first met her. She assured them of her plans to stay "a while."

Ella had no interest in policing young women's sexuality or preparing them for a domestic womanhood she herself had rejected. Instead, she sought to widen Black girls' perspectives. Once she took six members of the Typical Teens to dinner at Papa Milano's, a Near North Side Italian restaurant whose owner she had befriended, and then to her apartment at 1001 North Dearborn Street. She observed them as they gamely "tackled curling spaghetti on their forks" and sampled the restaurant's filling "Pizza Pie." At her apartment, she solicited the girls' opinions of the experience, tacitly offering herself as a model of sexually unconventional, financially independent, and racially self-possessed Black womanhood.[4]

Ella's desire to nurture confidence in her teenage charges took its most striking form in her creation of two co-educational after-school clubs that took advantage of the teens' interest in mambo and other popular Latin dances to introduce them to notions of the African "roots" of US music culture. In the Latin Dance Club, she combined weekly instruction in mambo, tango, and rhumba with programming related to Latin American music. In the Percussion Club, boys and girls alike learned to play the instruments that made Latin dance rhythms, notwithstanding the fact that drums were considered a "boys'" instrument. In both clubs she sought to share her own epiphany from hearing the Afro-Cubans at the Cable Car Village. She told the teens, "Why don't we go back to Africa, because this is where a lot of this music stemmed from."[5]

To Ella, who had spent the better part of the previous year and a half on a quest to teach herself to play Afro-Cuban percussion, the idea of going back to Africa must have seemed straightforward. But it was also deeply radical, coming at a time when US advocates of African and African diasporic arts and culture were still working to dispel widespread notions of the superiority of European "civilization." As Joanna Dee Das writes, when modern dance pioneer Katherine Dunham "first offered 'Negro' dance classes in 1930s Chicago, black parents had refused to send their children, seeing Africanist cultural practices as backward and shameful."[6] As Dunham garnered international acclaim and Black intellectuals increasingly embraced pan-Africanism, these attitudes began to shift. By the 1950s the *Defender* had begun to regularly cover news from Africa and the Caribbean, giving celebrity treatment to the diplomats, intellectuals, and social notables who visited Chicago from places like Liberia and Haiti. South Side branches of the Chicago Public Library hosted seminars and talks that explored African politics, society, and culture.

Yet during Ella's years at the Y, most young Chicagoans were still learning about Africa from American popular culture. In Hollywood films like *The African Queen* (1951) they saw Africa depicted as a place teeming with wild animals, exotic flora, and childlike, primitive natives. "When I was a child, I was ashamed of Africa," Margaret Burroughs wrote. "When I saw pictures in magazines and movies of strange black people who were so foreign to me, I certainly did not wish to be identified with them." The South Parkway teens were similarly unreceptive, as Ella told Studs Terkel, "because at the time they didn't want to be identified with Africa as their heritage."[7]

Through trial and error, she learned the stakes of a cultural or ancestral identification with Africa could be particularly vexed for Black girls. Once she arranged for the Percussion Club, which was mostly boys, to see a documentary about African culture. But when the teens saw the image of a woman with uncovered breasts, their "shouts of laughter and derision" forced her to shut the screening down.[8] And unlike Ella, many of the Y girls resisted drumming as a "masculine" endeavor. In her novella *Maud Martha*, published in 1953 while Ella was working at the Y, Chicago writer Gwendolyn Brooks depicted the interior life of a Bronzeville girl who tried to appear dainty to win the approval of adults as well as boys. The girls at the Wells Homes were similar; as much as they liked Ella, remembered Percussion Club member Beverly Lucas, they would not join the club out of fear of wear and tear on their hands. But Lucas was willing to suffer a few calluses to learn from Ella, a rare adult who really seemed to listen to her.[9]

Boys such as Dallas Browne and his two brothers faced fewer barriers to their participation than the girls. Browne, who had been a cadet in a local drum and bugle corps, recalled how transformative it was to learn from Ella about "those little dots on the map known as African countries." "She told us about our connection to these places and the richness of the music and the life of the people who lived there, people we had been taught to be afraid of," he later wrote. "Further, she pointed out how these instruments played an important part in the communities of our brothers here in. . . . the USA and 'Mother Africa.'"[10]

As Browne suggests, Ella's lessons in diasporic Black culture instilled self-pride in young Chicagoans. Her instruction may also have equipped them with the emotional and intellectual resources they needed to confront racism—whether pedestrian expressions of discrimination familiar to Bronzeville children or more flagrant and spectacular acts of violence. In August 1955, while Ella was working at the Y, whites lynched Emmett Louis Till, a fourteen-year-old boy from Chicago's West Woodlawn neighborhood, who had ventured to Money, Mississippi, to visit relatives. Black Chicagoans had come out en masse for his homegoing service at a Bronzeville church, which drew national headlines when his mother, Mamie Till, insisted on an open casket, to "let people see what they did to my boy."[11] Ella could not personally bear to pay witness to Till's ravaged body. Had white men not murdered him, Till might have learned to play conga in her Percussion Club or practiced the steps to the mambo in her Latin Dance Club.

FIGURE 4.1. Ella with Y-Teens, ca. mid-1950s. Photo by Jo Banks.

It was during her four years at the YWCA that Ella began calling herself a "rhythm specialist." The phrase gave an aura of legitimacy and professionalism to skills that pointed to no particular vocation and that she had developed largely on her own. To claim the mantle of a *specialist*, a term that arose from the twentieth-century invention of the assembly line and the proliferation of new scientific knowledge, was for Ella a bold act of self-invention. It was a boldness born of necessity. There was no language to describe Ella's talents or expertise on what were then still described as "primitive" instruments. She did not consider herself a musician, let alone a "children's musician"—and even if she had, the term fell short of describing what she was doing at the Y, which had less to do with drumming or Latin dance per se than with widening Black teens' horizons and inviting them to form positive associations with their African "roots." Implicit in these goals, moreover, was a concern with racial justice that Ella carried over from her more "political" work with CORE. The Black freedom struggle was not only a matter of marches and sit-ins; it required fundamental shifts in Black consciousness that could be explored and hastened through cultural expression.

Ella had more pedestrian reasons for dubbing herself a rhythm specialist. On evenings and weekends she was venturing out to clubs and coffee houses with her conga drum, offering performances of Afro-Latin chants and songs at folk clubs (or venues that had folk nights), where audiences were interested in "ethnic" musical traditions. Her repertoire at this early stage in her professional career likely included the compositions "Oye Mi Tambor" and "Yo Me Voy," Spanish-language songs of her own composition.[12] Both were simple but emotive paeans to Afro-Cuban percussion, especially "Oye Mi Tambor," in which Ella accompanied herself with ornamental rhythms (rather than standard Cuban conga patterns) while repeating phrases that convey urgency and need in abstract terms: *Oye mi tambor* (Hear my drum); *Es como el ritmo del Congo* (Like the rhythm of the Congo), *Estoy gritando / Estoy llorando, oye mi tambor* (I'm screaming / I'm crying, hear my drum).

Ella neatly copied the full lyrics, along with her English translation of "Oye Mi Tambor" on the inside front cover of her copy of *African Folktales and Sculpture*, a 1952 volume. Under the words, she drew a fanciful figure of a drum with a forlorn face, its downcast appearance translating the song's lyric about a "screaming" and "crying" instrument (or singer). The image captured the song's allegory of the transgenerational struggles of African and/or African diasporic peoples, suggesting the conga drum as a vessel of painful Black histories. And yet with its generous loops, the signature also conveyed her professional aspirations as a percussionist.

FIGURE 4.2. "*Oye mi tambor!*" Ella's drawing, ca. 1954.

Ella pursued these aspirations as she crisscrossed the city, her ears open to its sonic variety. Her receptiveness to a broad range of styles brought her into contact with an unusually diverse swath of people, both fans and performers. Just as she had toggled between the Cable Car Village and folk venues in San Francisco, in Chicago Ella followed the music. She did not allow herself to be limited to popular conceptions of "Black" sounds or to shy from places where she would have encountered few other Black patrons. She embodied the confidence of her signature: open, upright, receptive in mind and spirit.

Ella occasionally even took the bus to New York City to check out the scene at the Palladium Ballroom, Midtown Manhattan's mecca of Latin dance. On such trips Ella absorbed the musical vibrations and the energy of the mostly Cuban and Puerto Rican New York crowd. She found the Palladium to be a particularly welcoming space for an unaccompanied woman. "You didn't even have to dance with anyone, if you felt the music," she said. The moving bodies included people of varying skin tones and hair textures, and women dancing alone or together, one taking on the role of leader. There were teenagers and *abuelas* (grandmothers), because "you didn't stop when you got a certain age."[13]

Back in Chicago, with its more rigidly segregated neighborhoods, Ella frequented Bronzeville clubs that featured weekly Latin nights, including Roberts Show Lounge. It was likely at one of these venues that she encountered musician Sun Ra (then going by the stage name Sun Ray), sometime in the mid-1950s. Ra was then experimenting with the inclusion of a conga drummer in his jazz ensembles, leading Ella to recognize him as a kindred spirit. He "was always very excited and always talking about music," Ella remembered. "I used to see him at a place at Michigan Avenue around Twenty-Ninth or Thirtieth, not far from DuSable. We would get together with other folks. He loved to philosophize. Sometimes it would go on for an hour or two. Sometimes people would have instruments, and they would play." Ra would also have shared in Ella's interest in Africa and its diaspora, although where he pursued an experimental Afro-futurism, she would remain focused on roots.

In addition to Ra, Ella's Chicago Latin music circle in these years included dancers Vernon Duncan, Carmencita Romero, Neville Black, Jewel McLaurin, and Jimmy Payne. Duncan and Romero were alumni of Katherine Dunham's troupe. Duncan taught dance at Roosevelt College and performed throughout the city, incorporating elements of the West Indian ceremonial dancing he had studied on research trips to Haiti and Jamaica. Romero was born Lily Butler but "Latinized" her name at Dunham's suggestion. A specialist in Afro-Cuban styles, she had her own dance studio on West Roosevelt Road and taught modern dance at the South Parkway Y. Both the Jamaica-born Black and McLaurin trained with Martha Graham, and Black taught modern dance at the South Parkway Y on Thursday afternoons while Ella was Y-Teen Coordinator.

Ella worked most closely with Jimmy Payne, a pioneering teacher and performer of West Indian dance styles. Born in 1905 in Panama to a Cuban mother and Barbadian father, Payne opened his first studio in New York City in the 1930s, attracting a minor celebrity for teaching rhythmic tap to well-known students including Lena Horne and Bob Fosse. After relocating to Chicago in the 1940s, he taught generations of dancers African and Afro-Caribbean styles, performing with musicians including jazz saxophonist Sonny Rollins. When Ella met him, he was presenting a wildly popular "Calypso Carnival" show at the Blue Angel club. It featured a talented young woman named Grace Nichols—later known as actor Nichelle Nichols—and, briefly, a singer named Gene Walcott, who later changed his name to Louis Farrakhan.[14]

Ella even joined Payne's company on a 1957 national tour, alternately billed as "Below the Border" and "Afro-Cuban West Indian Ballet," that visited Southern Black colleges, including Arkansas Agricultural, Mechanical and Normal College in Pine Bluff, as well as theaters and auditoriums in places like Dayton, Denver, and Omaha. She would frequently open the program by singing "Babalú"—her old favorite by Miguelito Valdés—accompanying herself on conga and later perform her own chant, "Moon Don't Go." "I was so honored to be in that group," Ella said, noting that her role included dancing. "I was very free" as a dancer.[15]

Martin Yarbrough, a precocious young African American percussionist, moved in and out of the circle of these dancers, partly on account of his sister Camille, who danced with Payne's company. In the 1960s Yarbrough released a couple of albums of guitar-based folk material on Argo, a subsidiary of Chicago's storied Chess label. But when Ella met him in the early 1950s he was still a teenager who had become serious about Afro-Cuban percussion after hearing a drummer named Congo in a North Side neighborhood of Puerto Ricans and Cubans. Like Ella, Yarbrough recognized a

FIGURE 4.3. Jimmy Payne dance troupe, ca. 1957. Ella is kneeling
with conga on the right. Photo by Burnis McCloud. Courtesy
Denver Public Library, Western History Collection.

"home" in Congo's music and became determined to learn how to
duplicate it. After a week of practice, he received the master player's
blessing.[16]

Outside of Latin music, Ella made connections at various Chicago jazz, blues, and folk venues. During her four years at the Y she
befriended Pete Seeger, Gerry and George Armstrong, Bob Gibson,
Frank Hamilton, and Virginia "Ginni" Clemmens; pianist Mildred
Falls (accompanist to Mahalia Jackson) and the gospel group the Gay
Sisters (Evelyn, Mildred and Geraldine); scene-crossing musicians
like Big Bill Broonzy and Brother John Sellers; and figures who supported Chicago's folk-music scene, including Dawn Greening and
Studs Terkel.

At the College of Complexes, a modest venue at 1651 North Wells Street in Old Town, Ella discovered the Chicago equivalent of the folk-bohemian venues she had enjoyed with Jo Mapes in San Francisco. The College took a freewheeling approach to higher learning; its founder, eclectic entrepreneur Slim Brundage, called it "a playground for people who think." On any given evening, a visitor could listen to orators tackling issues both serious (the atomic threat) and silly (whether Freud had an Oedipus complex), observe a hypnotist put a patron in a trance, take in a poetry reading, or hear live music—including folk, jazz, and Latin styles. In 1956 it welcomed dancer Robert Wells, a protégé of Jimmy Payne, presenting a program of "exciting Afro-Cuban and Afro-Primitive dance rhythms," per the *Defender*, which also noted, "The recital marks a revival at the College of Afro-Cuban dance entertainment."[17]

The eclecticism of the College attracted a left-leaning, interracial clientele who embraced amateur as well as professional performers, cultivating a convivial atmosphere. Ella went there for inspiration as well as entertainment. The College was where you went "to find out what was happening musically," Ella said. "People weren't trying to show off, they were just up there trying to do what they could do and share. . . . People were always there writing or had their tape recorders. Because it was informal. People who had been very shy about singing could get into it quite easily."[18]

All of these connections were vital for Ella, but Big Bill Broonzy stands out for his professional mentorship and friendship. It is possible that Ella encountered him as early as July 1952 when he began a weekly gig as part of the "I Come for to Sing" folk review at the Blue Note jazz club in the Loop. Emerging out of a concert series at the University of Chicago in 1947, "I Come for to Sing" featured Broonzy alongside the white folk musicians Win Stracke and Larry Lane, each man selecting songs relating to the evening's motif, which could range from travel to drinking to work. Presiding over it all was the garrulous radio personality Terkel, his commentary knitting a narrative that bridged the different song traditions and styles. While not overtly political, the format was effective in representing music as a blueprint of interracial and transnational solidarity. At the time, the spectacle of an integrated folk revue carried a particularly potent charge for liberal white audiences.[19]

Previously Ella knew Broonzy through his jump blues discs on the jukebox in her aunt and uncle's apartment. After they met, and Broonzy discovered his "little sister's" musical passions and aspirations, he became both friend and mentor, introducing her around Chicago with the protective devotion of a favorite uncle. In accompanying her to music venues, Broonzy opened doors for Ella, both literal and figurative. "He would take me around to a lot of clubs, and I didn't realize how well known he was, but every time we had to go and open the door, they said, 'Hi, Bill!'" Ella recalled.[20]

Broonzy was also Ella's conduit to Local 208, the Chicago union for Black musicians. He made her promise to save money to afford the dues, and when she had enough he met her at the union offices to make sure she received her card. At a moment when Ella was beginning to receive invitations to perform, he demystified the protocols of professional musicianship, explaining that being in the union expanded the number and type of venues she could play and conferred certain protections. Ella recalled her first union meeting, at the Old Forum Hall on the South Side, as "one of my most exciting experiences," because it was where she met pianist Lil Armstrong, Broonzy's friend and one of Ella's jazz idols. She was also delighted to realize that union membership linked her to Black opera singers and orchestral performers.

Ella looked to "Big Bill" as a professional model. His command of a broad repertoire allowed him to travel across a wide range of musical circles. On stage, he struck a dignified figure of Black manhood, dressing in dapper suits to emphasize his professionalism. And he remained unafraid in his outspokenness about racism. Ella's favorite Broonzy song was "Black, Brown and White Blues," as overt an indictment of white supremacy as 1950s folk audiences were likely to hear on a stage.

They says, "If you's white, be all right"
"If you was brown, stick around"
"But as you black, oh brother, get back, get back, get back."

Broonzy claimed to have found inspiration for the lyrics after standing in an employment line and being turned away, along with a Black woman, after all of the white job seekers were hired. Having lived through exactly such a scenario, Ella enjoyed the thrill of freedom that came from hearing her friend expressing the truth, out loud and for everyone to hear.[21] Together Ella and Bill managed to find humor in the fact that Chicago maintained separate Black and white musicians' unions. "How can you call it a union when it's segregated?" Ella would quip, and they would fall out laughing. The joke, sadly, never seemed to get old.

Two years into her stint at the Y, Ella was in a financial position to move from her McCormick Y residence to a studio unit in Midway Gardens, a new seventeen-story "elevator apartment" adjacent to Washington Park. Located in a liberal bastion of the city, at the intersection of the Hyde Park and Woodlawn neighborhoods, the apartment was a magnet for Black middle-class professionals on the South Side and offered an ambiance welcoming of interracial couples and openly gay people. One of Ella's neighbors, *Defender* columnist Marion Campfield, recorded the exhilaration she felt looking down at the park from her three-room unit on one of the building's upper floors: "'Tis grandest feeling to gaze over treetops after spending almost quarter of a century looking at back doors!"[22]

Ella also felt grand. The unit was small, but it had the advantage of an unusually large closet, which she used as a makeshift recording studio. From her tenth-floor perch, Ella could look out toward Hyde Park and the University of Chicago. Like San Francisco State, the university was home to a growing faction of students drawn to folk music and its associations with progressive politics. A group of them—mostly young white men—had formed a Folklore Society that brought in speakers and musicians, including Ella, who in late 1953 appeared as part of a "wing ding," or sing-along, playing conga and sharing some of the same Afro-Cuban–style songs and chants she was teaching to the Y

Teens.[23] Although the details of her performance are difficult to pin down, the fact that the Hyde Park crowd had caught wind of Ella's reputation as a "rhythm specialist" attests to her growing reputation outside the Y, as well as to white folk enthusiasts' interest in the vernacular Latin styles that drove popular dance recordings.

Ella's formal introduction to these university folk audiences came in the spring of 1954 when she appeared on the bill of a Mandel Hall fundraising concert headlined by Pete Seeger, a hero of young folk revivalists—and of Ella herself.[24] Her first Seeger concert, in 1947 or 1948, had left a deep impression, especially the part where Seeger demonstrated the rhythms of a work song by chopping wood from the stage. As she recalled,

> I got my ticket early because I wanted to sit up front in the first seat. One of the songs he was doing was a capella and he had an axe and was chopping wood in rhythm while he was singing; there was wood all over me that first row! I think I fell in love with this natural music, because I'd heard a lot of blues in my uncle's jukebox.[25]

The show Ella was remembering may well have been one of the Hootenannies sponsored by People's Songs, the activist folk organization, and presented by Seeger with some regularity in Chicago in the late 1940s, including at the McCormick YWCA in June of 1947. By 1954, however, Seeger was a politically chastened folk idol, his career largely confined to the stages of college campuses, schools, and summer camps due to McCarthyite political persecution, specifically his refusal to testify when called before the House Un-American Activities Committee. The Mandel Hall concert proved a welcoming venue, as it was sponsored by the World University Service, a peace organization, and the proceeds were to go to Kenwood-Ells Nursery School, which served Black and Japanese American children.

Despite the fact that Ella was not the evening's main event, the *Chicago Tribune* advertised the concert with a photograph of Ella under the title "Folk Singer" and a caption that described her as an "interpreter of Afro-Cuban and Caribbean folk chants."[26] Ella appears in a black turtleneck, her head thrown slightly back as she sings and plays a conga drum hanging from a neck strap. The advertisement demonstrated both the mutability of the *folk* designation and Ella's own professional mobility through musical forms that sutured the divide between "Latin" and "folk."

Appearing with Seeger assured Ella a packed house. Writing in the *Maroon*, the student newspaper, a reviewer voiced measured but respectful praise for Ella. "Although not singing strictly Afro-Cuban music," he wrote, "she was quite enjoyable, and her explanations greatly illuminated a field of folk music which is almost unknown in the U.S. Her voice had little to recommend it, but the rhythms and inflections with which she carried the melody more than made up for this."[27] Especially given the tepid assessment of a University Folklore Society quartet that also shared the bill—"they were very nervous and self-conscious, and at times out of tune," the reviewer observed—it was a recommendation of which Ella could be justifiably proud. It had only been three years since she had run into Armando Peraza on the streets of San Francisco. With no formal lessons, and with no one blazing the trail for her, she had not only invented herself as a rhythm specialist, but had comported herself in the role with grace before an audience of 700 people.

Ella's reputation on campus took off from there. The following year, she was hired to provide entertainment at a "Hayseed Hoedown," a fundraiser for the university chapter of the NAACP. "The renowned folk singer and instrumentalist is but one of the well-known personalities who will appear at the square dance," the *Maroon* noted.[28] The next time she appeared at Mandel Hall was as the opener for an "I Come for to Sing" program featuring Terkel alongside Gerry Armstrong, Fleming Brown, and Big Bill himself. Once again, the student newspaper received her warmly, the reviewer writing that while Ella could not match Broonzy's "personality," confidence, or professionalism, she "was a completely charming person who can really play that drum."[29]

Through this stage charisma and her growing repertoire, Ella became adept at entertaining a wide variety of Chicago audiences. And just as Ella had carried her Percussion Club and Latin Dance Club repertoires from the Black working-class space of the South Parkway Y to the mostly white and middle-class leaning spaces of the folk scene, so she also brought songs from folk concerts and informal gatherings to the Y Teens. By her third year at the Y, Ella was increasingly associating herself with an international folk repertoire. For 1956, the *Y-Teener* reported, the Percussion Club would "try Middle East rhythms, which would take in countries like Lebanon, Arabia, and Israel. We are also going to continue learning new African chants."[30] Ella kept up this momentum outside of the Y by offering other rhythm workshops that spanned cultures and continents, reflecting her absorption of different styles via recordings and radio. At one of these workshops at the South Side Community Center on Cottage Grove Avenue, she taught boys and girls to "use primitive drums, rattles, gongs and other percussion instruments" to develop their sense of rhythm and to "stimulate their interest in the cultures of people in other lands."[31]

Her modest success on Chicago stages emboldened Ella to dream about whether "rhythm specialist" could be her full-time job. At the Y she had gained valuable experience, but she was ready to move on and curious to discover where her connections could take her. By July 1956 Ella felt ready to make a go of it. Following the Soviet economic model that was in the news, she launched what she jokingly referred to as her own "five-year plan." She would still be a rhythm specialist, teaching workshops and classes in Afro-Caribbean percussion, but she would also identify herself as a folk musician "working in the area of new group-singing techniques," including one she now explicitly dubbed "call and response." Recalling this juncture in her life, she joked that "freelancer" was not a job title that would get you points on a credit card application. "Ella, what do you mean *freelance?*" someone at the time asked her. "Well, you know that's feast or famine," she responded.[32] She was about to find out which one was in store for her.

PART II

RHYTHM SPECIALIST

Dear Ella,

I want to thank you for coming to our school for a free concert. I was very amazed that it was you.

I thot that is was going to be some one boring but it was you Ella Jenkins! When I saw you my eyes got so big.

The songs thy you sing was some of the songs you toll us how to sing we new mostly all of them.

From,
Sheire

(SAN FRANCISCO, 1987)

5

GATE OF HORN, GATE OF IVORY

1956–1957

The summer that Ella launched herself as a full-time rhythm specialist coincided with the return to Chicago of her friend and mentor Big Bill Broonzy, who had spent the better part of 1956 on an extended tour of Europe and North Africa. Earlier in the year, he sent her an encouraging postcard from Brussels, composed in his familiar galloping style: "Hello my friend I'm ok say hello to all of the folk singers and you keep up the drumming will see you in May."[1]

Ella had, in fact, kept up her Afro-Caribbean rhythms in a new club that had become the epicenter of the Chicago folk scene. It was called the Gate of Horn—an obscure name drawn from a passage in the *Odyssey*, in which Odysseus's wife Penelope distinguishes true from false dreams. Unlike the false dreams that pass through the gate of ivory, true dreams—the ones that come to fulfillment—pass through the gate of horn.

The Gate was the brainchild of entrepreneurs Albert Grossman and Les Brown, former Roosevelt College classmates who sensed a market for a nightspot that would cater to the growing folk audience.

They had in mind a "basementy" place, neither a coffeehouse nor a supper club, comfortable but not too comfortable. Above all, it would be a "listening room," a place where the music was paramount.[2]

The space the two men found was indeed a basement—on the lower level of the Rice Hotel on North Dearborn. Patrons descended a few steps from street level and proceeded down a hallway. Inside, they found a space that held about a hundred people, with round tables and a small bar offering beer and snacks. Ambiance-wise, it was less scruffy than the College of Complexes but still informal enough to appeal to leftists who had come up in the era of People's Songs and the Almanac Singers. "It's one of the more comfortable cellars around town, attractively lit, tastefully furnished, and apparently bent on producing an atmosphere of quiet informality," observed the *Tribune*'s nightlife reporter. "You can actually hear, and the music is worth hearing."[3]

Ella took to the Gate immediately. "I was always in there," she recalled, "sitting down listening and taking in the new sounds."[4] At the Gate "new sounds" meant everything from blues and spirituals to French chansons and English sea shanties. Such ecumenicalism was counted a virtue among folk audiences; so, too, was a long attention span. The new teen music of 1956 came in brief bursts of frantic energy, with Elvis Presley's "Heartbreak Hotel," the year's top pop single, clocking in at just over two minutes. By contrast, at the Gate's informal Sunday afternoon hootenannies, a listener learned to sit patiently through English ballads that could last dozens of verses.

Ella insinuated herself into the Gate's lively musical world early on with the same determined optimism she brought to declaring herself a "rhythm specialist": one afternoon she simply showed up and introduced herself to Grossman, volunteering to set up for that evening's performance. She calculated that she might be "paid" in the form of a bratwurst and soda, allowing her to save her money and avoid searching the neighborhood for a bite. The Gate of Horn welcomed all comers, but upstairs at the Rice Hotel Black patrons were routinely turned away, and the same was likely to be true for other area establishments.

Grossman accepted Ella's offer—and, as expected, reciprocated with the bratwurst and an invitation to stay for the early show. Two years older than Ella, Grossman had earned an economics degree from Roosevelt and had briefly dabbled in construction and real estate before becoming a folk entrepreneur. His ambition was not simply to own a nightclub but to scope out up-and-coming acts and sell their music to the masses. Within five years of meeting Ella, Grossman would be one of the most powerful men in American folk music, managing Bob Dylan and forming Peter, Paul and Mary.[5]

Yet even if the Gate served Grossman's self-interest, it still created a genuine folk community. Like other folk clubs opening at the time—mostly on the coasts, but increasingly in cities between them—the Gate was a harbor of alternative music and political expression in an era defined by anticommunism, nationalism, and the rollback of the wartime gains of women and racial minorities. With a clientele that mixed Hyde Park intellectuals and aging blues fans, members of the Old Left and college students, suburbanites as well as city dwellers, women as well as men, the Gate became an important social and political contact zone.[6] Ella was particularly drawn to what she called the "overlap between folk music and civil rights," an intersection that could be heard in the musical activism of artists including Pete Seeger, Josh White, and Paul Robeson. Many of the white people she met at the venue were directly involved in civil rights activism, supporting efforts to integrate stores, restaurants, and schools.

More discouragingly, at the Gate Ella occasionally confronted the nonchalant racism of people who limited their commitment to integration to their cultural appreciation of Black music, claiming virtue through their receptivity to artists like Broonzy. She bristled when white patrons of the Gate casually mentioned the "Negro genius" for rhythm or spoke of the inherent "musicality" of Black folk. In 1951 Ella had voiced her anger at the stereotype in "Negroes Got Rhythm," a poem that combined the blues lyricism of Langston Hughes's "The Weary Blues" with the bitter satire of "Strange Fruit":

Have you ever seen a Negro
 Who couldn't dance or sing
 Or do some musical thing?
He's got rhythm in his blood!
That's what some white folks say.

But, as she would later say, she mostly felt a sense of belonging within the Gate's progressive interracial folk milieu. At the club and, beginning in 1957, at informal get-togethers at the home of Dawn Greening in suburban Oak Park, she was able to shed some of her insecurity as an "untrained" performer. Among people who revered folksong as a treasured archive of the of the "common man," she found validation for her investment in Black song as Black history. Her vivacity made it easy to make friends. Before long she was emceeing the Gate's Sunday afternoon hootenannies, drolly keeping the musical traffic moving and holding her drum at the ready in case of no-shows.

Ella never performed from the mainstage of the Gate of Horn, but she did play a variety of other Chicago venues in the mid- to late 1950s, allowing her to observe how the populist spirit of folk revivalism was expressed differently in different spaces. At primarily white clubs like the Compass, a Hyde Park bar, and the College of Complexes, the freewheeling North Side free-speech forum, she played conga dressed in a distinctly ungendered bohemian uniform of a dark turtleneck and slacks.[7] In primarily Black nightclubs, she might perform the same music costumed in a straw hat and vibrant prints, appealing to Black Chicagoans' interest in Caribbean folk traditions. The internationalist spirit of the emerging folk revival, which embraced cultural pluralism, was also present in Black Chicagoans' growing African diasporic political consciousness.

In 1956, the year the Gate of Horn opened, Harry Belafonte's popularity suggested that there was a market for someone like Ella, whose repertoire also drew from Afro-Caribbean sonic cultures, connecting the people and cultures of the Black diaspora to the US-based movement for civil rights. That summer, Belafonte's *Calypso* LP was a fixture on the *Billboard* charts, competing with Presley's records for cultural and commercial dominance. To many industry observers, the message of Belafonte's success was that a sufficiently charismatic Black male singer might deliver musical critiques of racism and imperialism and still be embraced by white audiences—indeed, might even attract them. For a while, in fact, it seemed that "calypso"—like "folk," a name given to a range of musical styles—might overtake rock and roll as America's favorite music.[8]

The calypso revolution never materialized. But the Belafonte phenomenon—and the related popularity of Eartha Kitt, who launched her career with Katherine Dunham's dance troupe—undoubtedly caused Grossman to take notice of Ella's relaxed effervescence and novelty as a Black female drummer. "Al liked me," Ella said. "He knew I could sing and dance and play percussion." One day Grossman took Ella aside and proposed to become her manager and make her a "star." He pitched a world of wealth and permissive luxury, speaking with cocky confidence. He said she would be a fool to turn him down.

Other musicians found Grossman intimidating. Bob Dylan remembered his "enormous presence" and voice that sounded like "war drums." Joan Baez recalled her terror before Grossman's promises: "You can have anything you want. You can have anybody you want."[9] But Ella had no difficulty in turning him down—as she would later turn down a similar offer from Chicago music producer Frank Fried. To Ella, Grossman's promises were like the dreams that passed through the gate of ivory: fantasy with no substance. Above all, Ella rejected his dream of music as a vehicle of wealth and power. For Grossman, Ella saw, folk was an instrument of self-enrichment. To her it was a conduit of creativity, racial pride, and political expression. Ella wanted to use African drums, which historically had been martial instruments, to critique war and reimagine oppressive gender norms, represented by players who felt they had to beat drums into submission. In the terms suggested by the contemporary drummer Terri Lyne Carrington, she wanted to show that as a percussionist, "you didn't need an aggressive sound to have a purpose."[10]

Grossman took Ella's on-the-spot rejection personally and lashed out. "He told me I would never make a dime in the music industry if I didn't work with him," Ella recalled. "He said I would be a failure." Grossman's cutting remarks only confirmed Ella's gut-level activist impulse as a musician. "There may be more money singing in clubs, but I am not as happy there as I am working with young people and children," she recalled. "I want to achieve something more than a club date."[11] Her reasoning was analogous to that of gospel singer and Chicago icon Mahalia Jackson, who in 1960 published "Why I Turned Down a Million Dollars," a piece explaining why she had repeatedly rejected lucrative offers to sing blues and jazz. "I'm not going to pretend that offers haven't excited and tempted me," Jackson wrote. "I simply want to point out that you can achieve success and financial independence and still keep your word to God in the face of temptation."[12] Jackson's words resonated with Ella. She had seen what chasing dreams of ivory did to other musicians. With a manager and a commercial career, she recalled, "You had to be in a certain place. Then they told you how you had to sing, what you had to sing. That didn't seem free."[13]

By refusing Grossman's offer, Ella also acted on a deep-rooted instinct for autonomy and safety rooted in her precarious childhood, her mother's respectability politics, Christian Science lessons about the virtues of thrift, and a desire for sexual and personal agency as a lesbian. At thirty-two, she wanted what Bernadelle called a "day life," not a night life, and recoiled at the idea of playing the role of the sexually desirable chanteuse. In future years Ella would express this self-protective instinct in her observation that children "don't think too much about race, weight, years. If you're kind to them and you know some songs and respect them as people, that's all they care about."[14]

In 1956 Ella might have been mindful of the example of her favorite singer, Billie Holiday. Ella met Holiday twice, first toward the end of her time in San Francisco. She and her friend Earline Ehrlich had gone to see Holiday and lingered after her set, nursing the ice cubes in their Cokes in the hopes of meeting their idol. When she finally did appear, Ella mustered the courage to call out, "Hello, Billie!" to which Holiday, miraculously, replied: "Oh, can I come and sit with you girls?" and proceeded to order them food and a second round of Cokes. Ella, who had heard that Holiday "liked girls," boldly gave her a peck on the cheek. When a photographer came by offering to snap their picture, Holiday chipped in for three copies, so they could all have a keepsake. Holiday inscribed the photo in a looping script: "For Ella: Stay Happy Always if Possible. Billie Holiday." The words "if possible" stood out to Ella. The singer looked so radiant that night and seemed in such high spirits.[15]

Ella had cause to revisit these words in Chicago. In April 1956 she saw Holiday perform at Budland, a jazz club in the basement of the Pershing Hotel. She arrived early, carrying a copy of *A Pictorial History of Jazz: People and Places from New Orleans to Modern Jazz*. It was a Christmas present from her brother Tom, and Ella had taken to using it to collect autographs. On a single evening that January, she had scored signatures from Duke Ellington and his bandmates Harry

FIGURE 5.1. Souvenir photo of Ella with Earline Ehrlich and Billie Holiday, 1951. Holiday signed it, "Be happy always. If possible."

Carney, Johnny Hodges, Ray Nance, and "Cat" Anderson. Now she hoped to add Holiday's signature.[16]

But when Ella sighted the singer going into the venue and approached her, asking for her autograph and reminding Holiday of their meeting five years earlier, Holiday hesitated. "She says, 'Let's go down to the light, 'cause I want to see what I'm signing,'" Ella said.[17] Ella got Holiday's signature, but the encounter haunted her. Lady Day had been cheated and swindled, including by people who claimed to love her. Ella wished she could have made things better for Holiday. But if she could not protect the singer, she might at least take care of herself.

Six months after the meeting with Holiday, Ella encountered another brilliant Black female entertainer. Odetta Felious was a trained singer who had grown up thinking she would perform opera and oratorio but turned to folk music after hearing a recording of Lead Belly singing "Take This Hammer." She was a high school friend of Jo Mapes, Ella's folk-singing friend from San Francisco, but to that point Ella had never heard of her—or heard her remarkable voice.

That changed one night when Ella was listening to *The Midnight Special*, a folk variety radio show on WFMT, in her Midway Gardens apartment. The deejay played a recording of "John Henry," the ballad about the legendary African American railroad worker who battled the modern steam drill. Ella knew the song well; everyone from Paul Robeson to Belafonte to Stan Wilson had recorded a version. But Ella was struck by how this new singer's "John Henry" put flesh and bone on the familiar icon.

When the deejay announced that the singer would soon be headlining at the Gate, Ella made a mental note. "I thought, this guy has such a beautiful voice," she recalled. "I've got to go down there and see him." Ella did not realize her error until she arrived at the Gate and discovered that the talented "guy" was a woman. Compared to other female folk singers she knew, Odetta was in a league of her own. Ella was struck by the image of a regal, Black woman who wore her hair in a style that revealed its natural texture. Her voice, like Holiday's, was unmistakable, with a deep timbre that perched ambiguously in a contralto register. Between numbers, Odetta was soft-spoken, but when she performed, her voice made the microphone redundant. She sang with dramatic flair but almost no vibrato, choosing songs that fearlessly expressed the full range of human emotion.

At the time, Odetta was on the cusp of national fame. Her debut LP, *Odetta & Larry* (1954), recorded at San Francisco's Tin Angel club, had drawn attention in folk circles. At New York's prestigious Blue Angel nightclub, she had comported herself admirably before the likes of Belafonte, Josh White, and Pete Seeger. But she had not yet appeared in Chicago. To play it safe, Grossman had booked her to open for local favorite Bob Gibson, but within a week he promoted her to the headlining spot.

Odetta's voice, along with the authority and seriousness of her stage persona, struck Chicagoans as new. She was a stark contrast to Gibson, an entertainer known for his upbeat energy and lighthearted stage presence. The *Tribune*'s nightlife columnist Will Leonard called Odetta the Gate's "biggest 'discovery' to date":

> With a voice as deep as a well and as big as a barn door, she intones tunes (almost invariably on the pessimistic side) that cover a broader range than the folk singer's norm. There are those who say she sounds like Mahalia Jackson, when it comes to a spiritual. There are those who say she sounds like a man, when it comes to a work song. What she sounds like, to these ears, is an artist with a fine, distinctive sense of style, and an almost uncanny feel for phrasing and projection.[18]

When Odetta first arrived in Chicago, Big Bill and Josh White had been there to greet her—"to make sure," as Odetta later put it, that "their little sister was going to get on ok."[19] After being transfixed by Odetta's performance at the Gate, Ella set herself on a similar mission. She found her way to the club's small backstage area and introduced herself, offering to help Odetta with anything she needed. Before they parted, she gave Odetta a piece of paper with her phone number.

When Odetta telephoned a few weeks later to tell Ella she was returning to the Gate of Horn in January 1957, on the heels of the release of *Odetta Sings Ballads and Blues*, Ella went to work. She enlisted a Hyde Park friend named Gloria Thomas to host a Sunday afternoon house concert for the singer, and got her Midway Gardens neighbor Marion Campfield to publicize it in her *Defender* column. The sober hour of the concert ensured Odetta an attentive audience. More than one hundred people crowded into Thomas's home, where they "stretched yogi-fashion at [Odetta's] feet as she conducted, song-wise, a historical and animated tour of the nation's folk songs." Big Bill and Studs Terkel were there, mingling with the rest of the crowd enjoying a post-concert lemonade.[20] Ella had charged five dollars a ticket, yielding a tidy sum for the singer.

Shortly after, Ella received a thank-you note from Odetta, along with an unexpected enclosure.

> It has worried me greatly the work you've put out with no compensa-tion that one could count and add to the bank account. Therefore this money order. If I handed it to you—you'd give me some excuse that I wouldn't be willing to take—the amount arrived at equals 20% of the concert + 5 records sold by you. You are now a full-fledged promoter. 20% is the usual. This doesn't count out much—consequently most promoters go broke.[21]

It was a generous letter, conveying sisterly insight into the music busi-ness as well as an unexpected payment. If Ella's April encounter with Holiday was a painful reminder of the vulnerability of Black female entertainers to exploitation and abuse, Odetta's lesson was that Black women could thrive through networks of mutual care and support.

Ella and Odetta became lifetime friends. In Ella's folk scrapbook she gave the singer pride of place, right after Broonzy. Over the years she accumulated concert programs and clippings, photographs and personal cards. On one page, under a striking photograph of Odetta in profile wearing bold hoop earrings, Ella penned her enthusiasm in thick red marker: *"An amazing Artist! An amazing Personality! An amazing Woman!"*[22]

Buoyed by Odetta's example, Ella entered a tremendously productive period between late 1956 and early 1957. She presided over Sunday hootenannies at the Gate; sang calypso songs for the Faculty Wives Association of the Chicago Medical School; appeared at an "Evening of Modern Dance Expressions" at the Phillips Auditorium; entertained at the Spring Benefit Party of the South Center YWCA and for the Young Adults group of the Wabash Avenue YMCA; and demonstrated her skills as a percussionist at events sponsored by the South Side Boys Club, the Northside NAACP Youth Council, and Washington Park's annual "Negro History Week" celebration.

To supplement her income, Ella began offering Saturday afternoon rhythm workshops for the children of Midway Gardens, including Richard and Buzz Powell, the sons of elementary school teacher Eliza Powell. Richard, who would become an eminent art historian, remembered these workshops, which included chain-gang and work songs, as a gateway into African American history through folk music. And Ella herself left a deep impression. Her apartment, with its enticing collection of books, record albums, drums and other instruments, suggested that a "creative life" was possible for South Side boys like him. Even Ella's mode of dress—her pierced ears and peasant skirts—suggested alternatives to the images of Black success that appeared in Black print media.[23]

A color photograph taken around this time (perhaps by her friend Jo Banks) portrays Ella as Richard might have seen her. It shows her at home, posing with a collection of drums and playing a conga as she gazes upward at a poster depicting an African man's upturned face. The poster is an advertisement for the Belgian airline Sabena, then connecting Brussels to Belgian Congo. On its own, the Sabena poster is an unabashedly colonial image, showing a "primitive" Black man looking up at a modern jet airplane as though it were a mechanical god. But in the photograph the poster seems to imagine a sonic dialogue between Black America and Africa, diaspora and "homeland." At the center of this dialogue is Ella, elegant and contemplative, playing rhythms that connect her to the Continent.

The image is remarkable for picturing Ella's embrace of a diasporic sonic culture that rejected the division between Africa and African America, placing the US civil rights movement within an international frame. As historian Lonnie Bunch observed, while other Black American intellectuals in the 1950s and 1960s debated whether to focus their attention on the United States or on Africa, Ella "didn't engage that tension." Bunch said, "She grasped it all. She didn't feel she had to make a choice." To say that Black children in the 1950s needed to understand Africa was "very powerful and important," he continued. By using music to promote a consciousness of diaspora among young people, Ella not only conveyed the significance of their African ancestry, but assured Black children that their communities were not alone in their struggles for liberation from white supremacy.[24]

At the same time, and in the pluralist spirit of the folk revival, Ella wanted to catalyze Black children's curiosity about the rhythms of others. Ella had lived this musical dialectic in her formative years in the Bay Area, learning Jewish songs at the Emanu-El residence and Anglo-American folk songs at North Beach clubs, even as she was discovering herself in Afro-Cuban rhythms. "Life has given us lots of variety," she would say, and variety was to be embraced, not feared. In Chicago she spent hours in record-store listening booths, "traveling the world" through collections of folk music from Asia, Africa, and the Middle East. She consulted songbooks, from *English and Scottish Popular Ballads*, a standard source of British folk heritage, to American titles

FIGURE 5.2. Ella at Midway Gardens in front of Sabena poster.
Unknown photographer.

including Carl Sandburg's *The American Songbag* (1927) and *The New Song Fest* (1955), a collection published by the Intercollegiate Outing Club Association. She underlined passages in the long introduction to

The Book of American Negro Spirituals, James Weldon Johnson's landmark 1925 collection—especially those that spoke of the spirituals' "striking rhythmic quality," their African derivation, and their design for "group singing."[25]

Ella found the most resonant echoes of her inchoate ideas in Langston Hughes's *The First Book of Rhythms* (1954), a volume for middle-grade readers published at a time when McCarthyist political persecution threatened to derail the writer's career. The idea for the book grew from Hughes's 1948 residency at the University of Chicago Lab School. (Ella was in California when Hughes lived in Hyde Park, but Tom befriended him and carried on a years-long correspondence.) Vividly illustrated with ink-and-pen drawings, it explored rhythms both natural and human-made, from the rising and setting of the sun to the ingenious rhythmic practices of people at work and play. *The First Book of Rhythms* was ostensibly apolitical, but Hughes's investigation of the universality of rhythm led him to conclusions that cut against both Cold War–era nationalism and segregationist claims of Negro inferiority. It never mentioned race, and yet was pointedly inclusive, containing references to ancient African drumming, African American musical folkways, and contemporary jazz music.

Ella went through her copy of *The First Book of Rhythms* with a red pencil, her implement of choice for annotating important texts. She drew asterisks next to a passage where Hughes observed the relationship between rhythm and physical labor, a lesson of the work songs she often used in her workshops. "Rhythm makes it easier to use energy," he wrote. "Even sweeping a rug or raking a lawn is done better if the broom or rake is handled with a steady rhythmical motion." Where Hughes observed that "Rhythms go around the world, adopted and molded by other countries, mixing with other rhythms, and creating new rhythms as they travel," she wrote "like folk music" in the margins. Hughes's discussion of the drumbeat as a technology of unity—whether for waging war or for dancing—also caught her attention.[26]

Ella's discovery of *The First Book of Rhythms* led her to *The Rhythms of the World*, a 1955 album based on the book. Issued by Folkways, the source of many of the ethnographic recordings Ella was consulting at the time, it consisted of Hughes's spoken narration alongside snippets of field recordings from the Folkways catalog: the sounds of a child walking, the thumping of the human heart, the bleats and chirps of animals, and the organized sounds of music.[27] Anticipating Ella's later work, the album included a version of the children's chant "Miss Mary Mack" (from the Folkways album *Ring Games from Alabama*) and the sounds of ocean waves (from *Pacific Ocean: The Sounds of the Sea*). It also sampled sounds from albums Ella had likely studied, including *Haitian Chant: Drums of Haiti* and *Yoruba Dancing Rhythms: Drums of the Yoruba*. Lead Belly's "Julian Johnson" (sometimes "Julie Ann Johnson") illustrated the rhythms of work songs, and Sonny Terry, a favorite harmonica player of Ella's, showed how rhythms could made with everyday objects such as sticks and washboards. Like *The First Book of Rhythms*, Hughes's album conveyed a subtle yet distinct political critique. "Broken rhythms can be unproductive, unpleasant, startling or even harmful," Hughes narrated. "It is the same with men and women, and races and nations. When the rhythms of happy harmonious living are broken by quarrels or fights, wars or riots or disasters, people's hearts do not beat right, and their minds are worried, and their songs are troubled, and sometimes they cry."[28]

Hughes's work validated Ella's own developing notions of rhythm as a universal principle of human cooperation. "All the rhythms of life in some way are related," Hughes had said on *The Rhythms of the World*. "You, your baseball, and the universe are brothers through rhythms." Ella evoked a similar idea of rhythmic "brotherhood" in description of her rhythm workshops for boys from the South Side Community Committee, an organization for Bronzeville youth deemed at risk for "delinquency." In a caption she wrote to accompany a photograph of herself and six boys that appeared in the December 8, 1956, *Defender*, she articulated ideas that would serve as the ballasts of her musical practice for the next sixty years:

> The Workshop consists of experiments in various rhythms, chants and folk songs from around the world. They [the participants] learn to use primitive drums, rattles, gongs, and other percussion instruments. The purpose is to assist boys and girls in developing a better sense and use of rhythm, to stimulate their interest in the cultures of peoples in other lands and to provide an opportunity for creative expression. Under the direction of Miss Ella L. Jenkins, a specialist in Latin-American percussion instruments, the group is fast learning the values in producing musical harmony with others.[29]

Whereas her description emphasizes her facilitation of others' musicality rather than her own talent, Ella had begun to think seriously about recording her own album. She reasoned that an album would give her ideas wider reach and burnish her professional identity, perhaps even supplementing the modest income she was drawing from her rhythm workshops. But Ella had no models for the record she wanted to make. She knew only that she had worked out a method for using rhythm to bring people together and wanted to share it.

"Ella was making her own way," said her lawyer Linda Mensch of this period. "When I say 'her own way' I mean *her own way*. She was creating a path that nobody had made before."[30] The path led through the Gate of Horn and eventually to a boundary-breaking, multidecade performing and recording career. But first, she would need to meet Moses "Moe" Asch, the head of the Folkways record label.

I thank the P.T.A. for having Ella Jenkins come and sing for us. She had a beautiful voice. . . . Myself and everyone else had fun singing with her. Ella Jenkins wherever you are, I hope you come and sing for us again.

Louisa

(CHICAGO, 1970)

6
CALL AND RESPONSE
1956–1958

One night at the Gate of Horn, not long after Ella declined Albert Grossman's offer, she told her friend, record producer Kenneth Goldstein, that she wanted to record an album based on her rhythm workshops. Then working with jazz and blues musicians, Goldstein was not the man for the job, but he knew someone who might be: Moses "Moe" Asch, owner of the New York–based Folkways label. Goldstein suggested that Ella make a demo recording with three or four songs and a strong title—something that would "represent" her. He told her to bring it to the Folkways offices the next time she was in New York. No appointment was necessary, he said, because Moe was always there.[1]

Following Goldstein's advice, Ella booked studio time and recorded an acetate demo of four songs consisting of her vocals and conga accompaniment. She titled it "Call-and-Response Rhythmic Group Singing." It was not a phrase that rolled off the tongue, but it was Ella's precise summation of a methodology that drew from her Bronzeville girlhood, her San Francisco experiences of Jewish and Afro-Cuban music, and her immersion in the Chicago folk scene.

At its core was *group singing*, an activity that set music in a social context. *Call and response*, meanwhile, referenced an important form of African and Afro-diasporic music. And in the title's middle was a gesture toward Ella's specialization in all things *rhythmic*. Together, these terms described a *practice*, but said nothing of any specific style, genre, or audience. In focusing on a method rather than a sound, Ella's title proved both flexible and prescient. "Call-and-Response Rhythmic Group Singing" would embody her values as a recording artist for the next six decades, even as her repertoire, audiences, and approach to composition and performance changed.

Ella brought the demo to New York, taking care on the journey not to jostle the fragile disc. The address of the Folkways office, 117 West Forty-Sixth Street, was listed on every recording put out by the label, and as she walked there, Ella quelled her nervousness with positive thinking. Goldstein had said that Asch would appreciate her songs and chants. In her head she rehearsed what she would say when she met him.

Ella's mental discipline as she walked to the Folkways office was rewarded by a small miracle: there, on the very same street in the middle of Manhattan, was her friend Odetta. The two women greeted each other and spoke briefly. Odetta was busy with an album intended to build on the sales momentum generated by *Odetta Sings Ballads and Blues*. Although recorded in New York City, it was to be titled *Live from the Gate of Horn* at the insistence of her new manager, Albert Grossman. Ella showed Odetta her red demo disc, explaining that she was on her way to present the record at Folkways. In response, Odetta offered her friend a sisterly bit of advice: "If you're going to see Moe Asch, don't forget to ask about royalties."[2]

It was not the first time Ella had thought about the legal and financial details of a record deal. Schooled by Brother John Sellers and Big Bill Broonzy, she knew of hungry musicians who had negotiated with record-label owners for Cadillacs over royalties, allured by shiny emblems of success. But Ella had her eye on the long game, not the quick payoff. She had not forgotten the message of Odetta's earlier thank-you note: artistic labors, like all labors, deserved compensation.

She arrived at Folkways with Odetta's words still ringing in her ears. "So with my disc in my hand and thinking about royalties, I climbed up the stairs to Folkways' small offices," she recalled.[3] As Goldstein had predicted, Asch was there. With bushy eyebrows and a salt-and-pepper mustache, he had the slightly disheveled look of someone who spent most of his waking hours tinkering with audio equipment. In fact, Asch was something of a maverick in his family of highly intellectual Russian Jewish immigrants. As a young man, he had flouted the expectations of his father, acclaimed Yiddish writer Sholem Asch, to pursue studies in radio engineering, which the elder Asch considered a "trade" rather than a proper profession. In 1941 he fell into sound recording as a side hustle, founding Asch Records to supplement his main business installing public address systems. A couple of rough starts later, in 1948, he cofounded Folkways with his secretary, Marian Distler. By the time Ella arrived at Asch's doorstep, the label had already moved to the center of the incipient folk revival.

Their meeting was another touchstone in Ella's career, on par with both her discovery of Afro-Cuban rhythms and her decision to pursue a "day life" rather than a night life. The surroundings, however, failed to meet the occasion. Ella had imagined that the vaunted Folkways label would have a more impressive setup. For a man with a grandiose ambition to create an "encyclopedia of sound," Asch's office was contrastingly meager: a front room with a small desk and files, and a small studio and control booth beyond that.[4]

After Ella gave Asch her pitch, he took her acetate into the control booth. "I could see him in there, moving around and playing the disc," Ella recalled. "It seemed like he was in there a long time. Finally, he came out with the tape and said, 'You have something very promising here. Why don't you go back and record some more songs, then send me the tape and we can put it out as a record.'"[5] Because they were templates for improvisation rather than definitive performances, Ella's songs were short, so Asch floated the idea of a ten-inch extended-play (EP) recording, rather than a twelve-inch LP. He liked her conga playing, but recommended adding instrumentation beyond the one drum, to give the album more texture and variety. "But in the meantime," he concluded, "let's sign a contract."[6]

Asch took out a "standard contract," Ella recalled, with boilerplate language about the rights and duties of both parties. It covered three years and was non-exclusive, giving her the option of recording with other labels. Ella then made her request for royalties, and in response, Asch amended the contract to state that she would earn twenty-five cents on every album sold, to be paid out in semi-annual installments.[7]

In signing the contract, Ella entered into a professional and financial relationship with Asch that was unique in the history of Folkways.[8] Even Guthrie and Seeger, the label's gold-standard artists, relied on Asch's sporadic and irregular payments rather than regular checks based on a legal agreement for "mechanical" royalties, the assessable profits from record sales. But Ella had met the Folkways founder at a fortuitous time, when he was looking to build the label's children's catalog. And Asch was uniquely primed to understand the value of the spare call-and-response songs on Ella's demo disc.

Asch's interest in children's music went back to the early 1940s, when he released Lead Belly's *Play Parties in Song and Dance* on the short-lived Asch Records. That interest had solidified alongside Asch's disdain for the postwar consumer market for commercial "kidisks," which was dominated by Walt Disney Company fare and by popular Decca artists such as Danny Kaye and Burl Ives.[9] To Asch's ears, such recordings suffered from a patronizing false cheer that was mirrored in over-lavish production. He imagined Folkways as a home of "quality" children's recordings, defined by their simplicity and authenticity. Rather than treating children's music as an onramp to appreciation of the European classical repertoire (as in Kaye's popular voicings of "Tubby the Tuba"), they would appeal to young listeners' natural creativity and their predilection to learn through movement and play. And they would resist both the ersatz Americana of Disney's Davy Crockett and the racial regressivism of RCA Victor's *Little Black Sambo* (1955), conveying progressive values of pluralism, collectivism, and racial equality.[10]

By the time Ella signed with Asch, he had made significant progress in realizing this vision. Under the guidance of music educators
Beatrice Landeck and Charity Bailey, Folkways had released several
albums in a "Songs to Grow On" series, including two recordings of
original children's material by Woody Guthrie, and spirited children's
folksong anthologies that presented music on the themes of "American
Work Songs" and "School Days." In addition to Lead Belly's *Play Parties* album and Pete Seeger's *American Folk Songs for Children*, Folkways
produced spoken-word albums with Langston Hughes and writer Arna
Bontemps, including a Black poetry anthology and the *First Book of
Rhythms* album Ella had studied. It had published field recordings of
children's musical play in Indonesia and Africa, on Indian reservations
and in New York City streets.

As significant as many of these recordings were, they made up
a small percentage of Folkways' sales. By the time Ella stopped by,
Asch had begun to further develop an educational market for Folkways
releases. At the annual meetings of professional organizations such
as the American Library Association, he reached out to librarians,
classroom educators, and museum professionals, seeing them as a
"durable customer base." He pitched Folkways recordings as teaching tools of particular importance in an era of intensifying political
repression, when teachers could be fired from veering from Cold War
scripts. In "The Recording as Teaching Tool: A Bulletin for Parents
and Teachers," a 1955 pamphlet, he presented essays touting the ped-
agogical value of recorded sound as both supplement and corrective
to whitewashed textbooks.[11]

If Asch was willing to pay Ella royalties, it was because he recognized her as capable of carrying forward his aesthetic, political,
and business interests in children's music. Where Grossman acutely
misunderstood Ella's aspirations and ambitions, Asch recognized the
genius of Ella's "call-and-response rhythmic group singing." Where
the club owner promised her vague riches from a commercial path,
Asch promised her concrete royalties from new educational mar-
kets that connected musicians with teachers and librarians. And

where Grossman would control things like album titles (as he did with Odetta), Asch offered her final say over all creative aspects of her recordings, from the order of songs to cover art and liner notes.

In bringing her demo to Asch, Ella initiated a relationship of mutual benefit. Asch would give her artistic latitude, and she would produce recordings he could use to advance Folkways. He would give her a home for her career, and she would provide him with a revenue stream. Their virtuous cycle would last for nearly half a century.

Ella's agreement with Asch did not provide an advance to cover the fees of recording, which explains how Ella came to record the ten tracks of *Call-and-Response Rhythmic Group Singing* at the Howalton Day School, a private institution serving African American children, where she had connections and could be assured of access to a group of young performers and rudimentary recording equipment. For several weeks leading up to the taping of her album, she conducted a rhythm workshop with middle-grade students, aged eight to thirteen, teaching them songs and chants and offering instruction on maracas, wood blocks, tambourines, and claves. In preparation, she also listened to the 1953 children's album *Music Time with Charity Bailey*, which Asch sent to her as a point of reference. A Juilliard-trained pianist, Bailey headed the music department at the Little Red School House, the progressive Greenwich Village school that Moe Asch's son Michael attended. She was the first Black woman in the United States to receive certification in the Dalcroze method of early childhood musical instruction, which focused on movement and kinesthetic awareness. She had even hosted an educational children's program on New York public television.[12]

Despite admiring Bailey and her methods, Ella saw her own project as quite distinct. Bailey approached *Music Time* as a trained musician and classroom teacher; even the title of her album hinted at the organized division of the school day. And like most music educators of the time, she focused on the teaching of songs, assuming piano as the primary instrument. As a "good blues child," Ella was less interested in developing children's musicality, defined in Eurocentric terms. The title of Ella's acetate had omitted the word *music*, just as it omitted the sonorities of piano, the quintessential classroom instrument, and even the guitar, the quintessential folk instrument.

On the master tape Ella eventually sent to Asch, likely in early 1957, the only substantive "instructional" content comes at the beginning, as Ella concisely explains the "rules" of call-and-response rhythmic group singing. In a voice that is notably calm and free of overly cultivated diction or extravagant shifts in pitch, she explains:

> Many of you, I'm sure, have played the game "Follow the Leader." Well, you can play the same kind of game in song and sound. Here's how we play it. I simply sing or speak a line to you and you sing or speak it back to me, unless I instruct you to do something different. If I make a funny sound, you make one also. Sometimes, I may sing softly, sometimes loudly, sometimes fast sometimes slow. Whatever I do, you must follow. Remember, now, it's awfully important to listen.[13]

The ten tracks that follow are brief, totaling less than thirteen minutes. But in that short amount of time, they take the listener on a sonic journey akin to Ella's travels in the record-store listening booths. "Tahboo" and "Zeembah," the opening tracks, model West African–style chants through made-up vocalizations set to simple conga patterns. Then, "Moon Don't Go" and "Toom-Bah-Ee-Lero," each presented in both an a cappella and instrumental version, explore the rhythms of the African diaspora in the American South and Cuba ("Toom-Bah-Ee-Lero" approximates *tamborilero*, or drummer). The last four tracks—side B of the EP—display the cultural and geographic diversity of rhythmic chanting. Their titles are descriptive but not specific: "A Chant from West Africa," "A Love Chant from North Africa," "An American Chain Gang Chant," and "An Arabic Chant That Means Welcome" (the Muslim call to prayer). All but "An American Chain Gang Chant" are led by the Howalton schoolchildren, who, having practiced the role of followers in the game, now take their turns as leaders.

"Tah-boo" was Ella's oldest composition, dating back to Camp Reinberg. It was also a staple of her Chicago rhythm workshops, serving as a concise distillation of her theory of call-and-response rhythmic group singing in relation to the musical cultures of the African diaspora. On the album version, Ella introduces the tempo by tapping out a couple of measures of a simple pattern on the conga. She then leads the Howalton children through a call-and-response game based on her own made-up words, which she transcribed with precision in the album's liner notes:

> LEADER: Tahboo—oo—oo
> GROUP: Tahboo—oo—oo
> LEADER: Ee pah—ah—ah
> GROUP: Ee pah—ah—ah
> LEADER: Ee wahtah wahtah wahtah yeagah
>   (yea rhythms with say)
> GROUP: Ee wahtah wahtah wahtah yeagah
> LEADER: Bochoo—oo—oo
> GROUP: Bochoo—oo—oo
> LEADER: Ee pah—ah—ah
> GROUP: Ee pah—ah—ah
> LEADER: Ee changah changah changah yeagah
> GROUP: Ee changah changah changah yeagah[14]

After a first go-round, Ella leads the children through a variation in which the word-sounds are spoken rather than chanted. In a third repetition, she reverts to chanting but introduces several novel variations, challenging the children to pay close attention to shifts in tempo and volume. The song fades out, with increasingly soft repetitions of the closing phrase, "Boom boom boom boom hey," syllables evoking the opening sounds of the conga.

The use of made-up words is a central feature of "Tah-boo," reflecting Ella's wish to put her audience at ease. She had found that when she told the teens at her Y clubs and in her rhythm workshops that they were learning a song in a foreign language, they worried about sounding funny or pronouncing words incorrectly. By composing in made-up sounds—in this case, by evoking a "foreign" language without specifically representing one—Ella freed adolescents to be more fully alert to the pleasures of call and response. Instead of experiencing fear or anxiety over issues of pronunciation or recall, they could concentrate on opening their mouths wide to make the "Tah" sound and pushing the air through their puckered lips to make the "boo." If she vocalized "ee pah" in a staccato fashion, they could focus on making the staccato sound. As Ella observed, "The song or chant's very pattern causes the group to be attentive, to wonder what is to come next, and be willing to cooperate with the leader."[15]

"Tah-boo," a chant without linguistic content, could thus become meaningful for what it *did*, not what it *said*. It could introduce listeners to practices of call-and-response rhythmic group singing without purporting to "teach" them anything. It could immerse them in musical concepts without the baggage attached to "music" as a technical, specialized art form separate from everyday life. It could lead them to realize the value of cooperation without preaching to them about right and wrong. Through the rituals of its musical "game," it could model and amplify the elemental human need to speak and be heard in the company of another.

Although Ella had developed her use of made-up words as a helpful teaching tool, through songs like "Tah-boo" she risked reinforcing 1950s misperceptions of Africa as an undifferentiated "Dark Continent." Yet Ella justified her subordination of the details of specific African languages and musical styles to her goal of encouraging 1950s Black American youth to feel pride in African heritage, however inchoate their understanding. In this sense her album was part of a tradition of cultural consciousness-raising around Africa for Black American children going back to *The Brownies' Book*, an NAACP-affiliated children's magazine that debuted in 1919. It was a cultural expression of "diasporic consciousness": a means of connecting Black youth to ideas of Africa through notions of musical continuity as well as distinctiveness.[16]

Listeners at the time seem not to have been put off by Ella's approach. Journalist Era Bell Thompson was a major Black disseminator of knowledge about Africa in the 1950s through her reporting in *Ebony* magazine. She had just returned from a trailblazing tour of the Continent in 1953 when she attended a performance by Ella's Y-Teen Percussion Club that likely included the song "Tah-boo." She responded with a letter of support, praising Ella's "exciting teen-age Afro Cuban group" as "real gone" and enclosing a $25 check for the purchase of instruments.[17] In a different but complementary fashion, Chicago's *Liberalist* magazine viewed songs like "Tah-boo" through the lens of Cold War liberalism, in which intercultural understanding was a bulwark against nationalism and militarism. "Because some people are inhibited about singing, and yet because people get great joy out of singing together," it wrote, "Ella Jenkins began making up sounds to imply the moods of the music of Latin America and other countries."[18]

There is also evidence that in making *Call-and-Response Rhythmic Group Singing*, Ella was far less worried about "appropriating" Africa than about combating racial stereotypes of Africans and African-descended peoples as "naturally" rhythmic. Anticipating these misconceptions, which were at the heart of the late 1950s backlash to rock and roll as racially and sexually dangerous "jungle" music, she appealed strategically to the formal similarities of distinct musical traditions. As she explained in her liner notes, although "call-and-response" patterns dominated the "songs and chants of West Africa" and the "cult music of Cuba," they could be "found in songs of India, Greece, North Africa, and the Middle East" and were "common in churches and synagogues."[19] While her recourse to the universal obscured the significance of call and response as "the most fundamental principle of African form," in the words of scholar Kofi Agawu, it also set African music on a par with other music, including sacred forms in the United States. She used "sameness" to promote African peoples as no less valuable than those Americans who performed in a call-and-response style in the course of their weekly worship.[20]

Whereas the A side of *Call-and-Response Rhythmic Group Singing* introduces listeners to songs and chants whose meaning is inherent in the *form* of call and response, in the second half of her album Ella introduces music that derives meaning from its contents, particularly in the case of "An American Chain Gang Chant." It was Ella's version of "Another Man Done Gone," the chain-gang song that she had seen Odetta perform many times. At the Gate of Horn, Odetta would put her guitar aside and sing it a cappella, using hand claps to dramatize the sounds of an overseer's whip.[21] She discussed the song on Studs Terkel's radio talk show, explaining the history of the chain-gang as a post-Emancipation technique of extracting labor from African Americans at what were euphemistically called prison farms. And yet as the singer and her audiences understood, lines like "they killed another man," had resonances in the present, when white policemen could murder Black Chicago teenagers with impunity.

Ella had personal reasons for including her own arrangement of "Another Man Done Gone" on her debut recording. During her 1957 tour with Jimmy Payne's dance troupe, which visited the campuses of several Southern Black colleges, Ella had seen Black men in leg-irons for the first time. The spectacle was deeply shocking, making real something she had to that point only imagined. It brought home to Ella the reasons her parents and other family members had left the South behind.[22]

In her liner notes, Ella referred to "Another Man Done Gone" as "an old folk song from the South, from chain gang life," avoiding any reference to her own experience. "A chain gang is a group of prisoners who eat, work, and sleep chained together," she explained. "From time to time a man escapes the burdens of this life by escaping the chain

gang. The men left behind sing about 'Another Man Done Gone.'"
Yet while her description carefully avoided any mention of violence,
the song as Ella and the Howalton children perform it does not shy
away from its depiction of murder. It also follows Odetta's version by
substituting "He killed another man" with "They shot another man,"
a line that situated the chain gang within larger systems of state violence against Black men. Ella later varied the phrase to "They killed
another man" as though to dispel any ambiguity about the fate of the
injured party.[23]

Because Ella recorded it with middle schoolers, her arrangement
of "Another Man Done Gone" also ends on a note of relative hope.
Sleigh bells and tambourines represent the metallic sound of chains
while also sonically evoking jubilee. An opening and closing stanza
frame the story as one of liberation, picturing the escapee as he dis-
appears from sight:

> There he goes
> Way across the field
> They'll *never* catch him
> He's gone

Before he recorded *Play Parties in Song and Dance*, Lead Belly had
spent nearly twenty years on chain gangs in Texas and Louisiana.[24]
Precisely because it cut too close to the truth of his experience, and
because that experience had been exploited to serve Americans'
fantasies of Black male criminality, he could not have performed
"Another Man Done Gone" on his 1941 recording for children. But
more than fifteen years later, as the nonviolent civil rights movement
was asserting its strength, Ella could and did, passing on a chant that
conveyed both the history of African American bondage and the history of African American flight toward freedom. In 1957 these were
histories that even progressive teachers were not always at liberty to
share with their students. But following through on Asch's ideal of
children's recordings as teaching tools, Ella's "American Chain Gang

Chant" set forward a powerful lesson in Black history that projected hope for a liberated future.

The cover photograph Ella chose for *Call-and-Response Rhythmic Group Singing*, taken by her artist-friend Jo Banks, was similarly hopeful, showing Ella encircled by several Howalton middle schoolers as they sing and play instruments together. The image is closely cropped, giving it an air of immediacy and intimacy, and snapped from below, directing the viewer's gaze up at Ella as she sings with eyes closed and chin uptilted.

This image is analogous to the cover of Bailey's *Music Time* EP, which pictures her with two white preschoolers, but with differences

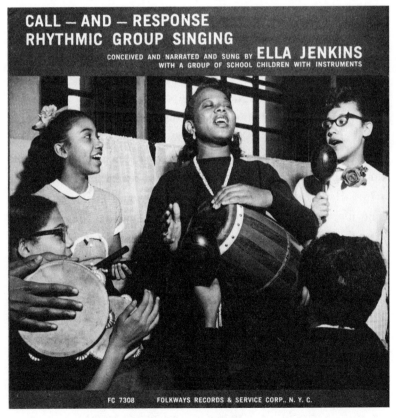

FIGURE 6.1. Cover of *Call-and-Response Rhythmic Group Singing* EP, 1957. Courtesy of Smithsonian Folkway Recordings.

that speak to the uniqueness of Ella's project. Bailey's album cover evokes the hierarchies of the music classroom, as the two little boys inspect a small guitar she is holding. Behind them, a piano—the "teacher's" instrument—is off-limits. In contrast, *Call-and-Response Rhythmic Group Singing* presents the hands-on nature of Ella's participatory method, as both adult and child tap, pat, shake, and strike their instruments. Additionally, Banks's photograph conveys a politically resonant message of pride consistent with the burgeoning civil rights movement's spirit of moral uprightness. If the cover of Bailey's EP telegraphs a politics of integration, the image of Ella with Howalton middle-graders suggests possibilities of Black collective self-definition that go beyond desires for inclusion and acceptance. In particular, it conveys the compatibility of middle-class Black children's simultaneous identification with Africa and America: the idea that they could simultaneously embrace "blackness" *and* US national belonging.[25]

Call-and-Response Rhythmic Group Singing reflected and anticipated the importance of music to the contemporary civil rights movement. Only a month or so before Folkways released Ella's album, her friend Pete Seeger introduced "We Shall Overcome" to Martin Luther King, at the twenty-fifth anniversary of the Highlander Folk School, an important training center for civil rights activists. "There's something about that song that haunts you," King was said to have mused about the repurposed pro-labor tune (and before that, a gospel song) that would become synonymous with Black activism in the 1950s and 1960s.

Ella, who had fallen under the spell of Armando Peraza's Afro-Cuban rhythms, understood well music's capacity to transport and transform listeners, especially when it was experienced in collective settings. She knew that the mastery of simple songs like "Tah-boo" could foster confidence and pride in children, just as movement anthems like "We Shall Overcome" could imbue singers with courage. In ways she could not then have realized, her music was preparing children for a future in which James Brown would declare "Say it loud—I'm black and I'm proud!" and Nina Simone would exalt the wonder of being "Young, Gifted, and Black."

As she waited for the EP to arrive, Ella corresponded periodically with Asch, her letters toggling between polite inquiry about process and more assertive requests for resources to market and publicize her work. When he came to Chicago on a business trip, she stopped by the Palmer House hotel to pitch him on the idea of buying bulk copies of her EP on credit so that she could market it directly to consumers. In August 1957 she wrote to him of "approaching schools, social agencies, and camp groups, as well as personal friends." In September she reached out again to tell him about her efforts to publicize the EP. "I've been selling a lot of people, organizations, institutions, etc. on the album and I have a feeling that it will sell with the kind of publicity, promotion, etc. I've been working on," she wrote.[26]

Asch agreed to Ella's request to buy copies of her album direct from Folkways' Midwestern distributor, the Chicago-based firm K. O. Asher. The arrangement was advantageous to both parties, but perhaps especially to Ella. She had realized that for *Call-and-Response Rhythmic Group Singing* to succeed, she would need to be able to sell it to attendees of her programs and workshops, not just refer them to the Folkways catalog or rely on the very few specialty outlets that carried Folkways products. (Record stores at the time did not stock children's music as a specific category.) Ella correctly reasoned that she would not only sell more records by avoiding intermediaries, but that through a direct-to-consumer strategy she would also earn more money, while keeping a close eye on matters of accounting.

Ella ordered fifty copies of the EP, as well as an additional twenty-five copies of the accompanying liner notes, to sell at a celebratory "autograph party" at the home of a Hyde Park friend, Jacky Lewbin, on November 17. Her brother Tom invited Langston Hughes, knowing that his appearance would contribute valuable publicity, but the writer sent his regrets. The guests enjoyed light refreshments as well as an "exhibit of percussion musical instruments," including the Chinese tom-tom Ella had acquired in San Francisco. "'Putting on the style' at an 'Autograph Record Party,'" is how Ella captioned a photograph of herself looking particularly radiant while playing conga for a group of young guests. She tucked it into her "Mostly about Folk Singers" scrapbook, next to a clipping from one of Marion Campfield's "Mostly about Women" *Defender* columns announcing a second autograph event, this one hosted by a group calling itself the "Friends of Ella."[27]

Tom showed up to toast her that afternoon, but Ella's mother was conspicuously absent. By 1957 Annabelle had quit domestic work and started a business selling baked goods to her former employers and their friends. But despite her own entrepreneurial bent, she put little

FIGURE 6.2. Ella playing at her *Call-and-Response* autograph party, 1957.
Unknown photographer.

stock in Ella's career as a rhythm specialist. As Ella explained, her mother was unable to see the value of a musical career for someone who was not "trained" in music. And she could not imagine that her daughter could be an educator if she were not a formal teacher. Annabelle's failure to support her dream hurt Ella, but she rationalized the pain away by reminding herself of her mother's painstaking labors in "maintaining" her and her brother.

Others were quicker to see the value in Ella's work. A few days after the Hyde Park gathering, artist and educator Margaret Burroughs sent a letter expressing her pleasure. "How much did I enjoy the record-autograph party Sunday," she wrote. "I met some old friends that I knew and saw a lot of others that I didn't know. I was happy that your 'baby' finally came out." She called attention to her own recent publication of a book of African American children's verse, and noted the parallels between Ella's project and her own: "Did you see my recent book 'Did You Feed My Cow?' That was a compilation of call and response children's folk rhythms and games. I'm glad to see that someone else picked up on the delightful and spontaneous character of this literature which came from our people." She noted the $4.25 price tag for *Call-and-Response Rhythmic Group Singing* (a $1.65 markup on the distribution price) while acknowledging Ella's need to earn "a few pennies." "It's a hard racket—this art business," she wrote knowingly. And like Odetta, she offered Ella sisterly advice:

The record should be played in schools, nurseries, kindergartens, and the like. However, the thing missing from the record—you are an audio-visual artist—and must be seen in action to be truly appreciated. A large part of your charm is your warm, lively personality. You know how one gets so much more out of *seeing* Danny Kaye on his programs for children than in merely hearing his records—So I think you should push more for personal appearances.

Why don't we organize a Christmas program for children—a sing and chant fest—might make some pocket change & could help promote the record. Let me know what you think.[28]

In distinguishing between the inert object and Ella's charming and "lively" presence, Burroughs was putting to words something Ella had already begun to understand. Interactions with audiences not only energized Ella, but inspired her to create. Without the constant stimulation of live events, she would not be able to make new albums. As she had promised Asch, she reached out to schools, community centers, and libraries, offering to conduct a workshop in return for the purchase of one or two copies of the album directly from her. Tom worried that his sister would not be able to survive on such paltry payments. But perhaps from her experiences in the folk world and in community organizations like the Y, Ella realized possibilities in "grassroots" marketing and distribution. The fact that she was a "recording artist," meanwhile, could only boost demand for her workshops and programs. In the fable of the Tortoise and the Hare, she was the Tortoise: patient and clear-sighted.

Ten days after her *Call-and-Response* autograph party, on November 27, 1957, Ella joined national stars including Odetta, Pete Seeger, and Mahalia Jackson at a tribute concert and fundraiser for Big Bill Broonzy, then facing mounting medical bills from his treatments for lung cancer. She appeared in the concert's first half, featuring local performers, and was introduced by emcee Studs Terkel as "a young teacher-singer-performer from town who . . . has been influenced and inspired by the blues of Big Bill . . . She's taught her students on the South Side . . . the beauty of the heritage and the richness through music." While Big Bill, who had suffered damage to his vocal cords during a surgery, sat silent, Ella played her conga drum and led the assembly through "Tah-boo," changing up the end of the chant to "Get well, Big Bill." Ella later managed to get a copy of an *Ebony* photographer's image of a smiling Bill flanked by Jackson, Seeger, and Odetta for her "All about Folk Singers" scrapbook, where she titled it "one of my real prizes . . . a kind of photographic folk classic."[29]

A few days later, Ella saw Big Bill again, this time headlining at the December 1 opening night of the Old Town School of Folk Music. The new folk institution emerged from the informal music gatherings that Ella and Bill had attended at Dawn Greening's home. Greening, together with the musicians Frank Hamilton and Win Stracke, had come up with the idea of a school that would use Hamilton's group-centered, "dining room" approach to teaching folk instruments like guitar and banjo. At 333 West North Avenue in the Old Town neighborhood, it would be a community center for folk fans, welcoming budding as well as experienced musicians, children as well as adults. Like the Gate of Horn, it would open its doors to musicians of diverse backgrounds and a variety of musical traditions.[30]

Ella was one of the first to arrive for the opening-night gala, queuing up with her friend, folk performer Ginni Clemmens, and donning a jaunty French beret. No longer able to sing, Broonzy played blues guitar, giving Hamilton the opportunity to demonstrate his teaching method. Ella never took lessons, but she became a regular at the school—leading children's programs and attending concerts and other events.

When Bill died the following August, Ella lost a father figure—an older man who had cared for her without self-interest. Bill had been the first star of the Chicago music world to take Ella under his wing. She had seen him in clubs and auditoriums, attended union meetings with him, and even sung with him under the trees in summers at the Michigan family camp Circle Pines. He was a link to the blues, the first music that mattered to Ella, and a link to the generation of Black migrants who had made her own opportunities possible. Big Bill's decline coincided with Ella's rise as a recording artist. She took comfort in knowing that although he was gone, the songs remained.

Dear Ella,

I liked your program. You have a nice voice.
It is a nice thing to do for us. You should go
TV. You are a good singer.

Tony

(BILLINGS, MONTANA, 1974)

7

ADVENTURES IN RHYTHM

1958–1961

For a slim EP by an unknown Black female "rhythm specialist," *Call-and-Response Rhythmic Group Singing* generated noteworthy attention. It was included in a *New York Herald Tribune* Christmastime round-up of albums for children and received a respectful notice in the *New York Folklore Quarterly*, which observed, "Her musical creations make young and old conscious of their own rhythmic and melodic capacities." It even received a brief but thoughtful mention in the jazz magazine *DownBeat*. "Miss Jenkins, concerned with group-singing techniques, works with a group of children in call-and-response and rhythmic group singing techniques that should prove fascinating to jazz listeners," wrote editor Don Gold. "In addition, the LP is of interest to parents who wish their children to become more rhythm-conscious, more aware of different sounds, and simply aware of the ease of singing."[1]

Meanwhile, and following from her performance at the 1957 Big Bill Broonzy benefit concert, Ella managed a busy calendar of rhythm workshops and public performances. "Miss Jenkins, a specialist in drums, rhythms and folk songs has an uncanny manner of getting people to sing along with her," raved *Defender* music critic Theodore Stone after witnessing Ella lead 350 people in call-and-response singing at a benefit for the Chicago Music Association, an organization that supported Black classical musicians. Ella and her conga drum were similarly a sensation as the after-dinner entertainment at a spring 1958 meeting of the World Congress of Religious Liberals. "When she left the platform," recalled one attendee, "there were lusty calls for 'more—more.'"[2]

Yet Ella's energetic promotion of *Call-and-Response Rhythmic Group Singing* had not yet been rewarded by a promised royalty check from Moe Asch. In April 1958 she took the matter up in a letter. "It has been a considerable time since *we* have corresponded, although I have dropped you a note or two now and then," she observed tartly, before moving on to the heart of the matter.

> I am writing at this time regarding whatever royalties I have coming, according to the contract made last year, which stated that I am to receive twenty-five (.25) cents per album sold after a certain time elapsed (according to contract). According to my record, the period of waiting for the first report is over. Believing that your company is thoroughly honorable and honest, I would appreciate an accurate account of albums sold and a simultaneous royalty check.[3]

But when Ella's first royalty statement did arrive, Folkways had deducted $15.60 from a total payment of $20.40, claiming as an expense copies of the EP that had been promised to the Howalton School children. Was this a misunderstanding or the shady side of the record business she had been warned about? In a follow-up letter, Ella chose the high road. "I was billed for records advanced to the children, which were to be without charge," she explained. "I would appreciate your sending me the check for that amount as early as possible; I will be touring camps beginning [in] August, promoting the album and teaching workshops in rhythm, and could use any extra spending money." As a show of good faith, she agreed to a two-month delay in her second royalty payment and assured the Folkways owner that she was "much concerned with doing a good job on getting my little album across to the right sources. I'm just learning about promotional ideas and hope to improve with your assistance."

But following this show of humility, her note took on a crisper tone. "I hope one day, perhaps in New York, I'll get to know you as a person—so many people speak well of you and tell me how wonderful you are to know. We shall see."[4] That sentence, with its use of the royal "we," put Asch on notice that Ella would not be pushed around.

Ella eventually did recover the $15.60 she had been erroneously billed. But her early sparring with Moe over unpaid royalties established a tug-of-war pattern that persisted over four decades. Ella would reach out, reminding Asch of what she was due, and after a period of delay and grumbling—with Asch often casting himself as the injured party—he would come through. It was a frustrating dynamic for Ella and the source of untold emotional labor. Once when she was annoyed with Asch, she used a Folkways Business Reply Card—the kind stamped "Postage Will Be Paid by Addressee"—to request overdue copies of her liner notes. "You've never been unfair," she wrote to Moe at another point, "however the negligence is rather confusing."[5]

Asch's difficult personality was familiar to everyone in the Folkways orbit. In addition to being stubbornly sure of his taste—a boon for those, like Ella, whom he liked, but a disadvantage for artists like Bob Dylan, whom he famously turned down—he had a reputation for anger and impulsivity. Where the business side of his operation was concerned, Asch took a kick-the-can-down-the-road approach, paying artists when he had the money, ignoring them when he didn't, and often "borrowing" from one to pay another. In this way he "took care" of artists like Guthrie and Seeger during difficult years in their careers: when Guthrie, beset by debilitating illness, could no longer appear in public, and when Seeger, hounded by anticommunists, was unable to perform in commercial concert settings. But as a freelancer who eked out a living on school and other community-based gigs, Ella could not afford to wait for Moe to square his debts. Besides, they had a contract.

Their dynamic took on the emotional resonances of a relationship between a tenacious but vulnerable daughter and a manipulative if ultimately indulgent father. When they were in the same room, Moe and Ella would have "horrible fights" that left both parties exhausted and in tears. "You're breaking me!" Asch would moan to Ella. "But I need the money!" Ella would shoot back. But the two somehow always made up—albeit on Asch's terms. "He would never let you go unless you kissed him goodbye," Ella's partner Bernadelle said. "I think he had a superstition about leaving him with bad feeling."

Despite Moe's concerning complacency regarding royalty payments, Ella had reason to feel optimistic about her career as a rhythm specialist in 1958. One sunny afternoon she was conducting a rhythm workshop near Sixty-Third Street and Cottage Grove Avenue, outside of the South Side Community Committee building, when a white male passerby asked whether she and her Latin percussion "group" would be interested in appearing on a local children's television show. Ella assumed the man had mistaken them for a professional ensemble. "We just do this because we enjoy it," she corrected him. But he persisted. "That's all we want you to do," he replied.[6]

The show the man had in mind was *Totem Club*, a daily half-hour production of WTTW, Chicago's recently founded outlet for educational broadcasting. Each weekday afternoon, *Totem Club* offered viewers aged seven to thirteen themed programming on topics from crafts to the natural world to sports. Like the members of network television's popular *Mickey Mouse Club*, "Totem Clubbers" had their own buttons and cards that attested to their membership in a "tribe" of viewers. The program's ersatz "Indian" theme—which originated in the honorary tribal membership of the show's original host—clashed with its liberal agenda of welcoming presenters and children of diverse backgrounds and abilities. Its producer, Rachel Stevenson, a trailblazing woman in public broadcasting, was particularly well known for accommodating hearing-impaired and deaf viewers.

Ella remembered her first appearance on *Totem Club*, with teens from both the South Side Community Committee and the Woodlawn YWCA, as a nerve-racking affair. In the studio both groups fidgeted self-consciously in front of the hulking cameras. Ella felt pulled in different directions, at once attending to the teens' nerves, minding the questions of host Joe Kelly, and interpreting the silent gesticulations of the director. But their assured performances put Ella's worries to rest. First, the Woodlawn teens demonstrated "Tah-boo," which Ella introduced as an "audience participation chant like they do in Africa, where . . . I say the first line and then the group comes in on the second line." The South Side Community Committee group followed with an Afro-Caribbean–flavored instrumental, accompanied by a dancer. As the teens settled into a rollicking groove, Ella called out "Baila!" ("Dance!"). Both performances elicited enthusiastic applause, but the pulsating carnival number got the bigger ovation, punctuated by an appreciative "Wow!" from host Kelly.

Stevenson, the show's producer, was so impressed that on the spot she offered *Totem Club*'s weekly Thursday slot to Ella. The job did not come with a salary, she explained, but WTTW would cover expenses— and Ella would have freedom to bring on guests and experiment with formats and themes. Perhaps more important, it would offer intangible dividends: experience in television and access to an audience of young viewers across the region. Ella immediately accepted.

This Is Rhythm, the weekly half-hour show Ella hosted from January 1958 to June 1959 (and periodically after that until 1962), established her as a pioneering Black female presence on Chicago television, second only to Mahalia Jackson, who had helmed a local variety program in 1955. While *This Is Rhythm* drew less attention than the famous gospel singer's show, it gave Ella a rare platform for self-expression. With Stevenson's encouragement, she hosted episodes that taught Black history, rewriting the narrative of Africa for children whose knowledge of the Continent came through popular caricature. She ensured that Black performers appeared regularly, and that Black children—including kids from public housing—were frequently on set.

Through Ella's thoughtful recruitment of musicians as guests, *This Is Rhythm* modeled ideals of democratic pluralism. According to the prevailing racial logic of the late 1950s, "integration" was something that Ed Sullivan achieved when he asked Lena Horne to sing on his popular program. But by inviting guests of all backgrounds to be on *This Is Rhythm*, Ella demonstrated that a Black woman could play the role of a broad-minded host. Each week she welcomed people to help her explore a different aspect of rhythm, curating episodes that spanned nations and cultures and that integrated elements of dance and visual arts. Programs covered Scottish bagpipe melodies, Japanese percussion, Appalachian dulcimer tunes, and Middle Eastern chants. She drew on the talents of local performers, including Big Bill Broonzy, George and Gerry Armstrong, and Jo Mapes (by then relocated from San Francisco), as well as visiting out-of-towners Odetta and the Black folk singer Stan Wilson.[7]

The first two episodes of *This Is Rhythm*—captured by a tape recorder Ella brought to the set—attest to the experimental, insurgent spirit of these children's broadcasts, which could be quite pointed in their overt embrace of Black freedom movements, both domestically and in Africa. On her January 9, 1958, debut, she and a group of children introduced viewers to the concept of rhythm and demonstrated the range of patterns that could be made with hand-percussion instruments, singly or in combination. Addressing herself to children who could not afford instruments or music lessons, Ella pointed out that old broom handles could serve as functional claves, the wooden sticks that laid the rhythmic foundation Afro-Cuban rhythm. In a segment where she displayed and invited the children to test out drums from her own collection, she noted which were from Africa, telling the children that Africa is "where we really get most of our rhythms from . . . it's often referred to as the Mother of Rhythms." She even managed to work in a brief lesson about recent African decolonization movements. After leading the children through a call-and-response version of "Bula-waya," a "chant in sounds" (like "Tah-boo"), she explained that she had chosen it to celebrate "a new country called Ghana," which had taken its own "big jump" in becoming independent.

For her second episode Ella ceded the spotlight to two accomplished friends, producing the groundbreaking spectacle of a television program helmed exclusively by Black women. In the first half, music teacher Geraldine Glover led a group of students from Carter Elementary School through several play songs, including "Bingo" and "The Mockingbird Song." In the second half Ella welcomed Odetta, explaining that her guest was a "very famous folk singer." With the children from Glover's school gathered at her feet, the folk star ran through "Three Little Piggies," Woody Guthrie's "Car Car" (with lyrics changed to reflect a female driver), and "The Fox," the English folk song that she had included in her recent solo album *Odetta at the Gate of Horn*. For the latter she drew from her operatic training to pantomime the voices of the foxes coming closer and closer to the geese that would be their dinner.

In both of these shows Ella translated the ideals of contemporary Black freedom movements into forms that children could both enjoy and grasp, nurturing their political consciousness through gentle and inclusive forms of music-making. In the world of *This Is Rhythm*, everyone had rhythm, and everyone's rhythms deserved attention; Black children were the proud bearers of a distinct cultural heritage; Africa was a continent on the rise, throwing off the shackles of imperialist rule; and Chicago, the hyper-segregated metropolis, was welcoming to all.

Ella's choices could be bold. In her reference to Ghanaian independence, for example, she implicitly referenced Martin Luther King's presence at the March 1957 installation of Prime Minister Kwame Nkrumah, where he challenged US Vice President Richard Nixon to "visit us down in Alabama where we are seeking the same kind of freedom the Gold Coast is celebrating."[8] But even apparently apolitical episodes, such as the one with Glover and Odetta, were

FIGURE 7.1. Ella and Odetta on the set of *This Is Rhythm*, Ella's weekly children's show on WTTW. Unknown photographer.

powerful in their visual representation of a world where the talents of accomplished Black women were taken for granted. In his correspondence with Langston Hughes, Tom proudly shared his sister's accomplishments. "Sister has a T.V. series of programs on WTTW here (educational station)," he wrote. "Through this program she is bringing to audiences (children, parents, et al) music and rhythms of cultures 'round the world.' You'd love it I'm sure." As WTTW would later observe, "In the late 1950s Ella Jenkins showed young Chicagoans a world of variety their own neighborhoods couldn't reflect and that commercial television couldn't portray."[9]

"Starring" on her own television show elevated Ella's public profile, lending her work a new sheen of professional legitimacy. At Midway Gardens Ella was greeted as a celebrity following in the footsteps of DuSable High School graduate Nat "King" Cole, whose pathbreaking NBC variety show had been terminated a few weeks before Ella kicked off *This Is Rhythm*.[10] She was featured in *Hue*, a monthly celebrity magazine from the publisher of *Ebony*. "Every week in an oak-panelled studio on Chicago's Lake Shore Drive," the article informed readers, "a cherubic faced young woman with a conga drum steps before two television cameras and begins chanting a series of foreign or made up words."[11] A series of accompanying "backstage" photographs showed Ella consulting with Stevenson, chatting with host Kelly, and reviewing details of the bagpipe episode with George Armstrong, decked out in Highland regalia.

Local press outlets also changed their portrayals of Ella. She went from being a "folk singer," a "rhythm specialist," and a "recording artist" to being a "television folk singer," a "TV rhythm artist," and a "TV and recording personality."[12] The press coverage of *This Is Rhythm* culminated in January 1959, as Ella entered the second year of her run as host, in the form of a *Chicago Tribune* article by esteemed African American journalist Roi Ottley. The first full-blown profile of Ella to appear in a flagship Chicago daily, under the impressive title "Ella Jenkins an Authority on Folk Music," it detailed Ella's formal education, her time living at the Emanu-El Residence Club in San Francisco, and her affiliation with the South Parkway YWCA.[13] The article misreported several details of her biography, painting a portrait of Ella's Depression-era childhood that hewed closely to 1950s ideals, complete with a nuclear family in which Obadiah was the main breadwinner before suffering an early death when Ella was four. It remains unclear whether the errors were Ottley's or, as seems more likely, the result of

Ella's revisionist representation, perhaps to protect her mother from judgment. In any case, she clipped the column and proudly shared it in publicity materials.

While it is difficult to assess the broad impact of *This Is Rhythm* on children in Chicago, one story illustrates the singular power of Ella's short-lived but pathbreaking show. Philip Royster, who hailed from the West Side neighborhood of Lawndale, was a young bongo player with Carmencita Romero's dance troupe when he received an invitation to drum on *This Is Rhythm*. Royster, who would later become a pioneering scholar of African American literature, never forgot the response of his father, a drummer who had set aside his own musical aspirations to support their family. "When I got back home from the gig, my father opened the front door to our apartment for me, which was unusual for him, because he usually slept days and worked nights," Royster explained. "When he opened the door I met his gaze, which was transfigured with the fiercest love I've ever seen. Blacks on television was still unusual in the late 1950s, and I believe he was overwhelmed with pride and admiration for this boy that he cherished."[14]

Royster's experience was unique, but the double validation that he experienced—first through his appearance on *This Is Rhythm*, and later through his father's pleasure—was emblematic of the effects Ella hoped her music could have on children. In this she was drawing on her own experience. "I came up in very poor neighborhoods," she once noted. "Poor in money, rich in music. Sometimes, it was music alone that kept us going and growing."[15]

A month after the Ottley profile, in February 1959, Ella attended a performance of a new play about a Black Chicago family. The Youngers, the protagonists of Lorraine Hansberry's Broadway-bound *A Raisin in the Sun*, were hardworking South Siders. Ruth and Lena Younger, the two matriarchs, dreamed of an alternative to their dingy and cramped apartment. Walter Younger, Lena's son and Ruth's husband, entertained visions of entrepreneurship. Beneatha Younger, Lena's intellectually ambitious daughter, juggled the attention of male suitors but felt weighted down by expectations of marriage. The end of the play saw the Youngers moving to a new home in a neighborhood where they would almost certainly face hostility from white neighbors. Their "victory" was as fleeting as it was unsettled.

Sitting in the Blackstone Theater, Ella saw aspects of her own experience spring to life on the stage. In the representation of the Youngers' apartment she was reminded of the many flats in which she and Tom had grown up. In Ruth Younger's desire for a home she recognized the strivings of her own mother, and of their annual quest for a "higher" address. In Beneatha she saw aspects of herself. Like Beneatha, who expressed ambivalence with marriage (and was in that sense a cipher for Hansberry's own bisexuality), Ella was more concerned with realizing a radical creative vision than with embracing conventional 1950s Black womanhood. She might have smiled when, in the play's second act, Beneatha appeared on stage wearing African textiles and with her hair shorn, in the style that some still called an "Odetta."

Ella was almost certainly intrigued by Hansberry's references to African culture and African independence movements, particularly through the character of Joseph Asagai, the visiting Nigerian student who pursues and influences Beneatha. Asagai's presence in the Younger household unsettles the family dynamic by igniting the characters' suppressed desires, not only spurring Beneatha to stop "mutilating" her hair, but also leading Walter Younger to briefly imagine himself as a powerful "African" warrior. Hansberry's play dramatized a certain Black American romance with a crudely idealized Africa, even as the character of Asagai introduced audiences to notions of transnational Black solidarity and struggle.

Ella was so taken by *A Raisin in the Sun* that she reached out to Hansberry (through Tom, who was friendly with Hansberry's older brother Perry) several months later to share a song she had written based on the play. Ella's composition "A Raisin in the Sun" borrowed the melody and mournful feeling of "Another Man Done Gone," and was arranged like a work song, with a call and response between Ella and a male chorus. As she explained in a letter to Hansberry (whom she addressed by her married name, as "Mrs. Nemiroff"),

> I was so completely moved and stimulated by the play; its message, that I composed a song, using your title and theme as a kind of tribute to you. At first it was only a poem—then I added the music. After several of my close friends and music publisher heard a little record "dub," I had made with four teen-age boys, they advised me to submit it to you.

Ella offered Hansberry the song for use in the forthcoming film of *A Raisin in the Sun*, set to star Sidney Poitier, suggesting that "it has possibilities to popularize your play to a greater extent among teens and young adults." She enclosed the lyrics and advised Hansberry of an acetate disc coming under separate cover.[16]

Ella's pitch to Hansberry did not pan out as she had hoped, but it illustrated the expanding scope of her ambitions as a composer. In mentioning a "music publisher," Ella was referencing Forster Music Publisher, which had an office on Wabash Street near Frank's Drum Shop, a destination for Chicago percussionists. She had recently struck a deal with Forster to publish *Fun with Rhythms and Sounds*, a songbook comprising five chants from *Call-and-Response Rhythmic Group Singing*: "Tah-boo," "Moon Don't Go," "Zeembah," "Toom-Bah-Ee-Lero," and "An Arabic Chant That Means Welcome." Ella had copyrighted these selections and acquired membership in the American Society of Composers, Authors, and Publishers (ASCAP). Joining ASCAP was like joining the Chicago musicians' union: for a fee, the organization monitored certain commercial uses of songs and saw to the payment of performance royalties, which were distinct from the mechanical royalties due to her from Folkways.

In essence, by publishing a songbook with Forster Ella increased the sources of the income she could earn from her creative labors and ensured that these labors were protected by intellectual property law.

She could also make a small profit by modeling the arrangement she had with Folkways, buying discounted copies of *Fun with Rhythms and Sounds* from Forster and selling them directly at her programs for their retail price of seventy-five cents. But *Fun with Rhythms and Sounds* was also personally significant, a means through which Ella established her identity as a composer as well as a performer. Like friends including Odetta, Brother John Sellers, and Big Bill Broonzy, Ella was keenly aware of the erasure of Black credit in the mid-century American recorded folk archive. Blues and spirituals, work songs and prison songs, lullabies and play songs: all of these expressions of Black creativity were claimed for America's folk heritage, and yet African Americans seldom if ever profited from the proliferation of this work by white recording artists, since legally speaking it "belonged" to no one.

The tradition of claiming arrangement as intellectual property had a particularly significant lineage among Black composers and performers. Since the late nineteenth-century tours of the Fisk Jubilee Singers, "concertized" Negro spirituals—songs from oral tradition reworked for concert presentation by formally trained a cappella ensembles—had played an important part in raising awareness of the art created by enslaved people and fostering sympathy for Black civil rights in an era of rising Jim Crow segregation. In mid-century jazz, too, inspired adaptations of American songbook "standards"—such as John Coltrane's famous version of "My Favorite Things"—were commonplace, part of a long tradition of "signifying" on European musical values.

Ella's move to copyright her work, both original compositions and arrangements, was thus a means of self-assertion as well as self-protection. The art of arranging was often misunderstood, but as jazz musicians knew, the creative reworking of sonic source material was an important category of composition. When Ella arranged "Miss Mary Mack," she was also critically interpreting the familiar Black girls' chant through her own artistic lens. Her "Miss Mary Mack" would be distinct from the innumerable improvised versions of children. But as a creation based on Black oral tradition, it allowed this tradition to be heard anew, and by new audiences.

Her confidence lifted by the publication of the Forster songbook, Ella invested in official-looking letterhead, announcing herself under a new title:

ADVENTURES in RHYTHM

PROGRAMS OF SONGS—CHANTS and RHYTHMS

—ESPECIALLY DESIGNED FOR GROUP PARTICIPATION—

The new name reflected Ella's evolving philosophy of music education. Where "rhythm specialist" had described Ella's area of expertise, "Adventures in Rhythm" conveyed the excitement of discovery she sought to instill. Like "fun" in *Fun with Rhythms in Sounds*, it cast music as sonic play. As she was increasingly recognizing, play was a powerful tool for eliciting musical participation, especially from children and adults who felt inhibited by notions of "good" singing.

In October 1959 Ella used her new stationery to correspond with a music professor who, after hearing Ella at a summer workshop, invited her to be a visiting Lecturer-Artist at Washington State University in Pullman, presenting to groups of adults (primarily college students in education, teachers, and recreational professionals) and to children at local elementary schools. Although Pullman, a predominantly white town near the border with Idaho, presented Ella with the challenge of unfamiliar audiences, during her time there she boldly retained the Africanist core of her Chicago rhythm workshops. As her notes reveal, by and large her presentations for adults as well as children followed the script of the debut episode of *This Is Rhythm*: first introducing the concept of rhythm, then elaborating on its history and variety, paying particular attention to African rhythms, and finally leading the audience through simple rhythmic exercises. In her choice of material, including spirituals such as "Come Out the Wilderness" and in her composition "Bulawaya," she explicitly aligned herself with the Southern civil rights activists and African decolonization struggles. To make the point visible, she came dressed for her workshops in African textiles.

Ella's personal warmth, cultural inclusivity, and identification with children gave her the foothold to pull off such audacious acts of fugitive civil rights pedagogy. The Washington State adults appreciated her workshops because Ella provided them with accessible models for incorporating songs and rhythms into classrooms and play spaces. Local children responded in more personal terms, expressing the intellectual and emotional imprint of Ella's lessons in heartfelt letters. One girl illustrated her letter with a drawing of Ella in her colorful African dress, along with her bongo and claves.

In the wake of her Washington visit, Ella set her sights on an album that would build on her rhythm workshops while appealing to older audiences. In Pullman and back home, in groups ranging from Black women's auxiliaries to Roosevelt College alumni, she had observed adults grappling with feelings of intimidation, embarrassment, or even shame around music performance. They would defend their reticence to participate, saying, "I don't have any sense of rhythm" or "I have two left feet" or "I can't carry a tune." The challenge of engaging such audiences was of course not unique to Ella; even Pete Seeger, the folk revival's leading advocate of group singing, occasionally struggled to entice audiences to join him. "Clear out your throat," he once told a Cornell University crowd, "don't let your neighbor look at you peculiarly if you sing too loud, just kick 'em in the ribs and get 'em singing too."[17] But unlike Seeger, Ella never asked anyone to sing. Instead, she instructed them to follow.

Ella's insight into the emotionally liberating power of musical play formed the basis of *Adventures in Rhythm*, her second Folkways album. Released in December 1959, the ten-inch EP looked a bit like *Call-and-Response Rhythmic Group Singing*, with a cover photograph again supplied by Jo Banks, showing her conducting a rhythm workshop with a group of Black students at George Williams College, a YMCA training school for recreation professionals. Sonically and conceptually, however, *Adventures in Rhythm* parted ways with her debut. As she explained in the album's liner notes, this record *is not* directed toward the small child, but rather toward *older children, teens and the, so-called inhibited adult.*

It is especially directed toward those persons who feel they have no rhythm in them (there *is* rhythm in you—we need only help you bring it to the surface), and those trying to improve their sense of RHYTHM.[18]

It followed that the album did not *model* a rhythm workshop, like *Call-and-Response Rhythmic Group Singing*, but presented polished versions of songs, mostly from Black folk tradition, as opportunities for participation.

With these ends in mind, Ella had recruited four accomplished friends from the Chicago folk scene as musicians: drummer Louis McDonald and guitarists Ted Johnson, Jean Curtis, and Valucha Buffington. She interspersed their skillful performances with instructional tracks demonstrating rhythms of increasing complexity, from a simple four-four rhythm to an asymmetrical clave rhythm. But she brought a light approach to technique. "Before we start our rhythmic adventure," she advised in the liner notes, "I would like for you to put aside, for awhile, all formal methods of learning music. We will emphasize clapping, tapping, snapping, etc. on the beat rather than off the beat, as this is easiest for most people. . . . My system is aimed at helping you feel and enjoy (not analyze and calculate) the rhythm within you. Now relax and have fun!"[19]

Lurking behind the cheer of such instructions was the unacknowledged risk Ella ran as a Black woman offering herself as a teacher of rhythm to the musically "inhibited." She had been confronting the stereotype of the naturally rhythmic Black person since childhood, watching movies at the Regal Theater that associated the "hot" and "intoxicating" rhythms of jazz with racial inferiority, bodily excess, and sexual promiscuity. She identified strongly with Langston Hughes, who had wryly observed that "in America most white people think . . . that all Negroes can sing and dance, and have a sense of rhythm."[20] As she was recording *Adventures in Rhythm*, America's moral panic over rock and roll evinced a new version of the old story in which a backbeat was a slippery slope to racial anarchy.

Ella intended *Adventures in Rhythm* as a rebuke to the stereotypes—both the "negative" notion of rhythm-as-primitive and the "positive" notion of rhythm-as-vitality advanced by anticolonialist African intellectuals like Léopold Senghor, who extolled the "rhythmic attitude" of the "Black man" as a source of "necessary energy" for anemic Western societies.[21] If rhythm could be learned, then there was nothing inherent to it, variations in aptitude notwithstanding. More powerfully, by inviting listeners to discover the pleasures of different rhythms Ella conveyed rhythm's historical dimensions, grounding in "culture" what was taken as "nature."

The album's spiritual "I'm Gonna Sing," for example, illustrated how enslaved people repurposed Christian teachings and European hymns to express alternatives to the cruel rhythms of lives lived as chattel. A version of "Miss Mary Mack" pointed to rhythm as a binding agent of Black children's culture and to Black girls as bearers of communal memory; whereas Ella's original composition, "No More Pie," a favorite of the children in Pullman, used rhythmic patterns to present a tale of deferred (and ultimately frustrated) desire in humorous terms. Songs like "I've Been Working on the Railroad" showed how Black people harnessed rhythm to survive coerced labor and economic hardship. To make her point about rhythm's universality, Ella contrasted it with "Zum Gali Gali," a work song associated with the kibbutz movement in British Mandate–era Palestine.[22]

Moe Asch believed in *Adventures in Rhythm*, notwithstanding the dim sales prospects for an educational record for musically "inhibited" adults. The *New York Times* music critic Herbert Mitgang was less open to Ella's audacious experimentation, however. "Ella Jenkins, who runs the show on this ten-inch long-play, is billed as a rhythm specialist, which is cutting it fine in an age of specialization," he wrote. "All sorts of instruments are banged and bonged here for 'teens and young adults,' among others. Here are Indian tom-toms, rattles from

Africa, and even a Royal Poinciana tree pod from Jamaica. It's good to know that these eternal verities are still around because, who knows? knowing how to beat a tree pod can come in handy some day."[23]

Mitgang's smug appraisal reinforced the very stereotypes about rhythm Ella's album sought to dispel. (He also seems to have mistakenly identified Ella's Chinese tom-tom as Native American.) His "joke" about "eternal verities" was particularly cutting, particularly because it assumed that readers of the newspaper shared his sense of the percussion instruments of non-European peoples as comically inferior. A different reviewer might have understood that tom-toms, rattles, and even Jamaican tree pods were in fact significant technologies, not merely of self-expression and play, but of nonverbal communication. As a piece of organic detritus, a tree pod was insignificant, but as a sound-making device for people denied access to drums it could be an important tool of expression, or even resistance.

If Ella caught wind of Mitgang's review—which, given the prominence of the *New York Times*, seems likely—then she put it out of her mind. (She had little reason to worry about Asch, who was indifferent to critics, believing in his own superior judgment.) In any case, by the time *Adventures in Rhythm* appeared, Ella had already landed on an idea for a follow-up album that would further explicate her thesis about rhythm as an expressive practice that revealed the suppressed history of Black people in the United States. *Negro Folk Rhythms*, released in late 1960, was another unconventional record, bridging audiences and musical styles. Unlike her first two albums, it was a collaboration, as reflected by the album's full title *Negro Folk Rhythms with Ella Jenkins and the Goodwill Spiritual Choir of Monumental Baptist Church*. Instead of picturing Ella or the choir, the cover image leaned into modernist abstraction, featuring an African mask from Ella's own collection alongside bold, modern lettering.

Side 1 of *Negro Folk Rhythms* featured Ella performing folk songs and original compositions inspired by folk tradition, some with her own percussion accompaniment, some with guitar accompaniment provided by her friend Shiz Hori, a moonlighting University of Chicago

FIGURE 7.2. Cover of *Negro Folk Rhythms*, 1960, featuring a mask from Ella's personal collection. Courtesy of Smithsonian Folkway Recordings.

engineer. As on *Adventures in Rhythm*, her selections included children's songs, from material she had sung growing up ("Who All Is Here?" and "Did You Feed My Cow?") to material she had learned as an adult ("That's All Right Julie," adapted from Maya Angelou's version); secular and work songs ("Who's Gonna Be Your Man?," "Hammer Song," "Cotton-eyed Joe"); and spirituals ("No More Auction Block"). All of these songs came from oral tradition, but Ella took care to produce arrangements that reflected her sensibility as a rhythm specialist. To make this point, the liner notes contained the phrases like "Arranged by E. Jenkins," "Written by Ella Jenkins," or "Melody by Ella Jenkins" in recognition of Ella's distinct forms of authorship.

The album kicked off with Ella's propulsive choral arrangement of "Wade in the Water"—actually a trilogy that bridged the title spiritual and "Didn't My Lord Deliver Daniel" with an original composition, "A Man Went Down to the River." On "Who's Gonna Be Your Man," Ella accompanied herself on bamboo drum, an instrument with a distinctive, airy resonance.

With the exception of "Racing with the Sun," a non-copyright-infringing revision of the song she had written for Lorraine Hansberry's play, Ella gave side 2 of *Negro Folk Rhythms* over to the Goodwill Spiritual Choir of Monumental Baptist Church. Directed by Arthur S. Logan, the choir was famous in Chicago for its technical proficiency in varying styles. It also enjoyed the distinction of being associated with one of Chicago's foremost social justice congregations by virtue of its pastor, Rev. Morris Harrison Tynes, who was close to civil rights leaders including Martin Luther King Jr.

On the album, the group performed "Rockin' Jerusalem," a Christmas spiritual; "Run and Help Us Tell," "This Is the Way I Pray," "All Over This World," "You Better Mind," "Get Away Jordan," and "Old Time Religion." The liner notes enumerated the differences in styles, from the "anthem" (or concertized) form, to the syncopated style of the gospel song form. To help listeners hear these differences, the last several tracks consisted of versions of the same song in different styles. "Old Time Religion" was presented in three ways: in a "traditional" version, a "classic" version, and a gospel version. To a broader American public that imagined "Negro spirituals" as an undifferentiated category of Christian slave songs, the album demonstrated the breadth of approaches taken by different performers for different audiences.

Although sonically and thematically distinct, both sides of *Negro Folk Rhythms* made the case for rhythm as key to Black history, and both were explicit in connecting that history to the civil rights movement. In many ways it was Ella's first "political" album, just as it was the first to explicitly refer to "Negro" rhythms. In the liner notes she alluded to the pivotal events of 1960, including the establishment of the Student Nonviolent Coordinating Committee (SNCC) and student protests and sit-ins. "Much attention is being focused upon the American Negro today as he struggles and fights, in a nonviolent manner, to achieve a lasting freedom," she observed. "People around the world are looking in on the progress of the Negro's fight for freedom; recognizing his dignity; sympathizing and supporting his cause." Ella also prefaced the track descriptions with the lyrics of a song that did not appear on the album: "Negra," an original composition dedicated to "UHURU" (freedom) "for the American Negro and the Negro of Africa." Like her early Spanish songs "Oye Mi Tambor" and "Yo Me Voy," "Negra" was a paean to diasporic Blackness. "Negra, si soy negra," it read. "Y no tengo miedo . . . Por eso es mi gran color." *Black, yes I am Black. And I am not afraid . . . For this is my great color.*[24]

Ella celebrated the release of *Negro Folk Rhythms* at the cavernous Hyde Park apartment of her friend Phyllis Courrier, a flamboyant free spirit who was well known in the Chicago folk world. (Her mother, Margaret Casey, was a co-founder of the College of Complexes, and Phyllis had worked as Odetta's secretary.) Courrier, her daughter Suzanne remembered, laid out a huge spread of food and soft drinks, relegating the cocktails to the butler's pantry out of deference to Ella. It was just as well, giving celebrants, including her brother Tom, more places to sit down or stand as Ella and various musician-friends, including Martin Yarbrough, the Gay Sisters, Willie Wright, Arvella Gray, and Sandy Paton, performed, and as her close friend, poet Elma Stuckey, read some of her verses.

Listeners appraised *Negro Folk Rhythms* according to their existing cultural agendas. In the *Bulletin*, an African American Chicago weekly, columnist Bernard J. Hayes used it to call attention to contemporary white appropriations of Black musical styles. *Negro Folk Rhythms*, he wrote, is "one of the true records on the market today that shows what a real artist wants to convey," noting that African American rhythms constituted the "backbone" of "modern" rock and roll. Writing in the *Journal of Negro Folklore*, folksong scholar D. K. Wilgus lamented that *Negro Folk Rhythms* lacked a "thorough and coherent explanation of what much of the recording is to illustrate."[25]

An obscure folk fanzine, the Minneapolis-based *Little Sandy Review*, was less measured in its criticism. The *Review*'s young co-editors, Paul Nelson and Jon Pankake, were upfront about their folk purism. "We are two people who love folk music very much," they had declared in its inaugural issue, "and want to do all we can to help the good in it grow and the bad in it perish."[26] In the case of *Negro Folk Rhythms*, that meant going for the jugular. "This album purports to be an educational survey of Negro folk rhythms," began the review by Barry Hansen, a young folk fan who would later gain fame as the late-night radio host Dr. Demento:

> Judging by the music it contains, the Negro is rhythmically a very unproductive race. The whole second side . . . sounds exactly like a recital of Negro Spirituals such as you can hear at any high school choral concert. The first side is a selection of hopelessly over-arranged and slickened performances which sound at their best like imitations of Odetta and at their worst are nauseatingly cute and completely phony.
>
> . . . This album will undoubtedly find its way into many classrooms whose teachers genuinely want to teach their children something about Negro folk music, but who are repelled from the real thing (such as that on the Lomax-Atlantic Anthology) because "it sounds too much like rock & roll" or something like that. Far too many performances of Negro folk music by educated Negroes such as Miss Jenkins bow to this kind of taste. Or perhaps the motive is a purposeful attempt by educated Negroes to remove the white stereotype of Negro music as something "barbaric" and to show these whites that Negro music is noble and good, *in the whites' own image.*

Negro Folk Rhythms, the review concluded, was "a complete negation of the greatness of Negro music."[27]

While Hansen's aversion to Ella's album is explained by the *Review*'s disdain for anything it saw as commercialized, watered-down folk music, the tone of his appraisal betrays an arrogance that goes beyond aesthetic judgment.[28] In particular, he and the editors seem ignorant of the standing of the Goodwill Spiritual Choir in Chicago. And they reveal their audaciousness as college graduates in assailing Ella's racial credentials on account of her own degree.

Unlike those white young men, Ella was not a folk purist. She liked Elvis enough to talk her way into one of his concerts in the 1970s. She embraced the smoothed-out sounds and wholesome look of the Kingston Trio, archenemies of the guardians of folk authenticity, pasting their August 1959 *Time* magazine cover in her folk scrapbook. The *Little Sandy Review* scorned Harry Belafonte for bringing calypso rhythms to the white suburbs, where folk authenticity went to die. But Ella had written to Lord Burgess, composer of "Day-O" and other Belafonte hit songs, offering him one of her own calypso-themed compositions. This "big tent" approach to folk music was not a liability to Ella—it was in fact central to her understanding of the music and to her educational mission.

Ella rarely allowed herself to publicly vent her frustration with such folk gatekeeping and policing of blackness. But in "A Lot of Singing Going On," an undated (and apparently unpublished) manuscript, she satirized this faction of the folk world.

> This interesting and remarkable resurgence of folk music and folk-singing has not restricted it self solely to the "Folksinger;" it seems almost every type of singer whether professional or amateur, ballad or "hillbilly," rock-and-roll or religious, each one is presumably trying, with relative sincerity, to revive *that old ethnic feeling*—in other words— everyone is bent upon being and sounding, to coin a word, "ethnicky." And the folk who label themselves FOLKSINGERS are the most *ethnicky* of all. They are the ones who endeavor to keep the "old" music pure; unchanged (a few modifications now and then), as opposed to the popular use of folk material for that grand old commercial "buck."

"The folk fever has taken hold of me also," she concluded, but "in [a] different kind of way. My interest lay in *feeling the moods of a culture through rhythms and sounds.*"[29]

What did "feeling the moods of a culture" mean to Ella? The phrase arguably cut to the core of her unorthodox approach to ethnography. Her musical education in the Black Metropolis had led her to embrace the communicative qualities of music—to see folk song as something people adapted to suit their needs, not as something trapped in amber. And while her language of "moods" was perhaps vague, it cautioned against making a fetish of origins and originals, rather than searching for meaning in changing practices of music-making.

Purists could forget the material conditions of the folk musicians whom they championed, and who lacked college degrees only because education was withheld from them. Ella, in contrast, lamented the uneven distribution of wealth and credit in the folk world, despite claims of reverence for the "old" performers. Repeatedly she saw opportunities flow toward white performers of Black music, leaving the careers of African American performers to languish. Her friend Brother John Sellers had been the toast of Europe in 1958. But at Gerde's Folk City, the hub of the West Village folk revival, he never attracted the same adulatory attention. Ella had similar concerns about Odetta, despite the singer's success under Albert Grossman, and Chicago songster Arvella Gray, whom she pitched, unsuccessfully, to Moe Asch. (She also repeatedly tried to persuade him to record an LP of poems by her friend Elma Stuckey.) And decades later, when Smithsonian Folkways updated the title of *Negro Folk Rhythms* to *African American Folk Rhythms*, she wondered whether that adjustment would contribute to the "forgetting" of Black history.

Ella saw these racialized dynamics of erasure play out time and time again. In December 1960 she took a trip to New York City to see Elizabeth "Libba" Cotten, a sixty-seven-year-old singer-guitarist making her debut at Izzy Young's Folklore Center in Greenwich Village. The Carrboro, North Carolina, native had recently released a Folkways album consisting of songs she remembered from her childhood and adolescence, including original compositions. After the show Ella asked for the older woman's autograph. Before they parted ways, Ella had gotten Cotten to promise that she would stay with Ella at Midway Gardens when she came for the first annual University of Chicago Folk Festival in February 1961.

When they met, Cotten was close to the age of Ella's mother Annabelle or her aunt Big Mama. Like them she had spent most of her life working in white people's households. And like Uncle Flood, she had played and composed songs for her own pleasure, until marriage, motherhood, and migration to New York City led her to put music on the back burner for several decades. She didn't pick up the guitar again until the late 1940s, while working in the suburban Maryland household of Charles and Ruth Crawford Seeger and their four children, America's First Family of folk music. One of these children, Mike Seeger, a member of the urban folk band the New Lost City Ramblers, took particular interest in presenting her publicly. Since the early 1950s she had been accompanying him and his band on the college folk circuit.

Yet for all that it inspired, Cotten's story of late-in-life success was also a cautionary tale for Ella, exemplifying the extraction of Black women's musical creativity for other people's commercial gold. In 1957 a British band, the Chas McDevitt Skiffle Group, released a version of Cotten's song "Freight Train," which she had composed as a precocious adolescent, after hearing it performed by Peggy Seeger, Mike's sister. It was credited to McDevitt, with no mention of Cotten's authorship, and greeted by the US music trade magazine *Cash Box* as "a refreshing and unusual item from England that could create a sensation in this country."[30]

Cotten lived and breathed music. While staying at Midway Gardens, Ella remembered fondly, she even snored musically. Ella was in the audience both times the older woman performed at the University of Chicago Folk Festival: on opening night, when she presented "Going Down the Road Feeling Bad," an Appalachian blues, and "The Vestibule in My Home," and the following evening, when she played six more numbers, including "Freight Train." The song's chorus portrayed the train as a vehicle of flight, but its verses spoke of the permanent repose of death, as the singer expressed her wish to be buried where "I can hear old Number Nine/as she comes rolling by."

Hearing Cotten sing "Freight Train," with its eerie, off-kilter undertow, Ella might have been prompted to think about the different trains in her own life: of a 1940s rail journey to Alabama with her cousin, when the two girls, rubbing the sleep out of their eyes, had been forced to move into a sooty Jim Crow car in the middle of the night; of the lonely trip accompanying her father's body to St. Louis, where she had been rebuffed by her church; and of long train rides that bookended her sojourn in the Bay Area, where she had gone looking for herself.

Ella had traveled a long distance since those train rides, and as a thirty-six-year-old rhythm specialist, she was only beginning to gather speed. A little like Cotten, she had followed an unconventional path to professional performance. Only four years into her five-year plan as a freelancer, she had launched a television show, published a songbook, and released three musically and politically adventurous albums. And while sustained by her many friends, she had done it alone, without a manager. But that last circumstance was about change—in the unexpected form of a woman who would be by her side for all of her future adventures.

Dear Ms. Ello Jenkins I liked it very much
but we missed gym but who cares this was
better than gym so I'm glad we missed gym
just to see you because I had fun.

Sincerely,
Mark

(1975)

8

CHICAGO FOLKS

1961–1962

Ella didn't notice Bernadelle Richter the first time they were in a room together, at an early 1961 party hosted by Shiz Hori, the Japanese American University of Chicago professor who played guitar on *Negro Folk Rhythms*. His Hyde Park home had been so mobbed with well-wishers that evening that, in order to be seen, Ella had performed from the staircase. Nor did Ella notice Bernadelle the second time they crossed paths, at the Old Town Holiday, the massive annual summer outdoor arts and crafts fair, where Ella was hawking tickets for another benefit concert she had organized for Odetta, while the singer was headlining at the Gate of Horn.

But they did meet the third time, at a small June 1961 dinner party hosted by mutual friends following the Odetta benefit. Ella was immediately drawn to the petite, brown-haired, and blue-eyed white woman who shared her enthusiasm for Odetta. Most twenty-one-year-olds found folk music boring, but Bernadelle, who dragged reticent friends to shows at the Gate of Horn, was uninterested in what was trendy among her peers. At a time when everyone was crazy about Elvis, she remained loyal to Buddy Holly. And while she liked folk, she appreciated German and Italian opera. Subtle signals—Bernadelle's slacks and boyish hairstyle—suggested that she also shared Ella's preference for women.

After that evening, Ella and Bernadelle spent time together. At the beginning of their relationship, perhaps because of the inherent perils, they rarely dated one-on-one. But they went out frequently with groups of friends, in which it was understood that they were a couple. Although neither woman, by their own accounts, had been in a "serious" relationship, within a couple of months they had fallen in love. "Your last letter was very sweet and I am truly happy that we are friends," Ella wrote to Bernadelle in an August 1961 letter from Bridgton, Maine, where she was working at the Maine Folk Dance Camp. "I've been lonely for so long. You make me realize how good it is to love someone with sincerity."[1]

That month Ella turned thirty-seven; Bernadelle had finished high school without definite plans and was taking classes at Roosevelt College while living on the North Side with her parents. Born in Chicago in 1939, she was the only child of Celeste Richter, an Irish American homemaker, and Joseph Richter, a brick worker of Austrian and Swiss extraction who eventually formed Richter Chimney Service, with Celeste running the business end. After Bernadelle graduated from Central YMCA High School, she worked for the family business while pursuing college in a desultory fashion. She tried real estate and insurance but could muster no interest in a business career. "Something was missing," she recalled. "I didn't know what it was but I wanted to find it."

Travel turned out to be Bernadelle's conduit to that "something." The summer before she and Ella met, she traveled to Europe for the first time, visiting Switzerland and looking for lost relatives on her father's side. Her wanderlust led her to get involved with a branch of American Youth Hostels (AYH), a group that promoted travel as a means of resisting Cold War nationalism while also detaching tourism from its elitist associations. Both in the United States and abroad, AYH was known for offering inexpensive group housing, creating conditions for cross-cultural interaction. Leftist politics were the bridge that linked AYH to the Chicago folk-music scene. The group had a Folk Song Committee and published a newsletter, *Folk Song Focus*, that dispensed gossip and information. Shortly after they started seeing each other, Bernadelle invited Ella to perform at an AYH-sponsored "Rhythm Weekend" in Ogelsby, Illinois. It gave them their first excuse to spend sustained time together.

Personality-wise, Ella and Bernadelle fell more into the category of "opposites attract" than "kindred spirits." Ella was extroverted and adept at casual conversation. By virtue of her mother's Christian Science faith, she had grown up understanding positivity and constructiveness as manifestations of Divine Spirit, and thereby tended to see her cup as half-full. Bernadelle, conversely, warmed up to people slowly and presented a more sober and serious exterior. Yet while she lacked Ella's outward verve, she was keenly interested in the world and quietly observant—traits that later led her to earn a graduate degree in photography at the Art Institute of Chicago.

This capacity for sensitive observance allowed Bernadelle to perceive aspects of Ella that other people missed in the onrush of her charm. For example, she grasped that Ella's social self-assurance was hard-earned—a skill acquired to endure a difficult childhood—and that her extroversion was partly a learned adaptation to standing out in white spaces. "Ella grew up knowing that no one else would be her advocate," Bernadelle said. "She had the confidence of putting it out there in the world that you get when you come from nothing." Such emotional intelligence endeared Bernadelle to Ella, who felt immediately "understood" by the serious, yet also gentle and open, younger white woman. "I just trusted her and felt comfortable around her" even though they were "different nationalities," she said, using a 1950s euphemism for race. "I loved that she was very patient, and very understanding, and that she was never embarrassed. When we walked down the street together, I was never frightened that she would pull away from me."

Figure 8.1. Photo booth image of Ella and Bernadelle Richter, ca. early 1960s.

Ella's memory was both a tender testament to, and a poignant acknowledgment of, the risks the two faced just for being together in an era predating both the modern gay and lesbian rights movement and *Loving v. Virginia*, the 1967 Supreme Court decision that struck down laws against interracial marriage. Even in the tolerant and socially fluid world of Chicago's interracial folk scene, their relationship tested social norms. Tom had discovered something similar in 1958 when he married Patricia Denton, a fellow sociology graduate student who was white and had been raised as a Christian Scientist. Ella served as the maid of honor at the ceremony, donning high heels out of filial love, but Patricia's parents stayed home. Their disapproval of her choice to wed a Black man, combined with Pat's relative indifference to Christian Science, contributed to her decision, within a couple of years, to leave Tom and quietly seek a divorce.

Annabelle, too, had voiced resistance to Tom's marriage on racial terms, albeit for different reasons. She had spent most of her life working for white women: ironing their clothes, cooking their meals, enduring their ignorance. She saw no reason why her handsome, well-connected, and accomplished son could not find a partner among the upstanding middle-class young Black women at the Eighth Church of Christ, Scientist. To Ella that preference smacked of hypocrisy. Mary Baker Eddy, the founder of Christian Science, had written of the material world as an illusion. Besides, "love doesn't work like that," she reasoned with her mother. "You love no matter what color."

It was an argument Ella and Annabelle would revisit when Ella became serious about Bernadelle. Annabelle received Bernadelle coolly at first—more, it seemed, on account of race than gender. But Annabelle did eventually "open up" to Bernadelle, Ella said, after coming to terms with the reality that Ella would never live up to her mother's ideals of respectable Black femininity. "She kind of liked me," Bernadelle said, "but it took a lot."

Bernadelle's parents, she and Ella agreed, displayed comparatively more warmth to Ella. Joseph and Celeste Richter "took Ella in as a person," Bernadelle said, exercising the same live-and-let-live ethic that had steered them to accept their daughter's lesbianism. Their openness reflected the fact that Bernadelle had grown up as a secure, doted-upon only child who did not have to worry about racism. "My father said you choose who you want to be with and that's that," Bernadelle remembered.

Ella said she never felt the tension of being an "exceptional Negro" with Bernadelle's parents, especially Joseph, who shared her silly sense of humor. But neither woman discussed their "friendship" openly—either with their parents or their peers. It was not unusual for women in their situation to live within a veil of protective privacy, if not self-censorship, at that time. As Bessie Smith had sung, it was "nobody's business." "I never felt that I had to account to anyone for what I did or didn't do," Bernadelle said. "And I don't think Ella did," she said. Ella was similarly resistant to submitting to anyone's definitions of her identity or her relationship. When asked what she wished to call Bernadelle, she was firm: "You can call her my dearest friend. People have lots of best friends, but she's my *dearest* friend. In life you only have one of those."

As Ella was falling in love, she was finding new audiences for her music. In October 1961 she became the Monday night host of *Meetin' House*, an hour-long folk program on radio station WSBC. It was a little like hosting Sunday hootenannies at the Gate of Horn. On the laid-back, free-form show she spun discs and aired live performances by friends including Arvella Gray, Ginni Clemmens, Jesse Fuller, LeRoy Inman and Ira Rogers, and Marie Ojenen, a Finnish singer. She also used *Meetin' House* to highlight Chicago's energetic blues scene, playing records by Muddy Waters, Sleepy John Estes, and others she had enjoyed at clubs around town. Occasionally, if she found herself with time to kill, she took the microphone and sang.

Around this time Ella also began work on an instructional album for children with disabilities. The idea was rooted in her recent experiences with blind children at a Chicago Park District summer camp, and with adolescents at the University of Chicago's Orthogenic School, a therapeutic day school for children with autism and emotional challenges. In both settings, Ella had been obliged to tailor her call-and-response technique to meet the children's different needs. With the blind campers Ella spent two days sharing her large collection of bells from around the world, encouraging them to take in distinctions in timbre and tonality as well as shape and heft, and using sound to teach them geography, history, and culture. At the Orthogenic School she combined the instructional approach of *Adventures in Rhythm* with the repertoire of *Negro Folk Rhythms*, using call and response to teach older children variations on spirituals like "Wade in the Water." Teens who struggled with social interactions and group activities took readily to her musical "games," moving quickly from imitation to the more complex tasks of creative improvisation and even composition.

With these varied students in mind, Ella began working on a series of drawings and poems to illustrate different instruments and different concepts of rhythm. One day she took them to her friend Betty Nudelman, a pianist and music educator in the northern suburb of Skokie. Ella first met Betty in 1957 at a Jamaica-themed soiree in Lake Meadows, where Ella provided the entertainment. Every year since, she had attended the Nudelman family Passover Seder, pulling out her harmonica for the post-meal sing-along. At Betty's recommendation she had also landed a part-time position at the new Niles Township Jewish Community Center (JCC) in Skokie, Illinois. When a JCC representative asked Betty whether Ella was Jewish, Betty pointed out that her Black friend had been offering "winter holiday" workshops at Chicago JCCs since the mid-1950s, and that her repertoire included excellent versions of "Shabbat, Shalom" and "Hatikvah."

As Ella recited her poems to Betty, Betty began improvising on the piano, translating the spirit of Ella's whimsical verses into musical forms. Ella liked their experiment enough to book them time in a downtown recording studio.[2]

The tapes they produced that day would form the basis for *This Is Rhythm*, Ella's fourth Folkways album. Released in late 1961, in the season of Ella's deepening connection to Bernadelle, it was much more intimate than her previous two albums, taking an inside-out approach that began with the child's sensory experiences of rhythm and moving outwards to show the connections between such experiences and established musical forms. Side 1 leads off with Ella's rhythm-instrument poems scored to Betty's simple but expressive piano riffs. Then the record moves to the concept of rhythm, drawing examples from the natural world and human culture. Following these rhythm tone poems, Ella demonstrates the sounds made by ten rhythm instruments, most associated with Africa, explaining the geographic and national origins of these instruments, their travel across cultures, their uses in musical ensembles, and their construction from natural or synthetic materials.

On side 2 of *This Is Rhythm*, Ella enlisted the help of children from Chicago's First Unitarian Church choir to illustrate songs with different rhythms and the different sounds that can be made through rhythmic combinations. For example, on "Let's Build a Rhythm," a highlight of the album, the children build a song of textural and timbral complexity using elements of "Are You Sleeping?," the familiar English version of "Frère Jacques." On the calypso-inspired "In Trinidad," Ella plays conga and is joined by the children's choir and Shirley Genther, the song's composer, on piano. The only original composition on the album was "My Dog Has Fleas," Ella's lighthearted take on a familiar problem:

> I bathed him, I shaved him
> O yes siree
> I rubbed him, I scrubbed him
> But my dog has fleas! My dog has fleas!

The stripped-down immediacy of the music on *This Is Rhythm* was mirrored in its cover image, an arrangement of Ella's own fanciful sketches of smiling, hand-holding rhythm instruments, including cheery bongos, contented rhythm sticks, and a mirthful tambourine. Composed using only the blue and red colors of a two-sided pencil, Ella's drawings hearkened back to her conga drum self-portrait of 1954 and portrayed a collection of instruments as a social ensemble.

There was a method behind Ella's decision to do her own illustrations: She wanted her rough-hewn sketches for the cover of *This Is Rhythm* to look like something a child might have drawn. "I am not an artist, as one might easily observe," she wrote in the liner notes, "however I feel that the manner in which I have handled the art work, the child can closely identify with his own dimensions in drawing and

FIGURE 8.2. Cover of *This Is Rhythm* LP, 1961.
Courtesy of Smithsonian Folkway Recordings.

printing."[3] The resulting image contrasted starkly with the cover illustrations of most children's recordings, which presented romanticized pictures of middle-class white childhood or forcefully effervescent designs. It gave visual form to the stripped-down sonic aesthetic championed by Asch, the graphic antithesis of blaring "kidisks" that he held in contempt.

Ella's concerns with the child's "own dimensions" also informed her decision to create an innovative companion book for *This Is Rhythm*.[4] Released by Oak Publications, an outlet associated with the political Left and with folk music, the book consisted of ninety-six hand-penciled pages, drawn in the same red-and-blue color scheme as the LP's cover. In a large and neat hand, Ella transcribed the spoken and sung content of the album, accompanying her text with large-format images so that nonreaders could follow along. With teachers in mind, she also made thoughtful accommodations in the book's design, such as a wire binding that would lay flat on a child's desk or a music teacher's piano stand. For these trained teachers she included carefully hand-drawn musical transcriptions of each song, with chords included.

Together, the LP and book surfaced the latent therapeutic characteristics of Ella's call-and-response method of music-making. Music therapy, a professional field that developed from the use of music to care for disabled veterans, was still in its infancy in 1962 and, in retrospect, it is clear that Ella, who had presented rhythm workshops at veterans hospitals, intuitively grasped its core principles. The nonperformative but participatory nature of Ella's approach—*I sing a line and you sing it back to me, unless I instruct you to do something different*—was especially useful to children who experienced anxiety or alienation in social groups. While it was simple, Ella's approach and sound required a great deal of professional self-discipline, observed noted music therapist Deforia Lane, revealing "a masterful teacher" who remained more focused on what children could do than on what *she* could do.[5]

The empathetic, therapeutic aesthetic of *This Is Rhythm* would endear it to generations of teachers and make it Ella's first project to receive notice in professional publications serving music educators and, later, specialists in early childhood education. Through Tom, it may have made it to the desk of Langston Hughes, whose *First Book of Rhythms* was a major inspiration, acknowledged in both the LP's and book's dedications and epigraphs. It even drew an endorsement from the *Little Sandy Review*, the purist folk-music zine that, only a year earlier, had accused Ella of "negating" Black music to make it palatable for square white audiences. Reviewer Barry Hansen did not let the reader forget his earlier takedown or spare Ella's new work from stabs at her racial authenticity—as, for example, in a petulant aside about her "perfect teacher voice." Nor, in the course of claiming that *This Is Rhythm* lacked "racial emphasis," did he acknowledge the album's emphasis on African rhythm instruments, its pointed inclusion of gospel and spirituals ("This Train," "These Bones Shall Rise Again"), or its citation of Hughes. But on her children's project, Hansen conceded, Ella "comes through pretty well." "I am no educational expert," he observed, in a rare moment of humility, "but it all sounds quite good to me."[6]

This Is Rhythm succeeded in large part because of its focus on children. In her two previous albums, Ella had been casting her net wide, hoping to lure older listeners, based perhaps on the popularity of her performances for adults in the Chicago area. Her decided turn to younger audiences on *This Is Rhythm* resulted in accessible, appealing, and innovative music as well as texts and images. Where the earlier albums had left some listeners confused about Ella's political "message," *This Is Rhythm* did a better job with Ella's articulation of sonic diaspora, cultural pluralism, and broadly democratic values of equality. The album's cover image of smiling percussion instruments, each unique and yet part of a whole, was hopeful but not sentimental, a picture of the world as it could be.

Ironically, a track from *Negro Folk Rhythms*, the LP that had caused the *Little Sandy Review* to accuse Ella of "whitewashing" Black music, resurfaced around this time—in a manner that revealed the disharmony of the world as it was. It happened in early 1962 when she and Bernadelle were attending the Chicago debut of *Revelations*, the visionary new dance work by a young choreographer named Alvin Ailey. Ailey based the dance on the spirituals and gospel songs he remembered from his childhood in small-town, segregated Texas in the 1930s, using startlingly new combinations of movement, spectacle, and music to tell an uplifting story of African American history that arced toward freedom. Ella had first heard about the dancer from Brother John Sellers, who worked with Ailey as a musician and arranger. Ever since high school, she had been drawn to modern dance. When Katherine Dunham and Pearl Primus performed in Chicago, she shelled out money to see them—not just once, but for every performance.[7] She likewise admired Ailey troupe member Carmen de Lavallade, whose solo dance, *Come Sunday*, was set to Odetta's recordings of spirituals.

Ella and Bernadelle sat transfixed through *Revelations'* first movement, watching de Lavallade and other dancers, costumed in muted brown tones, perform movements symbolizing African Americans' efforts to rise from the mire of slavery. But during the second section, which explored the "baptism" of Emancipation, they were jolted to attention by the familiar sounds of Ella's recording of "Wade in the Water" with the Goodwill Spiritual Choir. Ella was shocked to hear her voice. No one in the Ailey company had asked her permission to use the song.

By virtue of its roots in the nineteenth century, "Wade in the Water" was part of the public domain. But in using Ella's novel arrangement of the spiritual, which interpolated an original composition, "A Man Went Down to the River," into settings of "Wade in the Water" and "Didn't My Lord Deliver Daniel," the Ailey company had violated copyright law. Even if Ella's version had not been copyrighted, the Ailey company would still have been on the hook for "mechanical" royalties, from the public use of her recording. Either way, the intellectual property issues were straightforward.

Ella's wrangling with the Ailey company would ultimately be resolved to her satisfaction, but the legal back-and-forth over copyright and proper crediting dragged on tediously for several decades. At the time, however, the effect of discovering the company's use of her song would reinforce her desire to protect her "rights" as a Black female composer. Ella's grasp of the inherently political dimensions of her identity as an artist paralleled her sensitivity to the marginal place of children's music within the larger folk revival. She knew that some Chicago folk musicians regarded her artistry as inferior. In a sea of guitars and banjos, hers were among the only conga drums and bongos. More important, she didn't seek to play her instruments or sing with conventional virtuosity. Although the folk world harbored special and sentimental reverence for "untrained" musicians, like any professional music milieu (and as the *Little Sandy Review* made abundantly clear) it had its own pecking orders and rivalries, its own behind-the-scenes chatter about who was "good" and who was not. No one would ever choose an Ella Jenkins song to show off their musical chops. There was a profoundly democratic ethic to her music, insofar as it was designed to be singable or chantable to everyone, even nonmusicians; nevertheless, "children's" music occupied the low end of a continuum that tended to hold technical difficulty and complexity in high standing.

It was therefore heartening to Ella when student organizers invited her to be part of a children's concert at the second annual University of Chicago Folk Festival, in February 1962. The line-up for the Saturday morning show in Mandel Hall included Win Stracke and Ramblin' Jack Elliott, a Woody Guthrie acolyte who was part of the Greenwich Village folk scene. Like Ella, Stracke was well known to Chicago children, appearing as "Uncle Win" on a local kids' television show. But Elliott's main children's credential came from having recently released *Songs to Grow on by Woody Guthrie, Sung by Jack Elliott*, a track-by-track facsimile of Guthrie's well-loved classic, likely recorded by Moe Asch to generate income for the desperately ill singer.

There are distinctly divergent accounts of Elliott's performance, which followed those of Ella and Win. Bernadelle remembered it as disastrous, and that student organizers shut it down after children began running around the auditorium, with Elliott in hot pursuit. The *Little Sandy Review* remembered Ella and Stracke (curtly dismissed as "Chicago's Burl Ives") hogging the stage, so that by the time "poor Jack" appeared, "most of the kids were so tired and restless that he couldn't keep them in their seats." "Jack is fantastic with children, however," the magazine assured, "and he wandered right out into the audience with them, playing and singing while chasing them up and down the aisles."[8]

Whether Elliott was hounding frightened children or mischievously amusing them, the Chicago concert was a significant milestone. World War II had opened the door for the use of US folk music to express patriotism in American classrooms. As composer Henry Cowell told attendees of the 1944 annual meeting of the Music Teachers National Association, folk was the "music of the people, as democracy is a government of the people."[9] Yet in the Cold War era, two distinct approaches to children's folk music emerged. Music educators tended to see American and European folksong as a stepping-stone to children's appreciation of "serious" music.[10] Folk revivalists, in contrast, regarded folk music as an antidote to children's consumption of a mass-media music diet consisting of Madison Avenue jingles and banal commercial pop hits. To these folk fans, the suburban living room—with its hi-fi console and television set—was antagonistic to the populist spirit of the music. So, too, did they perceive an enemy in rock and roll, which by 1960 could no longer be dismissed as a passing fad. "Mass entertainment is murdering tradition and individualism," Mike Fleischer, president of the Chicago Folklore Society, told the *Chicago Tribune* in 1961. "Time was when a youngster who wanted to hear music would learn to play the fiddle. He would keep the old ballads alive and make up new ones. Now he switches on TV or radio and gets commercial junk with nothing to it but rhythm."[11]

Ella had an opportunity to enter the fray of such debates in a special 1962 "Folk Music and Education" issue of *Sing Out!*, the New York–based folk magazine, that featured her on its cover. In her essay "Rhythms for Children," she fearlessly critiqued a certain segment of the white folk Left. She began with a discussion of rock and roll. But instead of portraying the style as a popular scourge, she drew on her training in sociology and her experiences as a chaperone of Y-Teen dances to characterize the music as the latest "folk" expression of Black rhythms to gain a broad American audience:

> In the United States, within the past several years, there has been an increasing emphasis on the *rhythmic* aspects of our popular music. This has, subsequently, affected dance patterns of pre-teens, "teens," and young adults who have created rhythm-filled dances such as the "Madison," the "Continental," the "Slop," the "Watusi" (named after [the] African tribe), the "Pony," the "Roach" (this dance involves rhythmic stamping of the feet—the pretense of killing a roach), and the currently limelighted, "Twist."

From this impressive list, she went on to boldly defend the music on network television. "Even though the so-called TV 'Shoot 'em Ups' are weak, plot and content-wise, the musical background (which often-times overshadows the story) is, in most instances, Good Jazz, and the regularly intervaled singing and instrumental commercials show more musical creativeness than a lot of the 'best-seller' tunes. And *Rhythm* is still the protagonist."[12]

But if contemporary popular culture was not the antagonist of "good" music—in fact, if rhythmic pop might actually develop young people's musicality—then what or who was the enemy? In her liner notes to 1959's *Adventures in Rhythm*, Ella had broached the issue of the racial caricature of people of African descent by insisting on everyone's capacity to enjoy rhythm. Now, she sounded a wearier note, more in line with her unpublished sardonic poem "Negroes Got Rhythm":

> Time upon time I am approached, after a performance or demonstration, with: "Does everybody have rhythm? Don't you find that Negroes have a better sense of rhythm?—You people (meaning Negroes) have such natural rhythm!"
>
> I do find Negro people, as a group, highly rhythmic; however this does not include all Negroes—there are scores of examples I could cite but will not—here's a chance for a little research on your part.
>
> In addition to finding Negroes rhythmical, there are strong rhythmical traits among Arabs, Jews, Armenians, Indians (East), Africans and—well, you name some folk. I have observed also that children and adults from lower income groups respond better rhythmically—they are less inhibited.

Ella's impatience here jumps off the page. In particular, by claiming that she could cite "scores of examples" of Black people who are not "highly rhythmic" but "will not," she puts white readers—presumably people who feel comfortable in their liberalism and racial tolerance—on notice that she will not indulge their ignorance. Her gently facetious aside—"here's a chance for a little research on your part"—comes off as a bold challenge.

Once again, although she did not refer to the civil rights movement directly in "Rhythms for Children," Ella's irritation with the shallowness of white folk bromides about brotherhood reflects the times. The UC Folk Festival took place amid a coordinated campaign of student protest against racial discrimination in university-owned residential properties, not only on campus, but in the surrounding Hyde Park and Kenwood neighborhoods. The members of UC and South Side CORE chapters had joined together to occupy the University Realty office and the president's office. Just a few days before the children's concert, James Farmer, CORE's national chair, gave a speech at Hyde Park's KAM Temple, praising the students. Afterward, members of the audience of 500 sang "We Shall Overcome." On the day the *Chicago Maroon* previewed the festival line-up, it also contained front-page news about the release from jail of several CORE protesters.[13]

Other contributions to the *Sing Out!* "Folk Music and Education" issue—among them, other Folkways contributors—seemed oblivious, not only to such on-the-ground struggles, but also to Ella's perspective as an educated woman who identified with the Black working class. For example, Harvard musicologist Alan C. Buechner, a proponent of folk music in schools, lamented the disappearance of "oral tradition" in America, placing a measure of the blame on youth music and commodity culture. Similarly, the producers of the Folkways LP *American History in Ballad and Song*, which used music to teach suppressed perspectives, bemoaned "the recent juke box-debauchery," as though contemporary rhythm and blues contained no critical perspectives on racism, economic inequality, or urban life.[14] Yet Ella was making the case that "jukebox" music was *itself* a form of oral tradition—and, as evidence, had cited the dances that referenced contemporary urban life and consciousness. A sympathetic reader might well have wondered whether the "minor revolution" Ella was said to have launched had any hope of affecting music education as long as "experts" dug in their heels about contemporary Black popular expression.

A transcription of "The Old Rebel Soldier," a pro-Confederacy song, sounded a final dissonant note in this issue of *Sing Out!* It was offered as one of three Civil War songs collected by folklorist-musician Frank Warner and included on his album *Songs of the Civil War: North and South*, released to mark the centennial of the conflict. But while "The Old Rebel Soldier" possessed historical value, Irwin Silber's decision to publish a song containing the line "I hate the Freedman's Bureau with all its mess and fuss" was still jarring, given that Black Americans in the former Confederacy were at that very moment singing songs in protest of the unfulfilled promises of Reconstruction. It was yet another example of how the folk revivalists' drive to collect, document, and preserve the "old" could lead them to ignore the "folk" in their very midst.

Later that year, in May 1962, Ella, Bernadelle, and their friends celebrated when the US Court of Appeals voided the conviction of Pete Seeger, who had been cited for contempt of Congress for refusing to answer questions about the political affiliations of folk musicians. A seasoned children's performer and an icon of the 1950s and 1960s folk revival, Seeger had been a quiet advocate of Ella's work. And while he proselytized for string instruments, most famously through his book *How to Play a Five-String Banjo*, he was sensitive to Ella's conga drum playing, assuring her on more than one occasion that "for folk songs, you don't need a guitar."[15]

Nevertheless, Ella found herself in the early 1960s contemplating the advantages of a stringed instrument. Running to catch buses while lugging her huge conga drum made sense in 1956, when she started as a freelancer, but now it just seemed impractical. She had begun to see stringed instruments as a source of compositional possibilities that would allow her to avoid being boxed in solely as a performer of Latin and African diasporic music. And as the folk revival kicked into high gear, abetted by the popularity of guitar-based groups like Peter, Paul and Mary, a stringed instrument would open doors that remained closed to her as a specialist in Afro-Caribbean percussion.

The prospect of taking time away from her paid gigs to learn the guitar was daunting. One day, though, her friend and collaborator Shiz Hori suggested the baritone ukulele. Unlike the more popular tenor ukulele, he explained, baritone ukes were tuned like guitars, but with four strings rather than six, they were somewhat easier to learn. A baritone would be big enough to accommodate her large hands and long fingers, but light and compact enough to transport easily. A bit like the way Uncle Flood taught her harmonica, Shiz "taught me two or three major chords and I found out what the chord relationships were," Ella said. "I started investigating and discovered minor chords on my own. I thought the contrast between the major and the minor chords was just great."[16]

In Bernadelle's words, playing the ukulele made Ella "more central" to the folk world, removing the stigma she bore as a player of "primitive" percussion. On the other hand, the ukulele came with its own cultural baggage. When Ella first picked it up, the Hawai'ian instrument was riding a wave of popularity attributable to radio and television personality Arthur Godfrey, whose "ukulele evangelism" spurred a vogue in cheap plastic instruments. The oversize baritone ukulele was the invention of "Broadway Polynesian" Eddie Conners, and while it was initially received as a "Frankenstein" instrument—neither guitar nor ukulele but a hybrid—after Godfrey played it on his TV variety show it acquired its own following.[17]

Other musicians might have shied away from the baritone ukulele because of its déclassé status and ubiquitous marketing as a 1950s children's toy. "If a kid has a uke in his hand," Godfrey had quipped, "he's not going to get in much trouble."[18] Even Elvis Presley, who appeared in several scenes of the movie *Blue Hawai'i* playing a soprano ukulele, could not turn it into an instrument of youth rebellion. But Ella correctly intuited the instrument's appeal both to children and to educators. She liked that the ukulele allowed her to explore the untapped soprano register of her voice (with drums, she usually sang in an alto.) She also was drawn to its Hawai'ian roots, which gave her ways of introducing mainland children to the history and language of the fiftieth state.

Without fanfare, Ella had introduced herself as a ukulele player on *This Is Rhythm*'s "My Dog Has Fleas." (In a bit of an inside joke, the phrase "my dog has fleas" is a long-standing mnemonic device for the tuning of four-stringed ukuleles.) She was still associated with the conga drum, but that would soon begin to change. Following the positive reception of *This Is Rhythm*, she saved enough money to book a session at Maurice Seymour, a Chicago photography studio that was popular with African American musicians.

FIGURE 8.3. Publicity photo with drum, ca. early 1960s.
Photo by Maurice Seymour.

The images—two among several taken that day—offer different versions of Ella. The mood of the tom-tom portrait is alluring and mysterious, evoking the lineage of exoticized women-of-color female performers, from Carmen Miranda to Eartha Kitt. It is a "nighttime" photo, on the brink of sultriness, and sophisticated in a manner that suggests a club appearance.

In contrast, the ukulele portrait is approachable, wholesome, and, by virtue of Ella's wide smile, natural-seeming. It is a "daytime" photo, positioning her as a singer of songs. In the next several years Ella would continue to play the role of rhythm specialist. But increasingly, the ukulele would eclipse the conga drum as her signature instrument. Within the course of five years, she would be firmly associated with ukulele—and the only African American player of national prominence.

FIGURE 8.4. Publicity photo with ukulele, ca. early 1960s.
Photo by Maurice Seymour.

PART III
CHILDREN'S
ARTIST

Dear Miss Jenkins,

I think you're pretty.

Love,
Pamela

(MANNING, SOUTH CAROLINA, 1982)

9
ON THE ROAD
1962–1964

The CORE sit-ins and pickets of Ella's "rebel years" in the late 1940s had generally been small-scale affairs. She and her fellow protesters would enter restaurants, college cafeterias, and lunch counters in groups of three or four. But the mass struggles of the late 1950s and early 1960s—the Montgomery bus boycott, the Nashville student sit-ins, the Freedom Rides, and the Albany movement (associated with a wide-ranging civil rights campaign in Albany, Georgia)—called for new organizational tactics. These activists turned group singing into a potent tool of resistance. *We are not afraid*, they intoned from Mississippi prison cells, awaiting trial on trumped-up charges. *Ain't gonna let nobody turn me around*, they affirmed, infusing the traditional hymn with new meaning. For organizers, songs like "I Woke Up This Morning" were often as effective as any speech or flyer in communicating movement vision and strategy. "Woke up this morning with my mind stayed on Jesus," the people sang. "I'm gonna' walk, talk, sing, shout! / Hallelu I've got my mind on freedom!"[1]

Between 1962 and 1964 Ella engaged in her own freedom organizing through music, inspired both by ordinary people and by artist-
activists like Max Roach, Abbey Lincoln, and the Chicago-based
musician-composer Oscar Brown Jr. When *We Insist! Max Roach's
Freedom Now Suite*, the drummer's landmark collaboration with Lincoln and Brown, was banned by South Africa's Apartheid government
in 1962, Ella dedicated an episode of her *Meetin' House* radio show
to it. Using music to bring together domestic and global struggles
against racism, she juxtaposed tracks from *We Insist!* with selections
from *South African Freedom Songs*, a 1960 Folkways EP, and Big Bill
Broonzy's 1957 recording of "I Wonder When I'll Get to Be Called a
Man":

> They said I was uneducated,
> My clothes was dirty and torn;
> Now I've got a little education,
> But I'm still a boy, right on.

The South African government's censorship of a groundbreaking
civil rights album sharpened Ella's desire to make her own definitive
music statement about Black freedom. Although she explicitly referenced the civil rights movement in the liner notes to 1960's *Negro Folk
Rhythms*, the movement had in some ways outpaced even that lofty
project; for example, Ella was now regularly using the phrase "Afro-
American" instead of "Negro." The 1963 centennial of the Emancipation Proclamation presented an opportunity to make such an album.

In August of 1962 Ella wrote to Moe Asch, pitching her idea. She
proposed a collaboration with studio musicians and suggested a
recording targeted at older listeners. Showing her business acumen,
she proposed a retail price of five dollars, "an attractive price for the
Centennial." "If you're not interested in the project, please let me
know right away as I will try to peddle it elsewhere," she wrote. "I say
this because it is an album of conviction that I must make even if I have
to do it on my own and have limited copies." To make her urgency

crystal clear, she enclosed a stamped and pre-addressed envelope, along with the instruction to "please write yes or no."[2]

Asch never used the envelope. But neither did Ella follow through on her plan to record it with a different label. More precisely, travel got in the way—scrambling her plans and redirecting her creative energies. That fall she received an out-of-the-blue phone call from folk musician Sandy Paton. Personal circumstances, he explained, were compelling him to give up his work as a performer with the School Assembly Service, an educational booking agency. He thought Ella, especially given her expertise with young audiences, would make a fine replacement. The touring could be exhausting, Paton explained, but it was a source of steady income, and she could use her school visits to promote and sell her recordings and publications.

The School Assembly Service was exactly what it sounded like: an agency that offered educational programming to supplement regular classroom instruction. Particularly for children in small-town and rural schools, it provided key opportunities for exposure to the arts. Musicians sponsored by the service in the early 1960s included Merrill Nelson, a Minnesota trombonist and marching band director; a percussion trio headed by Harold Jones, a Black Chicagoan who taught at the American Conservatory of Music; and Charles King, a soloist and conductor with the renowned Ohio-based Wings Over Jordan Choir.

It took Ella two tryouts to convince the agency of the viability of her proposed "Adventures in Rhythm" program, modeled on her familiar rhythm workshops. The promotional flyer created by the Service to publicize it with school administrators showed Ella with her conga drum and wearing an African-style print shirt. It also bore the Langston Hughes quotation that Ella had cited in the *This Is Rhythm* liner notes: "Rhythm is something we share in common, you and I, with all the plants and animals and peoples in the world, and with the stars and moon and sun, and all the vast wonderful universe beyond this wonderful earth which is our home." The combination of image and words put principals on alert: while "Adventures in Rhythm" would be friendly and fun, it would not shy away from themes associated with Black Americans or civil rights.

Betty Carlson, the affable manager of the Chicago branch of the School Assembly Service, explained that she would provide Ella with a weekly itinerary and a per diem, but that Ella would be responsible for her own transportation. This created an immediate problem, since Ella had never learned how to drive. Once she had ventured a few lessons, but they had not gone well, and she had given up. Bernadelle possessed both a car and the fortitude for long road trips, but she was finishing her college degree.

As a result, during her two seasons with the School Assembly Service—from September 1962 through April 1963—Ella relied on a series of drivers. The list included Ginni Clemmens, Ginni's cousin's husband Jonathan, and Patty Jo Kelly, who was the nephew of one of Bernadelle's aunt's friends. Each eventually quit because Ella's itinerary was so demanding, hard on cars as well as people, particularly during the winter. "As soon as there comes a snowstorm, hailstorm, all kind of storms, unpleasant weather, [the drivers] said, 'I want to go back to Chicago,'" Ella remembered. After watching them perform car repairs in the bitter cold, she could not blame them.

Of all of Ella's drivers, Harold Hampton Murray, a twenty-one-year-old Wilson Junior College student, lasted the longest and had the greatest impact. A flutist and percussionist who would later record with Sun Ra, he had been a student of "Captain" Walter Dyett at DuSable High School and had picked up the conga after finding a cheap one at Frank's Drum Shop.[3] Around town, he occasionally played as part of a duo called Harold and Carl, but he also lent his talents to the Southside Community Committee center and had performed at a party celebrating the release of *Negro Folk Rhythms*. Harold was legally an adult, but Ella made a point of calling his mother and getting her permission for them to travel together.

Together, they undertook what Harold described as a "beautiful adventure," in which Ella brought her fugitive civil rights pedagogy to children and teens throughout the Upper Midwest. With Harold behind the wheel of a 1959 Pontiac and Ella giving directions, they embarked on tours that could last several weeks and include as many as three programs, at three different schools, in a single day. At each assembly Ella, who now performed with her ukulele as well as drums, would do a version of her rhythm workshop, with Harold lending a hand on flute or conga. "In twenty weeks with Ella I drove 28,500 miles," Harold, who later changed his name to Baba Atu, said. "Twenty-eight thousand five hundred! We would do all of our gigs, go to the next town, and then rest up to get ready for our next performances. . . . By the end, I didn't even need the map."[4]

Ella, who loved the sound of words, kept a tally of the names of the towns they visited. Some—including Nappanee, Wausaukee, Kaukauna, Escanaba, and Saginaw—had names derived from Native languages. Others, like Goodland, Star City, New Albany, and Richland, bore titles that expressed the idealism of the Europeans who colonized Native lands. Still others were named for fabled cities—Syracuse and Palmyra—as though the luster of these ancient places would somehow rub off on North Americans.

Harold and Ella were never sure what sort of facilities or audiences they would encounter. Sometimes they were shown to gleaming auditoriums. At other times they found themselves cleaning dingy, neglected spaces just to be able to perform in them. At some schools the teachers used the assemblies as breaks, depositing their students and then disappearing, leaving Ella and Harold to fend for themselves. At others the teachers and principal stayed and took notes. At majority African American schools they encountered children who sat "like statues," minding teachers who threatened punishment for "bad" behavior, Harold said; in those schools Ella would spend time drawing them out. At others, the children were unable to contain their energy and had difficulty focusing. But Ella always managed to win them over. "You could see it working—music soothes the savage beast," Harold joked. Eventually, even the rowdiest children "gave up on their aggression."[5]

The folk revival was filled with musicians trading war stories about gigs played in obscure coffee houses or to a handful of drunk patrons in a ratty basement bar. But they had nothing on Ella and Harold, who had to win over indifferent adolescents and high schoolers who would not hesitate to express their boredom. In such situations Ella relied on the interactivity of call-and-response rhythmic group singing. When most musicians performed in schools, they enforced the "rules" of the concert hall, demanding stillness and silence until it was time to applaud. Ella had no such rules; more than that, she expected children to raise their voices. She also paid attention to stagecraft, appearing in her African print dresses and shirts and laying out tables of exotic instruments to pique the students' interest. She appealed to their desire for forbidden knowledge, explaining that songs could convey histories that were not in their textbooks.

Ella was skilled at navigating the social dynamics of the assemblies. Knowing that some children avoided the spotlight while others

FIGURE 9.1. Ella and Harold Murray on the School Assembly Service tour, ca. 1962. Unknown photographer.

relished it, she chose volunteers strategically. "Certainly everyone enjoyed watching our top fullback play a cow bell while the audience sang a number of weird sounds over and over and over again," wrote a reporter from the *Preble High School Buzz*, a student newspaper in Green Bay, Wisconsin.[6] Back in Chicago Betty Carlson collected quotes from the letters of satisfied school administrators. From Rocky River, Ohio: "Miss Jenkins has the ability to get her audience 'with her' in presenting her musical program. We would be happy to have her back." From Rock Island, Illinois: "Fine Student participation, educational, well handled. Like to have her back again." "Well received and enjoyed by all. Very unique and educational," wrote a junior high school principal in Galesburg, Illinois.[7]

Whereas other people might not have lasted long with such lonely and demanding work, Ella gathered her resolve, approaching her performances as opportunities to plant seeds of tolerance and openness. She invited tow-haired children of Northern European ancestry to join her in singing spirituals that spoke of deliverance from the "Egypt" of slavery. By giving context to Black work songs, she countered textbook fictions of the contented slave and contemporary myths of the Black agricultural laborer. In some assemblies she decorated the stage with a cloth stamped with images of Léopold Senghor with the word "President" underneath. Maybe her audiences would not remember *Senegal* as the name of the African country that had chosen Senghor as its first leader, or maybe they would not be able to find Senegal on a map. But the powerful notion that Black men could be presidents might lodge in their minds.

Ella and Harold's "beautiful adventure" was also beset by the ugliness of racism, in an area of the country that infrequently made it into national headlines about civil rights. Not unlike the "real" Freedom Riders, they too were pioneers of freedom, putting their bodies on the line. Many of the children Ella entertained at her assemblies had never seen a Black teacher, or encountered a Black woman in a position of authority, within a school or any other setting. One white child confided that she resembled his family's Black domestic servant. In Hazel

Green, Wisconsin, Harold recalled, white people "rubbed my hand to see if the color would rub off." Even when their school hosts were courteous and welcoming, Ella and Harold ran the risk of being seen as "intruders" rather than as guests. A school principal once called the police on them for "loitering" outside of the school building, when they had merely arrived early for their performance.[8]

However, the schools were safe havens compared to the restaurants and hotels where they sought meals and lodging. Finding places that would serve them was a greater hardship than long days, endless drives, and inhospitable weather. Sometimes their only choice of lodging was miles from the schools where they performed, putting pressure on their already crowded schedules. Some restaurants refused them peremptorily, with only a look. "If the place was too racist we'd move on," Harold said.

Ella experienced such encounters as a form of bodily pain. As she would tell an interviewer years later, "I don't know if you've ever been discriminated against, if you've—if anyone had any prejudices against you—[but] there is something in your stomach that curls up. A knot gets into your stomach, and in your throat and you can hardly swallow, cause you don't know what to expect."[9] When she was dreading an unpleasant encounter, the ordinary friendliness of a waitress or hotel manager could make an average apple pie taste better and a thin mattress feel luxurious. But anxiety—of the sort Ella had written about in her 1951 college essay "My Sensitive Soul"—always loomed over the next interaction.

To manage the strain, Ella leaned into smalls acts of subversion. Once when the host of a restaurant refused them service on the pretense that the establishment was a "private club," Ella wrote "Does not serve colored" on a piece of paper and put it in the window as they were leaving. Humor could also take the sting out of sharp emotions. When the white people in small towns openly stared at them, Ella would joke with Harold, "Boy we're celebrities! Everybody's watching us."[10] At times when levity would not do, they took solace in each other. "We kind of talked to each other and therapized each other as we went along," Harold said. "We rationalized what they were going through, [saying] whatever it is, we're not carrying their baggage." In this, Harold and Ella closely resembled the civil rights activists who were trained not to respond to insult or even physical assault. Such strategies of mindful resistance to external stimuli (including physical pain) recalled Ella's Sunday School lessons at the Eighth Church of Christ, Scientist as well as CORE. Do not let mortal mind deceive or control you, her teacher Mrs. Rayford had instructed.

While on tour, Ella kept in touch with Bernadelle through chatty and affectionate postcards and letters. On one October evening, while Harold dozed at the Heim Motel in Connorsville, Indiana (they shared a room to save money), she wrote contentedly of their comfortable accommodations and the day's enthusiastic audiences. A week later she sent Bernadelle typed greetings from the Hollander Hotel in Nappanee, Indiana, where the proprietors were "especially kind and talkative," and shared her impressions of the Amish people who farmed the area. "I'd certainly like to visit their farms for I hear they are exceptionally good farmers. The men all have beards & the women wear bonnets. Instead of automobiles—they use horse and carriage . . . they use bicycles quite a lot also."[11]

It was Ella's practice to shield Bernadelle from "negative" news, although she broke her rule after a traumatic experience in Greencastle, Indiana, a town of about 8,500 people between Terre Haute and Indianapolis, in October 1962:

As tired and sleepy as I am I must sit up and write this letter or I shall explode.

This has been a trying night since arriving in this lovely (ha ha) town. People greet us with such hatred and suspicion! This is the first time since the tour that I don't feel enthusiastic about doing a program and yet I must because I am under contract and represent the agency.

. . . .

I shall never forget this humiliation, however, I am not going to spoil my daily preserve [*sic*] by keeping a chip on my shoulder. For one reason, I've got to help lift Harold's spirits and we must not lose faith in all white folks of Indiana for some have been nice and considerate.

In the same letter, she turned to Christian Science precepts:

> The beauty—the real beauty, I should say—of Indiana is its lovely country side—the many and varied trees—the grazing cattle and freshness—the air is good and clean. Mother nature is a beautiful personality if only mortal man could really take notice of her and reflect just a bit of that beauty. War would not exist in any form. We would learn to love this fellow man. So much for the thesis on brotherly love.[12]

Ella described the incident to Moe Asch in similar terms: "At present I am on tour of Indiana schools presenting school assemblies and learning very fast that Mississippi, Alabama, Louisiana, etc. are not the only states who are afraid and suspicious of the Negro."[13] And she wrote to Betty Carlson in Chicago, informing her that from that moment on, the School Assembly Service would have to book her hotels in advance, or she would break her contract.

Ella's tour concluded on April 10, 1963, a couple of days before Martin Luther King Jr. entered the cell from which he penned his famous "Letter from Birmingham Jail." In it he praised the courage and discipline of activists. Ella, too, had shown courage and discipline. "I know there have been difficult times," Carlson wrote to her in a parting letter of thanks, "but I hope the joyous ones will come out ahead and am sure that if you think in terms of what you have done for the young people, you will be gratified and feel it has been worth all the effort you have put into it."[14]

Ella had happier travels to look forward to. While she was out on the road, Bernadelle had been planning a two-month European trip. Fantasizing about the trip helped Ella manage the depression and loneliness of the school tours. Writing to Bernadelle from Paris, Illinois, she joked that "soon we'll be in *Paris, France*." In another letter she sketched the two of them relaxing on the deck of a Holland America ship. She even wrote to Holland America. "We wish to thank you for your kind consideration in sending us the circular pertaining to Miss Ella Jenkins' ability as a rhythm specialist," a company representative responded. "We are quite sure that our management will welcome her desire to perform . . . , and we have written to our New York office in full."[15]

Ella and Bernadelle sailed in June from New York harbor on the *SS Rotterdam*. Bernadelle was miserable with seasickness and took refuge in their berth. But for Ella the ship was a playground. She won its onboard table-tennis tournament, passed hours on the deck playing with children, and followed through on her offer to Holland America by leading a call-and-response sing-along from the ship's bandstand. She dashed off a happy postcard to thank her "Folkways family"—Moe, Marian Distler, and Irwin Silber—for the orchid they had purchased for her state room. "The flower was a most colorful bon voyage—thank you so much!" she effused. "The sailing is smooth, people are friendly, and the food the best ever!"[16]

Like other African American musicians who traveled abroad the 1950s and 1960s, Ella felt freer in Europe. With Bernadelle she strolled the streets of "Paris, France" without fear of being stared at or accosted. She visited restaurants in London and hotel rooms in Amsterdam with no "knot" in her stomach. Bernadelle had planned a varied itinerary—in France, Italy, Holland, Germany, Switzerland, Monaco, Belgium, Denmark, England, and Austria—and they did all of the typical tourist things. Both also documented their trip—Bernadelle with her cameras, Ella with a Hitachi tape recorder.

They also visited with two of Ella's old Chicago friends, both Black male musicians who had opened nightclubs in Europe. Jo Banks now lived in Copenhagen with his white American wife Karen and ran the Purple Door, a small but thriving folk and blues venue. Harold Bradley, an old friend from the Eighth Church of Christ, Scientist, had studied art in Perugia before settling in Rome and marrying a German Jewish

woman. He ran Folkstudio, a small art studio/folk club that drew politi-
cized, working-class Romans as well as visitors from around the world.
When they arrived there, Bernadelle and Ella spotted Bob Dylan at
Harold's club, although they never talked.[17]

Of the places that they visited, Ella ranked Switzerland, home of
Bernadelle's paternal ancestors, as her favorite. She was particularly
taken by the Kinderdorf Pestalozzi in Trogan, where war orphans were
cared for until they could be repatriated. The Kinderdorf's principles
of cooperative living and cultural exchange (children received instruction in their native languages while also learning German) greatly
impressed Ella, who shared her enthusiasm in a postcard to Moe:

> Yesterday I spend a little more than 2 hours in this amazing little vil-
> lage. Unfortunately most of the 200 children, representing 10 different
> nations, were on their summer holidays, however a sizeable group of
> children walked, ran and played throughout the grounds. I donated
> my latest little album to the children and staff and wish you could send
> them other records. I'll share more upon my return.[18]

Ella loved the stark beauty of Switzerland. But the highlight of the
1963 trip was her visit to the Salzburg, Austria–based music institute
of German composer Carl Orff, known internationally for his cantata
Carmina Burana. The opportunity to visit the institute, which backed
up to a mountain range later immortalized in *The Sound of Music*, had
come about through Ella's correspondence with Richard Johnston,
a University of Toronto musicologist who was also a leading North
American disseminator of Orff's *Schulwerk*, a novel approach to music
pedagogy. After discovering *Call-and-Response Rhythmic Group Singing* and noticing its resonances with Orff's work, he put Ella and the
composer in contact. An invitation to Salzburg had followed.

In the early 1960s US music educators were only beginning to learn
about Orff's *Schulwerk*, which he initially developed in the culturally
and politically protean period of the Weimar Republic in Germany. To
that point, most of them had been taught to drill children in skills of

sight-reading Western musical notation. Orff proposed to "liberate" young students from such a narrow and lifeless pedagogy: to give them instruments, teach them simple and accessible songs, and encourage movement. In North America his approach resonated with a broader 1960s-era questioning of restrictive social norms. As a flyer for a 1963 Orff-Schulwerk teacher workshop at Ball State University explained, "Music should grow in a child as it once developed in history. . . . Rhythm and melody are elemental forces which should be free to work their age-old magic before being artfully combined and shackled by harmony. . . . Children should be encouraged to make music on their own level, free from mechanical drill, free from adult pressure."[19]

Ella arrived in Salzburg with little idea of what to expect. But Orff, a spry sixty-eight-year-old, and his Institute colleagues Gunild Keetman and Lotte Flach, put her at ease. The room in which she presented her workshop (as Bernadelle watched, snapping photographs) was large and high-ceilinged, and filled with the instruments at the center of Orff's practice. Some, like cymbals, triangles, timpani drums, and glockenspiels, featured in German orchestral music. Others, including hand drums, castanets, tambourines, wood blocks, and specially modified xylophones and metallophones, were based on Orff's observations of Asian and African instruments. The metal instruments were attached to bases of various heights to accommodate different players.

At first Ella found presenting slow-going. Everything she said had to be translated for the international group, first into German and then into French. But the workshop, which she had titled "Fun with Rhythms and Sounds," took off as soon as she got everyone patting out cadences on percussion instruments and chanting "Tah-boo"—a song that, because it belonged to no particular language, required no mediation.

Afterward, Ella maintained a warm correspondence with Orff and his colleagues. "Back in our home we found your records and books and we are glad to have you with us whenever we want to hear one of your thrilling, lively performances," the composer wrote. "You must know already how honored I felt," she replied, "being called upon to

FIGURE 9.2. Ella in Austria with Carl Orff and Gunild Keetman, 1963.
Photo by Bernadelle Richter.

lead these sessions. It was, indeed, a new experience for me to have
sessions translated into other languages and I certainly appreciated
and put to good use my financial gift. I bought a lovely Swiss watch in
Bern and I call it my 'Orff' watch."[20]

Although Ella and Orff both centered on children's exploration
of rhythm and their creative improvisation, Ella's music pedagogy
was far more politicized than Orff's. From the onset of her career as
a "rhythm specialist," her commitment to civil rights had driven her
pedagogy, influencing everything from song selection to her grounding concept of call-and-response group singing. As Bernadelle noted,
music was Ella's means, not her end. In contrast, while Americans

inferred a politics of freedom in Orff's *Schulwerk*, the composer was notably and perhaps strategically "apolitical." The son of a Jewish man who had converted to Christianity, Orff survived the Third Reich by remaining largely silent in the face of horrors perpetuated by the National Socialists. In the postwar era his erroneous claims to having been an active part of the anti-Nazi resistance suggest the guilty conscience of someone who survived by sacrificing his better angels.[21]

And yet, despite their different orientations, Ella experienced Orff's enthusiasm as a powerful affirmation. It was especially meaningful to her as an "untrained" musician, who had enormous grassroots appeal to teachers but lacked standing in the world of professional music education. As Orff's method took off in the United States in the later 1960s, populating elementary school classrooms from Boston to Los Angeles with small-scale metallophones, glockenspiels, xylophones, and other "Orff instruments," Ella enjoyed the satisfaction of knowing how her own "little album" had so impressed the composer that he invited her to Austria. In 1963 no other US practitioner of children's music—let alone someone who had developed her method outside of music institutions—could claim such a distinction.

Ella celebrated her thirty-ninth birthday that August aboard the ship back to New York. As it passed Nantucket, she recorded the sounds of the Atlantic Ocean. In her girlhood, "traveling" meant moving to "higher" and more reputable addresses within Bronzeville. Later it meant sitting in a record-store booth and listening to songs from the Caribbean, Africa, and the Middle East. Now, it meant crossing the ocean on a luxurious ship, after traversing Europe with her dearest friend Bernadelle.

In 1953 James Baldwin published "Stranger in the Village," an essay reflecting on his experiences one summer in the remote Swiss hamlet of Leukerbad, the first Black man the villagers have ever seen. His sojourn there is both painful and illuminating, leading him to realize that although his own country would deny and oppress him, he is no "stranger" to America.[22] Ella's travels ten years later were in contrast exhilarating, but no less illuminating. They reinforced her belief in the universalism of rhythm and the tremendous variety of ways that humans made meaning with music. She did not naively believe that all peoples, or all popular forms of musical expression, enjoyed the same status or power. But the European trip did confirm her sense of the importance of knowledge of the wider world, especially for children without the means to travel. As she told Studs Terkel in December 1963, she used bells "from other parts of the world" in her rhythm workshops, because "oftentimes, some of these children have not gone far beyond their own neighborhoods or their own cities, and this is a way that children can have a traveling experience in rhythms and sounds and songs beyond their own experience and their own little areas."[23]

Ella pursued the idea of music as a "traveling experience" on two Folkways recordings released in the wake of her European trip. She conceptualized the first of these, *Rhythms of Childhood* (1963), an album mostly devoted to songs about nature and dance, while she was still traveling to school assemblies with Harold Murray, who contributes drumming and chanting on a track called "Rhythms of Far Away." In the liner notes Ella offered brief explanations of how and where she had learned particular songs, demonstrating the relationship between travel and cultural transmission or exchange. Some songs—like "The Cuckoo"—came to Ella via complex itineraries: a live performance on an episode of the *Meetin' House* radio show by singer-guitarist Jim Kweskin, based on a version he had heard by the Reverend Gary Davis. Others—like "Many Pretty Trees around the World," a song introducing children to the names of different trees—were inspired by Ella's own travels, in this case her summer visits to Bridgton, Maine.

A meandering album that reflects the experience of traveling without a fixed destination, *Rhythms of Childhood* is grounded by "Wake Up Little Sparrow," a song that Orff and his colleagues had singled out for praise.[24] On the surface it is a tender, blues-inflected meditation about a baby bird. "Wake up, wake up, little sparrow," Ella sings, fingering minor chords on the baritone ukulele. "Don't make your home out in the snow." But it is also a wistful love song, as Ella acknowledged openly in the liner notes: "I wrote it for a dear friend—Bernadelle Richter—who is as gentle as a sparrow." This gentleness comes through in Ella's sensitive solo performance of the melody, which repeatedly hovers and then descends, a bit like a bird in flight.

The words and sound of "Wake Up Little Sparrow" also carry an air of melancholic yearning, suggesting that Ella composed it while on the road for the School Assembly Service during the winter or early spring of 1962. "Hi, Little Sparrow," Ella had written Bernadelle, on letterhead from Sleepy Head Tourist Home in Fowler, Indiana. "Here I sit in a . . . quiet, quiet little Indiana town with nothing to do but read, write letters, sleep, eat and read, write letters, etc., . . . My transistor radio is playing—it keeps me company."[25] The loneliness of that particular period—and Ella's own sense of dislocation—come through in the rich ambiguity of the song's final two verses, which portray the vulnerability of the baby sparrow as well as the helplessness of the speaker, who can only watch as she sits alone in the snow:

> Little bird, O don't you know
> Your friends flew South, many months ago
> Your friends flew South, many months ago
> You're just a babe, you cannot fly
> Your wings won't spread against the sky
> Your wings won't spread against the sky

Ella recorded *Songs and Rhythms from Near and Far* (1964) after she returned from Europe. In contrast to the earlier album it finds Ella contemplating travel as a source of inner peace and spiritual growth. "We are all travelers in some big or small way," Ella elaborated in the philosophical statement that opens her liner notes:

> Some of our travelling experiences are quite similar, some are exactly the same and some of them are oceans and dreams apart.

The manner in which we travel is not nearly as important as the traveling itself, and what we learn from our travels and how we apply that learning to everyday living, is the most significant of all. Therefore, as we share SONGS AND RHYTHMS FROM NEAR AND FAR, let us keep before us, the *spiritual* as well as the physical concept of traveling.

Being at peace or at home with oneself and traveling beyond this point to a deeper understanding of others is one example of journeying in a spiritual way.

Good and worthwhile thoughts and attitudes can help us to travel far in life, reaching glorious heights, whereas negative thinking stunts out growth, keeping us hidden in dark, obscure places.[26]

Deeply influenced by Christian Science precepts, the statement seems to depict Ella's European travels as a source of spiritual sustenance, a balm to the "negative thinking" that clouded her earlier Midwestern journeys. In fact, Ella also reproduced her letters from Richard Johnston and Orff—all of them brimming with praise and excitement about her work. "I have been thinking of your work and how you do it . . . and my admiration has mounted constantly," Johnston wrote. "The discussions I had . . . this summer further made me realize I was right about you—not that I needed any more confirmation than I already had."[27]

In the liner notes, Ella published these letters in their entirety—chatty and business asides included—as a show of pride. But she also used them to attract attention in professional music circles. "These correspondences," she wrote, "should be of interest to music educators, and especially to those working in the area of music education for children, as there are many in the field, exploring new ways to help bring about richer and more enjoyable musical experiences to children."[28] Ella knew that the words of notable white men like Johnston and Orff were far more influential in professional circles than the most effusive praise of Black female YWCA officials, social service agency administrators, and small-town white school principals. Orff's imprimatur carried particular weight as a great living modern European composer.

Through its instrumentation and song selection, *Songs and Rhythms from Near and Far* routed teachers and children to the folk music of Western and Eastern Europe, the Middle East, and Black America. Some of the tracks, such as "A Little Town in Switzerland" and "Land of Canada," followed directly from Ella's experiences, while others drew from songs she had learned from others. She even included a documentary recording of the Greek "Yerakina," a folk dance, made during one of the Orff sessions in Salzburg. And although the hundredth anniversary of Emancipation had passed, Ella expressed her hopes for African Americans, in their journey "up from slavery" through the spirituals "Go Down, Moses" (listed as "Let My People

FIGURE 9.3. *Songs from Near and Far* LP with cover drawing by Peggy Lipschutz, 1964. Courtesy of Smithsonian Folkway Recordings.

Go") and "Joshua Fit the Battle of Jericho." Emancipation—as a state of mind as well as a political condition—was also expressed in Peggy Lipschutz's striking cover drawing, which transposed the image of a whirling globe over the image of the head of a pigtailed Black girl. It was an apt depiction of the Afro-diasporic vision Ella had been working toward since the 1950s.

Ella even found a use for her recording of the sounds of the waves off Nantucket, interpolating it into "I'm Going to Sea Now," an original song performed in three-part harmony by the Old Town School of Folk Music teachers Shirley Hersh and Ted Johnson. In a brief spoken introduction, Ella describes it as the "song of a young man who goes to sea." But it can just as easily be heard as her own reflections on her life's journey with Bernadelle:

> I'm going to sea now
> But I'll be back again . . .
> I'll travel this world over
> To see where the road to life will end . . .
> Perhaps I'll find me a loved one
> And she will be my bride

In June 1964 Ella took her first trip by airplane, accompanied by Win Stracke, Studs Terkel, and banjoist Fleming Brown. The four were returning to Chicago from an appearance at the Illinois Pavilion at the World's Fair in New York City. Soon after takeoff, their airplane ran into a violent thunderstorm. The three men hunkered down with drinks to calm their nerves, as lightning bolts stabbed the sky. But Ella gazed excitedly out her window. "Look how beautiful it is!" she exclaimed.

Only Ella could be so enchanted by something that others found so objectively terrifying. But that was part of her uncanny repose, on airplanes or elsewhere. Bernadelle, who also loved travel, nevertheless suffered in airplanes as she did on ships, trading seasickness for an interminable insomnia that left her exhausted upon arrival. But Ella would fall asleep promptly after takeoff, or perhaps after composing a couple of poems about the beauty of the clouds, and arrive at their destination refreshed. Every time she boarded an airplane, it was a reminder of how far she had come and, in the words of Nina Simone's 1967 civil rights anthem, a premonition of what "how it would feel to be free."

Dear Ella Jinkins

Thank you for calling me up on the stage.
I enjoid plaing the potato game and the bells.
I also enjoid the songs and I also thank you
for letting me say about the Volcano. That
was fun Ella Jinkins!

From Josh

(HUMBLE, TEXAS, 1989)

10

YOU'LL SING A SONG

1964–1968

Sometime after she and Bernadelle returned from Europe, Ella traded her apartment at Midway Gardens for an eleventh-floor unit at a new apartment complex at 2851 South Parkway, in Prairie Shores, a neighborhood south of the Loop. The move allowed for an easier commute to Bernadelle's parents' house and lower rent. At Prairie Shores, a room in a sparkling building with fresh paint and new appliances could be had for as little as thirty-five dollars a month. The most coveted units had views of Lake Michigan.

In moving to Prairie Shores, Ella took advantage of the postwar "revivification" of Chicago's Near South Side, which included the adjacent development, Lake Meadows. A city-led process of "slum clearance" reaching back to the 1940s had displaced thousands of low-income Black residents to develop real estate near Michael Reese Hospital and the Illinois Institute of Technology. The new high-rises were intended for middle-class Black Chicagoans, who had few decent housing options on the South Side, but also for white families. *Tribune* advertisements for Lake Meadows, the first and bigger of the two developments, read like a checklist of the American Suburban Dream: "100 acres of lawns and private tree-lined streets," "acres of free parking space," "safe play areas for children," "complete, modern shopping," and "Lake Meadows' own nursery school." In the *Defender* both Lake Meadows and Prairie Shores were touted for their affordability and outreach to a "mixed occupancy."[1]

By the time Ella moved there, the populations of Prairie Shores and Lake Meadows had broken down along racial lines, with Ella living among the mostly white residents of Prairie Shores. But while the forces of resegregation were beyond Ella's control, she did at least enjoy living somewhere that left her with a bit more in her pocket at the end of every month.

Living at Prairie Shores also eased Ella's weekly commute to the Niles Township JCC, where she continued to offer music classes. She found it interesting to see the world through the eyes of religiously liberal 1960s-era Ashkenazi Jewish American children, who (unlike some of their parents) were growing up confident in their Americanness— and their whiteness. One student likened her to a woman who worked in his house, recalling comments she had heard from children during her School Assembly Service tours. Others assumed that she was Jewish, or referred to her as Ella *Jacobs*. Once, after spying a harmonica Ella brought to class, a boy exclaimed, "It's a Hanukkah!" Ella used his adorable mistake as the inspiration for "Harmonica for Hanukkah," a novelty tune that still shows up in holiday playlists.

The harmonica-Hanukkah mix-up contained an important lesson about working with children who were still developing basic language skills, along with the dexterity to write with a pencil or skip to a song: to engage them, a teacher had to be willing to improvise, embracing the child's own point of view. At the JCC Ella created the song "It's the Milkman" to help children grasp the category of dairy products. "Look who's here, it's the milkman," her song began. "And I wonder what he's brought today." From there, the children could take turns responding. When one boy said the milkman brought him orange juice, instead of telling him he was wrong, Ella changed the prompt to "I wonder what *your* milkman brought today."[2]

Ella's JCC charges inhabited rich imaginative worlds.[3] Call and response was a launching pad for their own creativity—an entryway into composition. Once a child practiced imitating the words, rhythms, or sounds Ella modeled, she could make up lyrics, rhythms, and sounds of her own, and the game could continue until she tired of it.

As stimulating as the preschoolers were, however, they also presented Ella with unique challenges. Unlike self-conscious middle schoolers or defiant high schoolers, preschoolers were generally open to repeating new sounds or words back to her. (Their receptivity eventually led her to incorporate more foreign-language learning into her songs, departing from her earlier habit of composing with sound or "moods" in mind.) But the preschoolers required more help when it came to sharing and taking turns, skills that Ella would come to refer to as "group awareness." Sometimes a four-year-old would get so attached to a particular instrument that she would refuse to surrender it when it was time to move on to the next activity. At the same time, children's different abilities required sensitivity to wide variation within the group. A child might eagerly "respond" to Ella's call, for example, but still be unable to match her sound.

Through trial and error, Ella developed a distinctive approach to working with such preschoolers, subverting the expectation of young children's musical experiences as "preparation" for later performance or technical study. In 1964 teachers of kindergarten music classes approached song through the lens of their art training. They valued Stephen Foster songs, which entered the American canon through blackface minstrel shows, for their melodic complexity, assuming that such intricacy was good for children's development. Children learned such songs—as well as other material from Anglo-American, French and German tradition—to a teacher's piano accompaniment, and music educators expected children to "rise" to the contents of this repertoire.[4]

Ella, by contrast, fashioned a repertoire that was sensitive to young children's interests. Her songs for preschoolers were straightforward and short, with regular four-beat meters, and presented in a range that was accessible to their voices. Since children never tired of practicing their counting skills, she emphasized musical counting games like "One Potato, Two Potato," as well as memory games that challenged them to listen and recall words. She gave them maracas and rhythm sticks so they could create their own accompaniment and showed them how to manipulate the way they played to create different sounds (for example, making them louder or softer). She showed them how to use their bodies as instruments, like people in Africa and other parts of the world. All of these strategies were calculated to draw out what Ella called children's "creativeness from natural rhythm." "When I ask [young children] to do a dance I say to them: do whatever you think is a dance," she explained to the *Montreal Star*. "And they do. It's thrilling to watch."[5]

Ella's emphasis on creativity over "technique" would prove central to *Rhythm and Game Songs for the Little Ones* and *Counting Games and Rhythms for the Little Ones*, two 1964 EPs that established her as a preeminent figure in early childhood music education. Both albums conveyed the messy rambunctiousness and unashamed enthusiasm of young children, and Ella hoped that, in listening to her recordings, preschoolers would hear themselves. But she also wanted to encourage teachers to regard the inevitable "imperfections" of their sounds as intrinsic to their music-making. As she explained in the single set of liner notes that accompanied the albums, adults should not focus on "how well a child sings or plays an instrument or skips or hops but rather on the *doing* itself."[6]

For these recordings Ella reached out to her friend Hilda Branch Thornton, the owner and director of Lake Meadows Nursery School at 501 East Thirty-Second Street. An acolyte of pioneering Black Chicago educator Oneida Cockrell (who also influenced the early education program at Howalton, where Ella recorded her first LP), Thornton took a progressive approach to the early childhood classroom, emphasizing structured play over rote learning. And because of its location, Thornton's was a rare integrated Chicago preschool, drawing African American, Italian American, and Jewish American children from the surrounding neighborhoods.[7]

Ella and a group of Lake Meadows children recorded both albums at Chicago's Sound Studio, in a room arranged so the children would not feel inhibited about moving and breaking something. Ella instructed her engineer, Stu Black, to record the entirety of their interactions, from her initial conversations with the children to her feedback and questions after a song. "Mistakes," including coughs and hiccups, were to be part of the performance.[8]

Shawnelle Richie, a precocious kindergartener who was Hilda Thornton's goddaughter, arrived at the studio wearing the special dress her mother, a high school English teacher, had laid out for her the night before the session. Her hair was done just so. But despite

FIGURE 10.1. Ella leading a counting song, ca. 1960s.
Photo by Bernadelle Richter.

these extraordinary preparations, the recording sessions "felt just like the nursery school," she said. Ella "had a unique ability to make people feel comfortable, not only in a setting, but with their voices." Richie carried that musical self-assurance into other areas of her life. When she interviewed for a coveted spot at Chicago's prestigious Francis W. Parker School, then recruiting Black students, she approached the experience without fear. She got the spot—in part, she said, because of Ella's example.[9]

Counting Games and Rhythms for the Little Ones and *Rhythm and Game Songs for the Little Ones* had an outsized effect on children's music education, particularly as they were released at a moment when the value of preschool was beginning to take hold in the United States. Since the rise of mandatory public education in the early twentieth century, most US children entered school in first grade. Before that, they were cared for by family members or—if their mothers worked in factories or as domestics—sent to understaffed day nurseries, which saw mainly to their physical needs. Like the Sunshine Home, the public facility where Ella and Tom had lived while Annabelle labored as a live-in domestic, these nurseries were stigmatized as places of last resort. In contrast, cooperative "nursery schools" enrolled the children of middle- and upper-middle-class parents, who embraced them as educationally and socially enriching. The first such nursery cooperative in Chicago was established in 1915 by the wives of University of Chicago faculty members. Ruth Crawford Seeger developed the material for her 1948 book *American Folk Songs for Children* through her work at a cooperative nursery.

This picture changed rapidly over the next several decades. During World War II, the US government provided childcare for women who entered the paid workforce. After the war, as middle-class women retained jobs outside the home, demand was sustained for both nursery schools and day nurseries, the latter serving Black mothers who were more likely to be waged workers than their white peers. In Chicago Oneida Cockrell founded the Garden Apartments Nursery School and Kindergarten, in the Grand Boulevard development commonly known as the Rosenwald Apartments, and began serving the children of Black female educators. Nationally, kindergarten enrollment continued to climb through the 1950s, although most programs remained focused on custodial care, not, as in Cockrell's school, on their social, emotional, and intellectual development.[10]

The "preschool movement" of the early 1960s sought to merge the educational function of nursery school cooperatives with the caregiving function of day nurseries. Preschool advocates drew on social scientific research demonstrating the malleability of intelligence, which had previously been thought to be fixed at birth. As a result, more and more parents began to see schooling for three- to five-year-olds as an advantage, not a sign of neglect, and by 1965, 42 percent of five-year-olds attended kindergarten.[11] The shift was accompanied by the emergence of early childhood education as a professional field. In 1964 the National Association for Nursery Education, a group dating to the 1920s, changed its name to the National Association for the Education of Young Children, conveying the seriousness of the new "early childhood education" enterprise.

As social scientists produced evidence of the value of preschool on intelligence and as their findings took hold in practice, early childhood education also became a focus of efforts to rectify inequalities associated with poverty and racism. In 1962 in Ypsilanti, Michigan, psychologist David Weikart convinced local leaders to support a research initiative to determine which teaching methods and curricula would best prepare "underperforming" Black three- and four-year-olds for success at Perry Elementary School. The hypothesis was that two years of a high-powered preschool experience—with engaging and developmentally sensitive instruction for the children as well as support for their caregivers—would result in fewer of these Black children being shuttled into "special education" classes, as many of their older siblings had been.[12]

In 1965 data from what became known as the Perry Preschool Project was cited by the federal government to validate Project Head Start, a national preschool initiative. Civil rights advocates cheered the program, which included support for families as well as children. Writing in the *Defender* in June 1965, the National Urban League's Whitney Young predicted that Head Start would "break like summer lightning on the American landscape," raining "a torrent of educational vitamins on some 500,000 preschool children from disadvantaged homes."[13] Under the headline "To Be Equal," his editorial linked early childhood education to civil rights, noting that Black children experienced poverty because racism limited opportunities for their parents.

Taken together, these developments—Americans' growing embrace of school for young children; the rise of social science confirming the benefits of early childhood education; and the federal government's adoption of preschool as public policy—greatly expanded the audience for Ella's work, setting the stage for her emergence as a leading figure in early childhood music. A rising cohort of preschool teachers, newly sensitive to young children's distinct developmental needs, looked to her albums for ideas about how to incorporate music into their classrooms. They sang her "Hello" to start their pupils' days ("Children liked to be greeted cheerfully upon arriving in class," Ella liked to say), and learned how to use call and response to attract and maintain their attention. They squeezed money out of tight budgets to purchase child-sized rhythm sticks and maracas, and challenged the children to explore the different sounds they could make, individually or together. They also incorporated her music's lessons about social equality and cultural pluralism, introducing children to Ella's songs written in Spanish, Hebrew, and Arabic to conjure the worlds beyond their neighborhoods. And they used her arrangements of spirituals and Black folk songs to impart knowledge of Africa and of Black diasporic history.

Evelyn K. Moore, an African American educator who was one of the original four lead teachers of the Perry Preschool Project, discovered

Ella's recordings through a Folkways advertisement in a school supply catalog and was pleased to discover that she was a Black woman. In their efforts to connect with the children culturally, Moore and the other teachers used music by Black artists, from Odetta to contemporary jazz and rhythm and blues. Pete Seeger's unfussy renderings of folk material also went over well with children, Moore said. Ella's music hit a sweet spot, combining Seeger's straightforwardness with Odetta's use of folk song to teach Black history.

Ella's recordings of African American playground chants and children's songs—from "Miss Mary Mack" to "Did You Feed My Cow?"—also contained a subversive message, as they undermined concepts of the "culturally deficient" Black child that prevailed even in the most progressive early education circles at the time. In the "cultural deficit" model that Moore and her colleagues were taught, poor children of color entered preschool at a disadvantage because of dysfunction within their family and community culture. The purpose of preschool was thus to remedy that deficit, by providing children with "cultural experiences" they did not get at home. At the time Black early childhood educators embraced this model because it pushed back against blatantly racist ideas of Black children's inferior intelligence. "We thought we wanted to bring the children 'up to par,'" Moore said, looking back critically on that era. The idea that Black children possessed their own forms of cultural knowledge "did not permeate the education sector."[14]

Against the deficit model, Ella's body of work offered a powerful argument against the notion of Black children's—or any children's—cultural deficiency. She had grown up with economic struggle but not cultural poverty. If anything, she had taken for granted the cultural richness that was her birthright as a Bronzeville girl in the 1930s, realizing only later that her childhood had been scored to rhythms that bore the sonic traces of her ancestors. As Ella later wrote, "If you were poor and living in the black belt in those days—when I was growing up—if you didn't have a record player at home or a juke box—you could always stand outside the small, local record shop that blasted the latest discs through the loud speakers. There were lots of spots and many corners where one could turn to get some 'musical Training'—to get some 'cultural background.'"[15]

As the preschool movement suggests, inequities in education remained at the heart of the civil rights project a full decade after the historic *Brown v. Board of Education* decision. Occasionally schoolchildren themselves were at the forefront of protesting exclusions and inequalities. In May 1963 one thousand Birmingham, Alabama students, aged seven to eighteen, skipped school to march for integration— and were met by dogs and city police wielding clubs and firehoses. In Chicago, too, African American children marched to call attention to the impoverishment and overcrowding of their neighborhood schools. In October 1963 more than 200,000 students staged a massive "Freedom Day" school boycott, accusing Chicago Public Schools superintendent Benjamin C. Willis of thwarting school integration by erecting makeshift buildings—derided as "Willis Wagons"—at majority-Black schools even as nearby majority-white schools suffered under-enrollment. Mahalia Jackson made headlines for supporting the action.[16]

When Martin Luther King made a historic visit to Soldier Field in June 1964, 70,000 people, mostly Black, turned out to greet him; many marched to the rally carrying signs calling for Willis's removal. Ella, who had briefly met King at a 1963 Chicago expo celebrating the hundredth anniversary of Emancipation, was among a handful of local musicians and dancers invited to entertain the crowd at a pre-rally concert. The ninety-minute program featured an array of talent, from the classically trained singer (and *Chicago Defender* fine arts reporter) Earl Calloway and members of the Chicago Philharmonic Youth Choir to the Jazz Interpreters, a young sextet that included Ella's likely former drum student Tom Washington, to her Old Town School of Folk Music comrade Win Stracke.

Ella counted the Soldier Field rally as one of the highlights of her life—although perhaps because of the excitement, she has forgotten whether she sang "Guide Me" or "The Wilderness," her two favorite freedom songs. Only two days earlier, on June 19, the US Senate had finally passed the Civil Rights Act. King might have used the rally to take a victory lap, but instead he spoke of the pressing need to confront "subtle segregation in the North"—issues of unemployment, job discrimination, substandard housing, and inadequate city services.[17]

In *Stride toward Freedom*, his 1958 memoir of the Montgomery bus boycott, King wrote of the necessity of meeting physical violence with "soul force," his translation of the Gandhian concept of *satyāgraha*.[18] *Soul force* was also an apt phrase to describe what Ella understood to be the power of music. Soul force was manifested when thousands of people sang "We Shall Overcome" at Soldier Field. But soul force could also be part of mundane interactions. Making the world peaceful for children is "something I feel very strongly about," Ella said. Music was one way of creating that peace.

That summer and fall of 1964, when the weather was nice, Ella and Bernadelle would drive around, looking at real estate. They did so "for kicks," Bernadelle recalled, in the manner of a couple feeling their way to a deeper commitment. Their fantasy of homeownership rested on a rickety foundation, however, since they had no savings. Their situation changed in early 1965, when Bernadelle inherited $5,000. The previous Christmas, while he was out shopping for presents, Joseph Richter had suffered a fatal heart attack at age fifty-six. The money came from her mother's sale of his businesses, Richter Chimney Service and Richter Building Maintenance.

Bernadelle and Ella knew other lesbians who bought houses and lived together. One day, returning from a visit to one such couple—the television and radio producer B. J. Ross and her girlfriend Linda, who lived off of Armitage Street in Lincoln Park—they stopped to look at a new development of brick townhouses on the 1800 block of North Mohawk Street, in an area then undergoing urban renewal. The model was spacious, with four bedrooms, and featured a modern split-level design. It was in a predominantly white but still "mixed" neighborhood that they associated with artists and performers, including folksinger Bonnie Koloc. Ella's attention was drawn to a nearby Cuban restaurant on North Sedgwick Street near Wisconsin, where she would later catch late-night sets by Celia Cruz, her favorite singer after Billie Holiday. (In those days, they had "tremendous stamina for going out," Bernadelle recalled.) They decided then and there to buy it.

But no bank would issue them a loan. They assumed it was because Ella was Black, but they also understood that they faced discrimination as a couple of "unmarried" women. Bernadelle, twenty-five and naive, was unprepared for such outright bigotry. But Ella knew the lengths to which white people and institutions would go to prevent Black people from living in "their" neighborhoods. The experience inspired her to write "A Friendly Loan," an unusually biting song she would later record with Brother John Sellers and singer Joseph Brewer.

It took the intervention of Ella's friend, prominent Black attorney Calvin Campbell, to finally secure a mortgage. Once they moved in, Ella was able to spread out for the first time in her life. She chose an upstairs bedroom as her office space and found plenty of room elsewhere for her collection of instruments, including drums, harmonicas, and ukuleles. Bernadelle turned a basement crawl space into a darkroom, leaving the rest of the lower level to Ella as a home studio for lessons and workshops.

Ella would not get to revel in her new space for long. Soon after they moved, in the summer of 1965, she received an invitation to conduct summer music workshops for teenagers enrolled in the pilot of a federal program called Upward Bound. Like Head Start, the new precollege initiative grew out of the Johnson administration's War on Poverty. It provided week-long enrichment programs on college campuses, including a handful of historically Black institutions, for academically talented high schoolers and recent high school graduates from low-income families. Local staff would determine the curriculum. Programs serving Black students were to emphasize "culturally relevant" materials and explore modes of instruction beyond rote learning.

Ever since 1943, when she and her brother Tom—then awaiting his deployment and wearing his Navy uniform--were arrested for "walking while Black" while on a visit to Tom's friend in Alcoa, Tennessee, Ella had avoided travel to the Deep South.[19] In March, while she and Bernadelle were trying to find a lender for their house, a white mob led by state troopers viciously attacked civil rights marchers crossing the Edmund Pettus Bridge in Selma, Alabama. They had watched the footage of "Bloody Sunday" on television. But Ella put aside her fears for the opportunity to work with Black high schoolers on the campuses of Fisk (in Nashville), Morehouse (in Atlanta), Dillard (in New Orleans), and Texas Southern (in Houston). In a way, she felt, she would be contributing to the Southern movement.

They set off in late June with Bernadelle at the wheel. Traveling from Morehouse to Dillard required them to briefly traverse Mississippi, where they thought anxiously of the three CORE volunteers—two white, one Black—who had been murdered there the previous summer. But while the trip to Dillard passed without incident, when they ventured off campus to a French Quarter restaurant a waiter refused to serve them. Ella fought back with the tactic she had last used in Indiana in 1962: She found a piece of cardboard, wrote "NO NEGROES" on it in big letters, and placed it in the establishment's front window.

Other moments were memorable for the pleasures they brought. On one of the campuses, Ella met the young SNCC activist John Lewis, a leader of the "Bloody Sunday" march. When she asked him to share a song, per her practice of "collecting," he offered "You Better Leave Segregation Alone," a freedom song that emerged from the 1960 Nashville sit-in movement. Student activists there had cleverly refashioned "You Better Leave My Kitten Alone," a popular rhythm-and-blues hit by Little Willie John, as "You Better Leave Segregation

Alone," a satire of white resistance to civil rights. "You better leave segregation alone," the students sang, "because they love segregation like a hound dog love a bone."

The song Lewis shared was not new to Ella, who had heard "You Better Leave Segregation Alone" on documentary recordings of the student sit-ins.[20] But she never tired of hearing it. She found a powerful commentary in its lyrics, which cast segregationists as slavering hound dogs. Singing it, young activists would repeat and elongate the word "bone" so it came out sounding a bit like a dog's howl.

Twenty years after Lewis sang it for her, Ella performed "You Better Leave Segregation Alone" on *Free at Last: A Musical Tribute to Dr. Martin Luther King, Jr.*, a 1985 Chicago children's television special hosted by LeVar Burton. "A bo-o-ne, a bo-o-ne, a bo-o-ne," she sang, emulating the style of the student activists, as an interracial group of boys and girls, all born in the wake of King's assassination, clapped along. Normally when she performed Ella addressed her energy outward, toward children. In this performance, however, she briefly goes inside herself, half-closing her eyes and barely smiling, savoring the memories the song evokes.[21]

That fall, back at her new home office, Ella worked on two projects that were to make 1966 a defining year in her career. One was *The Ella Jenkins Songbook for Children*, a collection of sheet music from Irwin Silber's Oak Publications; the other was *You'll Sing a Song and I'll Sing a Song*, her most enduring album. At seventy-two pages and with illustrations by Peggy Lipschutz (who sketched the cover for *Songs and Rhythms from Near and Far*), the songbook represented a significant upgrade of 1959's *Fun with Rhythm and Sounds*. The dominant themes of Ella's music to date were all represented. There were songs to introduce US children to different languages and cultures (the made-up "Nigerian" song "Caney Mi Macaro," as well as material in Hebrew and Spanish); songs to teach Black history ("Pick a Bale of Cotton," the chain-gang song "Long John," and spirituals); songs from Ella's own childhood ("Did You Feed My Cow," "Miss Mary Mack," and "Sifting in the Sand"); and songs from her nursery school albums ("Hello," "It's the Milkman").

The Ella Jenkins Songbook for Children was a landmark achievement: a collection of children's material, both arrangements and original compositions, by an African American woman. By putting her name in the title, Ella not only embraced her renown in the field of children's music, but established herself as a songbook author alongside such figures as Ruth Crawford Seeger and Beatrice Landeck, the trailblazing women behind *American Folk Songs for Children* (1948) and *Songs to Grow On* (1950). At the same time, she distinguished her songbook from these earlier, piano-based collections of folk material by calling attention to her distinctive approach to music as an accessible social practice. "As you use the book you will observe that *all* of the songs and chants have been organized into call-and-response, follow the leader and echo form, and that they are rather simply written but the material is challenging and is aimed at a variety of age levels and singing experiences," she wrote in the preface. Her intention was for each child to find a place in the sound or song (or rhythm or whistle) and follow it at their own pace.[22]

The Ella Jenkins Songbook for Children contained a song that Ella had not yet recorded. "You'll Sing a Song and I'll Sing a Song" was an elegant précis of her political and aesthetic sensibility. In some ways, it was a blueprint for understanding all of her creative output. Exceedingly simple, it consisted of variations on a rhyming couplet:

You'll sing a song
And I'll sing a song
Then we'll sing a song together
You'll sing a song
And I'll sing a song
In warm or wintry weather

The lyrics encapsulated Ella's core belief that music—singing—was about human communication and human relationship. When *you* sing a song and *I* follow, we engage in musical dialogue. When we sing a song *together*, we affirm the social and cultural value of listening to each other. Through song, we model an ideal of nonhierarchical human reciprocity, in which you and I recognize each other as equals.

Those who knew Ella's earlier work might have noticed the new song's formal similarity to her earlier, African-styled call-and-response songs. In fact, "You'll Sing a Song" was both endlessly adaptable and universally accessible, a template that linked it to songs going back to "Tah-boo." Children, Ella found, generally caught on to the game after one repetition. For variety, the lyrics could be altered—to "You'll whistle a while/And I'll whistle a while" or "You'll hum a line/And I'll hum a line"—or instead of singing, children could play the melody with kazoos or harmonicas, or mark its rhythm with sticks and drums. Song leaders could cue differing styles of vocalization, varying volume or timbre. If a child forgot a line or missed a cue, the group was always there to carry them along. There was almost no way to feel alone when singing it.

Fittingly given its compact statement of her core principles, "You'll Sing a Song and I'll Sing a Song" became the title track of Ella's ninth Folkways album, her other landmark project in 1966. She recorded it early in the year, after assuring Moe Asch of "another good seller"—a reference to the success of her *Little Ones* albums. In a March 1966 letter she also questioned the accuracy of her Folkways royalty statements. Her checks from Asch did not reflect the fact that she was "constantly being told at workshops, record distributors, and stores that hundreds of my records are being sold—around the country." After the usual grumbling and delay, Asch revisited his books and came up with additional earnings, as well as money to cover recording and artist expenses for the new album.[23]

For *You'll Sing a Song and I'll Sing a Song* Ella partnered with the Urban Gateways Children's Chorus, a group combining children from Chicago's First Unitarian Church and Urban Gateways, a philanthropic arts initiative that partnered with Chicago Public Schools. The work she had described to Asch as "a teaching as well as entertainment album" was an immediate success. Teachers found that they could play the disc for students, who related to the voices of the children's chorus; but they also felt encouraged by what she called her "strictly informal approach," which invited creativity and improvisation. In her liner notes Ella emphasized the teacher's autonomy, drawing attention away from her own recording as definitive. "When using this record," she wrote, "don't *just* use my ideas, but combine them with your *own* techniques and personality. This record is designed for listening, as well as for participation. It is structured for imitating, as well as for creating. The album takes you only so high on the ladder. Your skills and the children's contributions will take you the rest of the way."[24] To demonstrate that no one recording of a song was definitive, the album included two different iterations of "Miss Mary Mack" she had published in her songbook—one from her own childhood, the other a Southern version titled "May-ree Mack"—as well as two tracks of "Did You Feed My Cow?" The repetition—which recalled Ella's presentation of spirituals in different styles on *Negro Folk Rhythms*—was a means of recognizing that folk songs were subject to variation, reinvention, and appropriation, depending on their social and cultural setting.

The biographical note Ella wrote for the liner notes of *You'll Sing a Song and I'll Sing a Song* reflected her awareness of her growing prominence. "Ella Jenkins is known to teachers and parents throughout the United States for her contributions to the teaching and enjoyment of folk music and rhythmic activities for children," it read. "Miss Jenkins' records and teaching methods are used in many preschool programs, and in elementary and high schools. Her records are also being used in many federally funded programs for education (including Project Head Start)."[25]

The success of *You'll Sing a Song* and its title track, particularly among educators, was not inevitable. In many ways, the album represented Ella's most overt critique yet of prevailing music-education orthodoxies, and for this reason it took significant risks. The ideals of her album were consistent with progressive educational approaches going back to the early twentieth-century theories of John Dewey. But it also contributed important variations on the "whole-child" approach. In 1966 it was still radical to imagine that children's musical education should work toward the fostering of their individual creativity within a context of mutuality and sharing. So, too, was Ella's practice of looking to Black diasporic musical practices as models of classroom practice.

In later years, Moe Asch spoke openly of the importance of Ella's 1966 album to Folkways, particularly as the novelty of the Folk Revival began to wear thin. When he took the reins of Smithsonian Folkways, the label formed by the Smithsonian Institution's acquisition of Folkways, Anthony Seeger reckoned that *You'll Sing a Song and I'll Sing a Song* had played a role in keeping Folkways afloat through Asch's death in 1986. The album's reputation as a trailblazing work of American children's music was solidified by its 2007 induction into the Library of Congress's National Recording Registry, which highlights "the richness of the nation's audio legacy."[26] The honor also cemented the reputation of *You'll Sing a Song and I'll Sing a Song* as an album representing the entirety of Ella's career.

You'll Sing a Song and I'll Sing a Song launched Ella as the most significant and successful independent voice in US children's music, a field dominated in the mid-1960s by commercial film soundtracks (*Mary Poppins*), classical albums for children (Leonard Bernstein's *Bernstein Conducts for Young People*), and what Asch had disparaged as "kidisks" (*Let's All Sing with the Chipmunks*). While such titles reaped profits and won Grammy Awards, educators and adults seeking alternatives clamored for Ella's work. Her monthly date books grew crowded with engagements—as many as six a week, at fees ranging from $40 to $125. She taught and performed for the children at JCCs, as well as for children at Chicago's Muhammad University of Islam, run by the Nation of Islam. She entertained the middle-class members of Jack and Jill, a national organization for Black children and teens. She drew large, appreciative audiences at professional organizations, from the American Camping Association to the Association for Childhood Education.

In their house on North Mohawk Street, Ella and Bernadelle settled into a cheerfully chaotic domestic life. They rarely used their kitchen for anything but coffee, subsisting on cheap grub from local restaurants and fast-food joints. Their oven served as storage space. But that did not stop them from hosting friends and family, from Brother John Sellers to Ella's brother Tom, who after earning a master's degree in city planning at Harvard had taken a job with the Boston Redevelopment Authority.

Ella's mother was silent about her daughter's decision to buy a house and live openly with Bernadelle on the North Side. Yet even if she disapproved of Bernadelle and had no interest in "white" neighborhoods, it stands to reason that she was proud that her daughter was now an owner, not a renter; and further, that she had climbed the mountain of homeownership in part by adhering to Mary Baker Eddy's precepts regarding thrift. In the late 1960s, when Ella's old friend Armando Peraza came through town on tours with jazz musician Cal Tjader, he and his musician-friends would hang at the North Mohawk Street house after gigs. Peraza was impressed that Ella was earning enough from her music to pay her share of the mortgage. Few Black female solo musicians could claim to have done so well.

In the face of the demands on Ella's time, Bernadelle stepped up to help, eventually taking on the role that Albert Grossman had once proposed to play. In some ways, watching Ella struggle to keep up with her booming business, Bernadelle felt she had no choice but to become her manager. The breaking point came when she discovered that Ella had filled a whole suitcase with unopened mail and thrown it down a garbage chute. "I said, 'Ella, you can't do that!,'" she said. "That's when I started helping her." The arrangement worked out for both of them, even though Bernadelle, by her own account, was not the "ideal person" for the role. Their business relationship also gave them cover from prying questions, particularly when Bernadelle joined Ella on the road.

Ella's happiness during this period spilled over into her correspondence with Asch. In August 1967, shortly after her forty-third birthday and as she and Bernadelle were about to set out for another European trip, she composed a warm letter:

> This year marks my tenth with Folkways and I feel like celebrating, because I still enjoy making records, because some fresh thoughts keep a-coming my way and because the Folkways family has, during these ten years, been especially nice to me. I remember quite well how nervous I was upon approaching your office and studio with my ten-inch disc in hand and what anxieties I experienced while waiting for you to tell me whether or not my "Call-and-Response—Rhythmic Group Singing" made any sense and how pleased and encouraged I was when you told me you liked my ideas. Well, the ideas, fortunately, are still flowing and within the last couple of years I have realized a sizeable monetary boost, which helps to inspire me to work harder.

She went on to request a renewal of her recording contract with Folkways as well as $1,000, from royalties or paid as an advance. "I would just like to celebrate my tenth anniversary with a hundred dollars for each year. That's why I want to make my tenth album this year. Kookie? That's all a part of it."[27]

Asch signed the check, and Ella responded with *Play Your Instruments and Make a Pretty Sound*, an instructional album for preschoolers and early elementary-aged children. Released in early 1968, it featured music by the Original Jass All-Stars, a Chicago outfit run by the well-regarded reed player Franz Jackson. Just as *Peter and the Wolf*, Leonard Bernstein's best-selling recording of Sergei Prokofiev's symphonic fairy tale, introduced young people in the early 1960s to orchestral instruments, *Play Your Instruments* introduced children to the harmonica, ukulele, and jazz instruments, through tracks including "Harmonica Happiness" and a delightful New Orleans–style version of "You'll Sing a Song and I'll Sing a Song." Moreover, unlike most popular musical "guides" to orchestral music—or even forward-thinking compilations such as *A Child's Introduction to Jazz*, narrated by Julian "Cannonball" Adderley—it was interactive, encouraging children to dance, play-conduct, and experiment with simple rhythm instruments.[28] And it incorporated thoughtful touches for teachers, such as "Put Your Instruments Away," a track in which Ella, perhaps unconsciously, made good on her long-ago promise to herself never to misplace another harmonica.

Ella's exuberance on *Play Your Instruments and Make a Pretty Sound* would be tempered by loss. In November 1967, while she was working on the album, her aunt Willie Mae "Big Mama" Walker died after an extended illness. By the time Big Mama became sick, she and her husband, "Flood" Johnson, had separated, and she had moved in with Annabelle. She passed away at Cook County Hospital.

Ella's loss of Big Mama, who at times had been more of a mother to her than Annabelle, cut deeply. Their bond was based on Big Mama's caretaking of Ella, but it was also physical. While Annabelle was naturally slender, Ella and her aunt were full-bodied women, and looked so alike that "you almost wondered," Bernadelle said.

Annabelle and Ella's shared grief over Big Mama's death might have drawn them closer, but instead it led to a deeper estrangement when Annabelle declared that Bernadelle was not welcome at the funeral. Ella tried to shield Bernadelle from knowing her mother's reason, but it was obvious. Ella was furious, as was Tom; but he was both out of town and averse to conflict, leaving Ella to fend for herself. There was a big fight, Bernadelle said, after which "Ella fell apart."

Within a year of Big Mama's death, in October 1968 Uncle Flood passed away. In the last years of his life, particularly after he and Big Mama split up, he struggled with alcoholism. "Uncle Flood always gave [Big Mama] his whole paycheck but he had an inclination to drink. He never missed a day of work and on the weekends he never stopped drinking," Ella said. Drink eventually cost him his job and home. Periodically, Ella and Bernadelle would go searching for him in liquor stores and bars. Ella despaired over the tragic ending of the life of a man who had been her first and best music teacher. She no longer attended Christian Science church, but in such difficult times she still returned to Christian Science teachings, looking for solace in Mrs. Eddy's precepts about the eternal soul.

Ella's personal losses were compounded by the April 4, 1968, assassination of Martin Luther King. That day she was working with children at Burke Elementary School, not far from the Washington Park fieldhouse where she had learned to play table tennis. After finishing up, she returned home but did not think to turn on the television or radio. Bernadelle, meanwhile, was driving to Mohawk Street from the School of the Art Institute when "all of a sudden, the horns started and traffic was stopped." She was the one who told Ella. For the next few days, they were glued to their television. At some point Ella went back to her datebook and penciled "Martin Luther King" into the square for April 4. She had long since renounced violence of any kind, but she understood why, in the wake of King's death, some people felt a need to break and burn things.

Dear, Ms. Jenkins,

Thank you for everything that you have done for us at 92nd Street "Y." I really liked the show very much.

I liked the song that goes like this: Ms. Mary Mac Mac Mac all dressed in black black black. With silver buttons buttons buttons up and down her back back back back back and so on and on.

So thanks again and have a great time in Chicago. By now.

Sincerely,
Victor

(NEW YORK CITY, 1981)

11
A LONG TIME TO FREEDOM
1968–1979

The summer after King's assassination, in July 1968, Ella made her first appearance at Ravinia, the storied music festival held annually on a former amusement-park grounds in Highland Park, Illinois. For many Chicagoans in the late 1960s Ravinia was a ritual of the season, on a par with baseball games at Wrigley Field and sunny-day jaunts to Lake Michigan beaches. From the downtown Loop, concertgoers could take a train that delivered them to Ravinia Park in under an hour. Those holding lawn tickets could spread a picnic blanket on the wide Ravinia grassland and from there enjoy a concert in the soft summer air.

Ravinia got its start in 1904 as a classical festival: the "summer opera capital of the world."[1] In 1936 it became the summer home of the Chicago Symphony Orchestra. But by the 1950s it had greatly expanded its offerings, supplementing concerts of "serious" music with "lighter attractions" by jazz, folk, and pop musicians. Louis Armstrong set an attendance record in 1956, only to be outdone by the Kingston Trio in 1959, and then by Peter, Paul, and Mary in 1963. Ravinia also had long featured Family Pop concerts, which introduced children to orchestral music. But Ravinia had never featured a musician who composed and performed primarily for children. Taking a gamble, festival organizers booked Ella into their largest venue, an open-air, covered pavilion seating more than 3,000 people.

On evenings when the symphony orchestra played, the Pavilion stage brimmed with musicians neatly sectioned by instrument families. On the afternoon of Ella's show, the stage was empty but for a single microphone and a table holding several rhythm instruments. Ella had settled on the bare-bones setup following Bernadelle's advice to pretend that the Pavilion concert was just "a very large school assembly." She also began in the same way she had taken to kicking off many of her performances, with "You'll Sing a Song, and I'll Sing a Song." The song had become her trademark, and its familiarity relaxed the crowd and set the stage for their participation. It would have been easy for her "just to stand up and do a concert" at Ravinia, but a group sing-along was more satisfying. That way, she said, "everyone has a chance to get in there and get involved and feel that he or she is making a contribution."[2]

Tom was seated among the young families in the Pavilion that afternoon. Although he had seen his sister perform countless times, he was once again reminded of Ella's skill in attracting and *holding* children's attention. With few props and no stage spectacle to speak of, she kept her audience rapt for an hour. "They were jumping off the rafters," he said, landing on a phrase that would capture the children's enthusiasm and engagement. The folks at Ravinia were also impressed—both by Ella's ticket sales and by the calls for encores. Later that summer, when orchestra conductor Seiji Ozawa had to bow out of a planned Young People's Program, they booked Ella's "Hootenanny" for a return date. As a local newspaper put it, "By popular demand the nationally famous folk singer will repeat her enthusiastically received program."[3]

Ella would return to the Pavilion stage annually for the next thirty years (and periodically thereafter), joining the Chicago Symphony Orchestra in turning Ravinia into her own unofficial "summer home."

The scale of her concerts there solidified her reputation as a nationally preeminent performer of children's music, not just a darling of Chicagoans or a niche favorite of teachers. Such universality was exceedingly rare for a Black female musician to achieve. In popular music Black women who scored Top 40 radio airplay were said to have "crossed over"—the metaphor emphasizing the barriers to their success. At Ravinia Ella had also shown that she could draw a large white public without significantly diluting her message. In the wake of King's movement, there was now a cohort of liberal white adults who brought children to see Ella precisely because they valued her social justice advocacy. Given the rise of Black Power, she may well have been valued by white audiences in 1968 for her unflagging commitment to interracialism.

In almost single-handedly creating an audience for socially progressive children's music, Ella was part of a groundswell of post–civil rights progressive children's culture, from the television shows *Mister Rogers' Neighborhood* (1968) and *Sesame Street* (1969) to the album *Free to Be You and Me* (1972), Marlo Thomas's musical celebration of racial egalitarianism and gender parity, to *Ebony Jr!* (1973), a publication aimed at Black children growing up with afro puffs and Stevie Wonder. Her efforts also anticipated calls for "multicultural" education from groups like the American Association of Colleges for Teacher Education, which in 1973 affirmed that "being different connotes neither superiority nor inferiority" and called for "programs that help different minority students understand who they are, where they are going, and how they can make their contribution to the society in which they live." Even the culturally conservative field of music education was waking up to the messages of Ella's work. In the 1968 Tanglewood Declaration, for example, the Music Educators National Conference called for the incorporation of rock, jazz, American folk music, and "the music of other cultures" into classrooms, conceding that the field would have to change if it wanted to stay relevant.[4]

Ella welcomed the boldness of young people inspired by newly politicized concepts of Blackness in the post–civil rights era. In her visits to Chicago schools, she observed children and teenagers flaunting their Africanness. In defiance of Eurocentrism, they wore dashikis and other garments fashioned from African textiles, embraced unprocessed hairstyles, and even took a quiet pride in darker skin tones. Emboldened by calls for Black Power, young people *talked* and *walked* differently, conveying confidence and self-knowledge in the swaying rhythms of their speech and carriage.[5] Ella took pleasure in being greeted on the streets as a "Sister" and in receiving nods of recognition for her afro, now flecked with patches of gray.

The new pulses and intonations of these post–civil rights children inspired Ella's creativity in the late 1960s and 1970s. "RHYTHM is a repetition of PATTERNS and RHYTHM is a network of CHANGE," she wrote in an August 1968 description of an "Adventures in Rhythm" workshop. Rhythm for Ella had always been a means of accessing Black history, but now it was also about present-day collective Black-self-definition. Just as they could create new rhythms, so people could manifest a new sense of self through changes in their physical cadences. Soon after she wrote these words, students at her alma mater of San Francisco State College initiated a five-month strike that led to the creation of the nation's first Black and Ethnic Studies departments in higher education. "When I first started going on tours around the country visiting high schools," Ella recalled, "I would sing spirituals or gospels, or blues and black kids would sink into their seats, ashamed because I was singing about their heritage and history." Now Ella's rhythm workshops were in vogue, supported by a growing body of research demonstrating that children of color benefited from "culturally relevant" material.[6]

The folk revival, which had helped to launch Ella's career and inspired so much of her music, was in the rearview mirror by the time she appeared at Ravinia. Even at the height of the revival—sometimes cited as 1963, the year ABC television debuted *Hootenanny*, a short-lived folk variety show—folk music had been a minority taste, attracting left-leaning college students who expressed their displeasure with the contemporary order through old songs and "old-timey" sounds. But within a few years, these same young people would begin to feel that their experiences and political aspirations were better expressed by the thunderous sound of electric guitars than the gentle plucking of acoustic instruments.

The decline in folk's popularity was even more rapid than its rise, chastening once thriving institutions. John Cohen, a member of the New Lost City Ramblers, recalled departing the 1967 University of Chicago Folk Festival—only six years after its confident debut—with the feeling that its days were numbered, "since most everything else is going rock." Commercial record labels were among the first to see the profits of forgoing folk for rock. In 1967 Elektra, once known for such urban folk singers as Oscar Brand, Phil Ochs, and Tom Paxton, released the debut LP of a Los Angeles group called The Doors, and followed the single "Light My Fire" to industry dominance. "The 'boom' is over, and a part of our musical history has disappeared (in terms of a mass scene) along with calypso and the twist," declared folk musician Happy Traum in *Rolling Stone* in 1969. "Millions have traded in their 5-string banjos for a Fender, and the work songs and ballads from out of our collective past have been replaced by the Now sounds."[7]

The dimming of folk's commercial clout coincided with a fraying of the relationship between the folk revival and the civil rights movement, as even before King's death, young Black activists increasingly saw white liberals as a liability to their struggle. At the Newport Folk Festival in July 1963, an interracial group of singers, including the SNCC Freedom Singers, Bob Dylan, and Joan Baez, had joined hands to sing "We Shall Overcome." But the festival's suturing together of the civil rights freedom song with the image of interracial harmony would not hold, especially in the wake of the violence of assassinations and state surveillance. Despite their African derivation, banjos had always been a hard sell for Black folk revivalists, retaining the ugly stain of the blackface minstrel show. But by the late 1960s banjos and Black Power salutes were worlds apart—the former suggesting a past defined by subservience, the latter gesturing defiantly toward a liberated future. This quarrel was illustrated in Julius Lester's *Search for the New Land* (1969), in which the Fisk University alumnus ridiculed the folk veneration of Negro spirituals as the romanticized appropriation of Black oppression by privileged white youths. At such a moment, Ella's ukulele might have looked decidedly old-timey (despite its very different lineage than the banjo). But the commodification of the "teenager" in the 1950s and '60s had also produced a cultural distinction between "youth" and "children," which assured Ella's continuing relevance. While not leaving adolescents behind, she stepped gladly into this space.

Post–civil rights culture also illuminated growing class divides within the Black community, as middle-class children and adults became the primary beneficiaries of post–Civil Rights Act policies of "affirmative action." In his editorial launching *Ebony Jr!*, publisher John Johnson cited Lorraine Hansberry: "I hope you will remember that to be young, gifted and Black today is an honor and an opportunity."[8] Middle-class children were pictured as beacons of the world that civil rights activists had birthed. Meanwhile, poor and working-class Black children continued to be understood as "problems": by government agencies, in education, and in popular culture. In the same breath as it called for more expansive music curricula, going beyond Western classical music, the Tanglewood Declaration spoke of "inner city" and "culturally deprived" youth, reiterating tropes of the cultural "lack" of Black as well as Hispanic students.

Ella responded to the jagged rhythms of the post–civil rights era by expanding her music into new contexts. In 1969 she wrote and performed the soundtrack for a series of short educational films aimed at low-income urban preschoolers. Directed by Gordon Weisenborn and made in consultation with the Chicago-based Erikson Institute for Early Education, the films featured a mixed-race cast of children and adults inhabiting a sensory-rich world of noisy buses, tall apartment buildings, and colorful fire hydrants. Experimental and dreamy, and free of instructional narrative, they were visually, aesthetically, and politically innovative.[9]

One of these films, *Water Is Wet*, also afforded Ella her first experience of acting, as she appeared in it as a mother who lives with her preschool-age son in a small apartment. At one point the boy spills a large cup of tempera paint, dousing himself and their kitchen table. Both he and the viewer feel anxious: What will the mother do? Will she be very angry? But Ella's character takes him to the laundry room, making the spill into an occasion for learning. As they watch the dirty clothes go around in the drum of a washing machine, Ella's song plays in the background:

> If you're playing with a friend
> And you're having a lot of fun
> If clothes get a little dirty
> When your playing's all done
> Now don't you worry
> Please don't you worry
> No don't you worry, little one
> Because the washing machine can have a lot of fun
> Because the washing machine can have a lot of fun

It is a lovely moment, easing the child's anxiety that his play is "bad" and introducing him to a home appliance that creates its own fascinating underwater world. It is also a moment that rewrites the script of Ella's own childhood. Where Annabelle made Ella feel ashamed of dirtying the hems of her dresses while playing with boys, Ella's character consoles her son, assuring him that his play—and his still-developing mastery of his body—are nothing to fret about; in fact, they give the washing machine a chance to do its important work.

Ella was also putting the finishing touches on a new album, *Seasons for Singing*, based on her music workshops with middle-grade children at St. Pauls, a Lincoln Park church that ran a well-regarded summer camp. One of those children was a ten-year-old Black girl named Aqua-netta White. Like Ella, Aquanetta lived on North Mohawk Street, but south of the de facto racial dividing line of West North Avenue. Each weekday morning she and her cousins were picked up at their local church, Olivet Baptist, and driven to St. Pauls. The "sister" churches were less than two miles apart, but they occupied different worlds.

When Aquanetta's father heard that his daughter would be part of a camp group performing on Ella Jenkins's next recording, his first response was to ask whether she was getting paid. But Aquanetta and her mother countered that it was an "honor" to be selected to sing in a studio with Jenkins. What they did not anticipate was that Aquanetta's unusual name—inspired by the early twentieth-century actor Acqua-netta, an "exotic" beauty whose tumultuous love life and rumored African American heritage drew attention in the *Defender*—would have a prominent place in *Seasons for Singing*.[10]

Even Ella did not foresee this. On the day of the recording session, after the children performed all of the songs they had rehearsed, she realized that they were still one track short. That was when Aquanetta blurted out, "Why not 'Go, Aquanetta, Go!'"? She was referring to a Chuck Berry–style jam composed by assistant counselor Kathy Grif-fin, who originally used a different name in its title. But one day at camp Aquanetta, who liked to show off her dance moves, convinced her friends to sing it with her name, which had a pleasing, percussive rhythm to it. After that, she had come to think of it as "her" song.[11]

Like the boy in *Water Is Wet*, Aquanetta feared that her spontaneity in the studio would get her in trouble, even if she meant no disrespect. But Ella surprised her by embracing her idea. In the bit of studio time that remained, they recorded the song, along with its revamped cho-rus: "Go Aquanetta, go go go! / Show them how to rock 'n' roll / Now go, Aquanetta go go go!"

Months later, when Aquanetta finally got her copy of *Seasons for Singing* and saw "her song" on it, she ran home to show her parents. Her father put the disc on his stereo so they could listen together. Once he placed the stylus carefully on the vinyl and heard her name and voice, he called a temporary truce on their running argument about being paid. Aquanetta was giddy with happiness. "You could not tell me anything," she said. "I had to walk onto the bus on the side, that's how big my head was swollen. I had just cut a record with Ella Jenkins!"[12]

Not unlike the experiences of the young drummer Philip Royster when he appeared on Ella's television show *This Is Rhythm* in the 1950s, or the nursery schooler Shawnelle Richie, when she sang on Ella's *Little Ones* albums, Aquanetta's experience making *Seasons for Singing* with Ella made her feel that she mattered. It was a feeling that she could return to when, not long after recording the LP, she was bullied by a white boy at Oscar F. Mayer Middle School, where she and her brother were two of only four Black students. Ordeals like Aquanetta's revealed the unfinished project of civil rights in the "post"-civil rights moment. For many Americans the legislative and legal victories of the mid-1960s represented the culmination of a noble struggle. But these achievements had neither eliminated racism nor significantly changed the material conditions in which children like Aquanetta lived, as King himself noted toward the end of his life, when he became more outspokenly critical of American empire and American capitalism. The 1960s civil rights movement was one aspect of a longer and broader freedom struggle that was now taking on new forms. Or as Ella put it in the liner notes of *A Long Time to Freedom*, a 1970 LP memorializing King, "The grandiose struggle is very much alive today and Black men and White men and Yellow men and Red men are taking part in it all—perhaps because more of us are beginning to realize that to make a country truly free—all men must have their freedom."[13] Notably, Ella's language reflected new forms of late 1960s political solidarity—especially around opposition to the Vietnam War—that linked disparate groups of Americans together under monikers like "Third World."

A Long Time to Freedom is an outlier in Ella's catalog, neither a children's album nor an instructional album nor even an album for sing-alongs. With substantial contributions from Brother John Sellers and operatic tenor Joseph Brewer, it is not even simply an "Ella Jenkins" album. But it is Ella's most deeply personal recording. In the liner notes she wrote passionately about the sonic richness of her South Side girlhood, revising her own longtime self-identification as an "untrained" musician. She reflected on her growing consciousness, in young adulthood, that this childhood had immersed her in "true folk idiom." She acknowledged her mother as the inspiration behind the title composition, "A Long Time to Freedom."[14]

Bernadelle and Tom knew the album was the statement Ella had wanted to make since 1963 when she wrote to Moe Asch about an Emancipation centennial album. With their encouragement, on *A Long Time to Freedom* she ventured into uncharted musical territory. On "Soft Pedal Blues," a song popularized by Bessie Smith, and her own composition "If You Ever Get Down," she displayed her training as a "good blues child." And on "A Friendly Loan," an acerbic send-up of her ordeal in trying to buy a house with Bernadelle, she demonstrated her capacity for satire:

> If you've got money troubles
> Just like my very own
> Walk down the street
> And get yourself a friendly loan
> . . .
> You don't have to write
> Why you don't even have to phone
> If you've got your credit
> You can get a friendly loan.

Ella's vocal delivery on the track was intentionally smooth, a foil to its sardonic critique. But that critique surfaced in the way the melody dipped down on the last line of each stanza. Channeling musical satirists like Big Bill Broonzy, Nina Simone, and Oscar Brown Jr., she sang the word "friendly" at the low end of her register.

"A Friendly Loan" revealed the tenacious inner fibers that supported Ella's smooth and pleasing exterior. Odetta had become famous for igniting musical fires with her voice. When she sang about John Henry, audiences felt the heaviness of his hammer. "Folk songs were the anger, the venom, the hatred of myself and everybody else, and *everything* else," she explained. "I could get my rocks off with those work songs and things, without having to say, I hate you, and I hate me."[15] Ella was less inclined to let it all hang out. Among the many reasons she had pursued children's music was it allowed her, in Bernadelle's words, "to stay focused on the good," as she had been taught at the Eighth Church. Even Ella's version of the chain-gang song "Another Man Done Gone" emphasized escape, the dream of a better day.

As Margaret Burroughs had once observed, Ella had a knack for communicating optimism and joy. Her graciousness and "focus on the good" put people at ease—including white people who were not used to interacting with Black women. Moreover, by virtue of her orientation to children, her activism was never perceived as "angry." But as songs like "A Friendly Loan" showed, Ella's cultivation of a "positive" persona involved unrevealed emotional labors. She drew the curtain aside on these labors in the liner notes to *A Long Time to Freedom*, describing why she had decided to open the album with "The Wilderness":

> I like the Wilderness so much, I think, because it seems to sum up some very basic attitudes about life with other humans. In other words—expressing it in the language of today—you work out your own "hang-ups," your own kind of wilderness first then you can extend this understanding to other people—in fact you can free yourself to such a degree that you can "love everybody."[16]

Melding Christian Science critiques of materialism with 1970s popular psychology, this passage is as close as Ella would ever come to publicly expressing the effort and discipline that undergirded her warm demeanor. "Life with other humans," it said, was trying, even as it was both desired and necessary. The psyche was its own wilderness, littered by "hang-ups" that had to be confronted to become fully open to "other people."

A Long Time to Freedom was not a big seller, even if critics responded warmly, calling it "a truly outstanding album" and "one folk buffs shouldn't miss."[17] In many ways the album defied trends. It was a folk recording made after the sunset of the folk revival; a civil rights album released in the era of Black Power; an "Ella Jenkins" album that handed others the microphone. But like Moe Asch, Ella never paid much attention to the flavor of the day. She was offended by the reduction of long-standing struggles for freedom and equality to "opportunities" for cashing in. As she told a reporter in 1974, "You know, I almost resent it when a company says this is a 'good' time to do a black record, a Spanish record. Why I've been doing black music and Spanish music right along with other things for years."[18]

Against such commercial demands or broad political or cultural trends, Ella looked to her experiences with children as a source of creative inspiration. A number of the albums she released in the 1970s, her most prolific decade, furthered her ongoing exploration of music for and with preschoolers. The songs she wrote for the Weisenborn films became the basis of *My Street Begins at My House* (1971), graced by a cover photograph of Ella taking Patty and Doxie, her beloved miniature poodle and dachshund, for a walk in the alley behind her house. *And One and Two* (1971) addressed preschoolers' love of counting songs, as well as their need to move their bodies as they learned. *Nursery Rhymes: Rhyming and Remembering* (1974) collected familiar songs like "The Muffin Man," "Little Miss Muffet," and "Humpty Dumpty" to support children's language learning. "If you remember the words [to 'The Muffin Man']," Ella instructed in the album's whimsical, hand-drawn liner notes, "sing the words. If you remember the *tune* only *hum* or *la la* or *loo loo* or any other PLEASANT sound you can think of."[19]

Some of Ella's 1970s albums were more introspective. In *Growing Up with Ella Jenkins* (1976), she took stock of the longevity of her influence. "Many times I will meet a young person who says, I used to hear you sing at our school when I was in kindergarten," she wrote. "Now I'm teaching kindergarten using your records in my classroom. As a result of these kinds of remarks, I decided to make an album . . . because it seemed that many people were growing up with my music."[20] And on *Songs Rhythms and Chants for the Dance* (1977), she returned thematically to the time she spent dancing mambo and cha-cha-cha to the sounds of Armando Peraza's band at Cable Car Village, producing an innovative album that paired dance music with interviews of notable Chicago dance professionals, including her old pal Jimmy Payne. In the liner notes she reproduced the page from a program for Alvin Ailey's *Revelations* that correctly credited her as the composer of the music for its "Wade in the Water" sequence. (To be certain she caught the reader's eye, she inked in a large asterisk next to her name.)

As ever, travel—both real and imaginative—remained an important springboard for Ella's music over the decade. *Little Johnny Brown* (1972) contained songs in Spanish and Navajo, the latter of which she learned on a visit to the Navajo Nation. A week-long tour of Tennessee schools led to *This a Way That a Way* (1973), recorded at a studio in Nashville, and titled for the way "the little Tennesseans" sang the lyrics to "This Way, Valerie" as "This-a-Way, Valerie."[21] And a 1973 trip with Bernadelle to Kenya and Tanzania inspired *Jambo and Other Call-and-Response Songs and Chants*, an album that introduced American children to Swahili words—and in that sense was a significant departure from her earlier practice of composing from made-up sounds. Released in 1974, the *Jambo* LP joined other mid-decade cultural homages to the East African language: from Kwanzaa, the Afrocentric winter holiday; to *Jambo Means Hello: Swahili Alphabet Book* (1974), the pioneering picture book by Muriel and Tom Feelings; to *Star Trek: The Animated Series* (1973–74), in which Nichelle Nichols, a former dancer with Jimmy Payne's troupe, revived her breakout television role as the graceful and brainy Lieutenant Uhura (whose name was based on the Swahili word for "freedom").

The most important of Ella's "travel" albums of the period—and one of her best of the decade—emerged from a three-week residency with New Orleans schools. Released in 1976, *We Are America's Children: Songs, Rhythms and Moods Reflecting Our Peoples' History* was inspired by the city's unique culture, which bore traces of Indigenous, African, and European influence. While the Bicentennial celebration of that year centered Philadelphia and Boston and defined freedom in terms of the self-emancipation of colonial Americans from the British monarchy, Ella's album offered New Orleans–born music as the expression of a different American story, in which freedom was an ongoing project. Whereas the LP's cover drawing, by Peggy Lipschutz, channeled the pro-labor iconography of the Popular Front left, in her liner notes, she distinguished national ideals from contemporary realities, writing that she had made the album

> out of a deep concern for the role children must play when celebrating the bicentennial of our country. . . . It is they who will carry on our musical traditions, share our heritage with people of the world, and see to it that the words "freedom," "justice," "integrity," "liberty," and "equality" be exercised daily in thought and action . . . all the while expanding and strengthening these principles we say we believe in.

It was an anti-triumphalist celebration, vested in aspiration rather than exceptionalism. As the children sang in the opening track, "We are America's children. We hope we are number one."[22]

FIGURE 11.1. Ella at home on North Mohawk Street, ca. 1970s.
Photo by Bernadelle Richter.

Building on the momentum of *You'll Sing a Song and I'll Sing a Song*, Ella's diverse 1970s albums boosted her national profile. But nothing brought her to greater national attention in this period than her 1974 and 1975 appearances on *Mister Rogers' Neighborhood*, a nationally distributed program seen by millions of children. Ella experienced the power of Fred Rogers's mass audience almost immediately. Walking through Chicago, or in the airport, she was suddenly recognizable to children and adults as "that singer from *Mister Rogers*'!"

Ella and Rogers had an immediate chemistry. They hailed from starkly different worlds—Rogers was from an upper-middle-class household in the white hamlet of Latrobe, Pennsylvania, on the outskirts of Pittsburgh—yet they were "neighbors" in disposition, philosophy, and love of music. Both possessed an intuitive gift for communicating with children. Both regarded their work as a conduit of ethical, political, and spiritual values, and both taught children compassion, neighborliness, and helpfulness—not so that they would be "good," but because these qualities were the requisites of a just and peaceful world. Finally, both were skilled musicians. On his show Rogers used songs to render emotionally complex ideas accessible to children and to help them navigate transitions, beginning and ending each episode with familiar songs. He also employed a crackerjack jazz trio, which improvised to scenes set both in the "Neighborhood" and "The Land of Make Believe."[23]

At first glance, *Mister Rogers' Neighborhood* might seem to have had less in common with Ella's work than another PBS children's show, *Sesame Street*, on which an interracial cast and a colorful array of puppets spoke with knowing fluency about urban experience. The world of Mister Rogers was white and evoked small-town or suburban life through detached houses with green lawns. Yet Rogers's approach to the television *experience* was more closely aligned with Ella's approach to musical performance than that of *Sesame Street*. Where *Sesame Street* revolved around short, high-energy segments designed to stimulate children's interest in reading and numeracy, *Mister Rogers' Neighborhood* had a leisurely, almost languid, pace, emphasizing children's social and emotional development. And where *Sesame Street* had a hip, self-referential vibe that endeared it to adults and older children. *Mister Rogers' Neighborhood* spoke directly and exclusively to preschoolers, giving no thought to their caretakers. *Sesame Street* was a television show. Rogers called *Mister Rogers' Neighborhood* a "television visit."[24]

For her first visit to Pittsburgh, Ella accepted Rogers's invitation to stay the night before the taping at the large home he shared with his wife and sons in the affluent Squirrel Hill neighborhood. The next day, he incorporated this detail into his introductory monologue:

Hi Neighbor! I have a treat for you today. A friend of mine is coming. She's been staying with my family and me at my real home. You know, *this* [*gesturing*] is my television home. But at my real home is my friend Ella Jenkins. This is a picture of her [holds up photograph]. And she is a musician who loves to work with children. Look down here on the picture, and see that little drum? I have that drum right here. I brought her instruments over so she wouldn't have to carry them all. Here's the drum, see? [*shows the drum*] . . . That, and this baritone ukulele which she plays. Oh, she plays it so well and sings so well! *Listen* [*plucks the four strings*].

On cue, Ella knocked at Rogers's door, and the two settled down—Ella on a sofa, Rogers perched on a table across from her—for an informal conversation and sing-along. He was a curious and eager participant, asking questions about her musical background, following Ella's lead on "You'll Sing a Song and I'll Sing a Song," and tapping on the drum while she performed "Harmonica Happiness," the camera offering close-ups of the dramatic fluttering of her fingers as she played. On "Animals in the Zoo," a song with a challenging melismatic phrase, he joined her on the "oo-oo part." "Well, you certainly sing well. I enjoyed singing with you," she said encouragingly when they finished.[25]

The entire segment, from Ella's opening "Oh, hi Fred!" to their goodbyes, lasted about seven minutes. But in that time it pictured a relationship between a white man and a Black woman as a friendship of equals. Telling children that Ella had been a houseguest at his "real" home was a "'Fred Rogers' way of communicating to children about race," said the ventriloquist (and frequent Neighborhood guest) Susan Linn, whose puppet Audrey Duck would sing with Ella the following year. It echoed an earlier memorable moment in the series: a 1969 episode in which Rogers and Officer Clemmons, the singing police officer played by African American opera singer François Clemmons, seek relief from summer heat by soaking their feet together in a wading pool. Broadcast at a time when white backlash to civil rights was spurring the closure or defunding of public swimming pools, the 1969 segment offered viewers an unapologetic image of racial integration. The 1974 episode with Ella, aired at a time of "white flight" from the "inner city," updated this image for the post–civil rights era. The episode made a powerful impression on the famous TV host. "I don't believe I've ever seen Fred look so happy and captivated," wrote Nan Wheelock, the show's associate producer, to Ella.[26]

In the 1980s and 1990s Ella would appear on *Mister Rogers' Neighborhood* an additional six times. (Although it aired videos of her singing, she never appeared on *Sesame Street* and visited *Barney and Friends* only once, in 1993.[27]) She dazzled with "Go Down, Moses" on the harmonica, showed off her collection of children's tops from around the world, and gave Rogers a lesson in singing the blues. And in a 1985 episode that entered show lore, Ella taught Rogers and regular cast member Chuck Aber how to do "Head and Shoulder," a Black girls' chant she recorded on the 1971 *Little Johnny Brown* LP. Rogers struggled to keep up with Ella's syncopated rhythms, to the point of laughing and saying, "It's hard, isn't it?" Rogers could have retaped the scene but decided to keep it so children could see that adults, too, learned new things and made mistakes.[28]

Ella's mid-1970s appearances on *Mister Rogers' Neighborhood* generated new demand for her performances. In the second half of the decade, she traversed the country from Philadelphia to San Francisco and New Orleans to Washington, DC, where she appeared at the Kennedy Center. She voyaged to Brisbane, Australia, as the guest of the state of Queensland, which incorporated her work into its preschool curriculum. And she continued to crisscross the Chicago region, negotiating its diversity as she had in the 1950s, when she shuttled between South Side jazz and Latin clubs and North Side folk venues. While Sunday Sings at the Old Town School of Folk Music and summer concerts at the Ravinia Pavilion remained staples of her performance itinerary, attracting primarily white and middle-class audiences, she also continued to work with the predominantly Black and Latino schools and libraries on the South and West Sides.

In addition to paid work, Ella continued to lend her talents to various causes and organizations, increasingly including those associated with women's rights and gay and lesbian liberation. She appeared at fundraisers for the National Organization for Women and other feminist organizations and with Jo Mapes donated her labors to the first Annual National Women's Music Festival, held in 1974 at the University of Illinois's flagship campus in Urbana-Champaign. Ella's Children's Music Workshop drew "encore after encore," according to the campus newspaper, but she was turned off by heated arguments over the participation of men and boys in the festival.[29] As someone who had participated in CORE actions on that campus in the late 1940s, Ella was put off by talk of separatism and would not abide the exclusion of boys from her workshops. The paucity of Black women at the gathering (she never overlapped with her friend Bernice Johnson Reagon, who would also perform on the women's music circuit) also gave her pause.

Ella never returned to the National Women's Music Festival. But her public advocacy of women's rights endeared her to the small but culturally significant world of 1970s feminist cultural organizations, from the music quarterly *Paid My Dues* to the *Ladyslipper* mail-order catalog, which included her albums in its recommendations of "music for children that doesn't insult their intelligence or bore them." In 1979, when Ann Christophersen and Linda Bubon opened the pioneering Chicago feminist bookstore Women and Children First, Bubon made sure to stock copies of Ella's albums, valuing their "consciousness of inclusivity." Ella and Bernadelle became frequent customers, popping over to visit while walking their dogs.[30]

At this detail suggests, in Chicago Ella and Bernadelle made no special effort to hide their "friendship"; yet neither did they talk openly about it. They continued to value their privacy, remembered sculptor Richard Hunt, who regularly met Bernadelle and Ella at Salt and Pepper, a diner near his studio. But the two women were keen to talk about other things, especially their travels. It always seemed that they had "just come back from somewhere or were about to be on their way somewhere," he said.[31]

In 1978 Ella decided to return to the theme of travel for a new LP that would teach children about language and languages. She had taken to opening her performances by asking children how many ways they knew to say *Hello*. That single prompt was usually enough to get the children excited, and from there she could use songs to encourage further inquiry. Where did people say *Howdy*? Where *Bonjour* or *Nihao*? Had they ever heard someone use the greeting *What's happening*? "We can all travel far in friendships if we just extend a polite hand—a smile or a friendly greeting to someone else," she would tell the children.

In September 1978 she entered a San Francisco studio with a group of children and a violin accompanist to record the album. But she missed her Chicago engineer, Stu Black, and brought the tapes home for re-editing. The following month, on October 12, she wrote to Moe Asch to assure him that the record was forthcoming. "The title of my new album is TRAVELLING WITH ELLA JENKINS (A Bi-Lingual Journey)," she informed him. "I think it's a fine album."[32]

Below the signature, she typed a terse postscript: "My Mother passed away yesterday—she lived [a] full, energetic life and I shall miss her very much." Whether Asch ever responded directly to this news, included as an afterthought, is unknown. He might have interpreted the stoicism of her tone as a signal that Ella was still

FIGURE. 11.2. Ella captured by Bernadelle, ca. 1970s.
Photo by Bernadelle Richter.

in shock. Or perhaps he intuited that she wished to speak no further
of the matter and required no condolences. Either reading would
have been correct.

In the fall of 1978 Annabelle had checked herself into Hilltop Sanatorium, a Christian Science facility in Lake Bluff, Illinois, where she had once worked. She did not alert Ella or Tom to the fact that she was preparing to die. Mary Baker Eddy's faith held that embodied illness was not to be discussed, and that in matters of health and healing Christian Scientists required the care of spiritual healers, not doctors or nurses. Annabelle was married to her fifth husband, a barber named Haywood Skinner, but he was not a believer. The sanatorium afforded her a place where she could comfortably rest, "shielded from the material thought of the world."[33]

Ella and Bernadelle rushed to visit Annabelle as soon as they found out she was at Hilltop. Soft music played in her room as she slept; but communication between mother and daughter was sparse. They did not think Annabelle looked particularly ill—but then again, she was not surrounded by medical equipment, the beeping machines that Ella vividly remembered from her father's bedside at Hines Veterans Hospital. When she died a day or two later, sanatorium officials listed the cause of death as "Natural." Under "Conditions," they noted that she suffered from "acute coronary insufficiency."

The days immediately following Annabelle's death were a disorganized blur. Tom, then living in Cincinnati, had not had time to visit Annabelle and "completely fell apart," Bernadelle said. Everyone was pulled in different directions. Bernadelle was heading out on a European trip with a cousin, and Ella was facing a string of out-of-town obligations, which she could not (or would not) miss. Haywood Skinner was not stepping up. It was therefore left to Bernadelle's mother Celeste to oversee the details of Annabelle's wake, funeral, and burial. Over the years, the two had become friendly, even joining their daughters on one of their summer European jaunts. The service took place at Griffin Funeral Home, on the Bronzeville thoroughfare formerly known as South Parkway, but since 1968 called Martin Luther King Drive.

When they finally got around to sorting through Annabelle's affairs, Ella and Tom would find that in Christian Science fashion, she had taken care to put everything in order. She left Tom and Ella the details of her insurance policies and bank account, along with documentation of the satin-lined mink coat and matching fur stole that were her prized possessions. She had purchased the $2,000 coat on the installment plan at Marshall Field's in 1972 and stored it and the stole in the off-season at a fur retailer in the Loop.

Fur was on its way out by the time Annabelle purchased her pieces. Activism associated with animal rights organizations meant that the public wearing of animal hides was regarded as gauche at best, at worst inhumane. But Annabelle was unconcerned by rows over minks and sables. It had taken her the better part of seventy years to afford a fur coat, an extravagance claimed both proudly and defiantly by affluent Black women, from Bronzeville society matrons to entertainers like Billie Holiday. The greatest pleasure of her last years had been on cold days, when she could wear her fur while her husband drove her around town on errands.

Ella had no use for her mother's coat—and even had she wanted it, it would not have fit her fuller figure. But she held onto her mother's Bibles and Christian Science literature; her letters, peppered with references to helpful passages in Eddy's *Science and Health*; and the newspaper clippings she regularly sent Ella, on all manner of interesting subjects. Denied an education in her native Mississippi, Annabelle earned her eighth-grade diploma by attending Chicago night school in the early 1960s, when she was in her sixties. The documents would be Ella's reminder of the "full and energetic" life her mother had lived.

Dear Mrs. Forsman,

Thank you for letting Ella Jenkins sing too us. She's the best singer I know! I bet she knows more than two billioun songs! I only know a couple or a few. Well I have to go now. bye!

YOUR friend,
DeWayne

(GREAT FALLS, MONTANA, 1975)

12

LOOKING BACK AND LOOKING FORWARD

1979–1999

The summer before Annabelle died, Ella and Bernadelle embarked on their most ambitious adventure to date: an extended voyage to China, a country only recently opening to US tourists. The visa applications required them to indicate what they proposed to share with the Chinese people. Bernadelle cited her photography and filmmaking, while Ella wrote of her extensive work as a children's musician-educator.

Unofficially, Ella was also excited about the idea of going to a country that was known for its preeminence in table tennis. Ever since Mao Zedong, an avid player, had elevated the game to a national pastime, China had moved up in world rankings. In 1971 table tennis attracted global attention after a friendly encounter between US and Chinese competitors at the World Table Tennis Championships. Members of the US national team—including Ella's one-time opponent Leah Thall—visited China after the tournament, spurring a reciprocal invitation to the Chinese national team. The American press had dubbed these tentative steps toward a thawing of Cold War tensions "ping-pong diplomacy."[1]

Ella was so excited about the trip that she even penned a short poem, riffing on the ubiquitous television advertising campaign for the perfume Enjoli, which featured a song based on Peggy Lee's 1962 hit "I'm a Woman." Ella's version went:

> Travel Agency Man
> I've got a major plan
> I'm going to China
> and then to Japan
> Because I'm a travellin *woman*[2]

It was a clever send-up of the advertisement's appeal to a liberated American woman who could "bring home the bacon" and "fry it up in a pan," while also retaining her sexual allure for men.

For US travelers used to certain comforts, China in the late 1970s required fortitude and patience. Rice shortages affected their meals, and even Peking, as Beijing was then known, lacked basic tourist infrastructure. But hotels almost always had public table-tennis tables, giving Ella a chance to socialize with locals in the Esperanto of ping-pong. She communicated with Chinese children through music. On a visit to an elementary school near Canton (Guangzhou), Ella traded greetings and songs with students, while Bernadelle snapped photographs. And after taking in a concert at the Children's Palace in Peking, she showed some young performers how to play harmonica blues and snap their fingers on the offbeats.

Travel had always been a source of renewal for Ella, but when she returned from China, she faced a new round of legal arguments with the Alvin Ailey American Dance Company over *Revelations*. In January of 1980 she wrote to Asch, informing him of her impending costly "legal entanglement" with "a New York Dance company" and asking for $5,000 in back payments. To sweeten the request, she described ambitious plans for a series of "VERY MARKETABLE" new albums for the educational market. But under her breath, she made her expectations very clear. "You know, Moe," she wrote, "since I started writing a lot of songs, people, publishers, have tried to take advantage of me—it's very disappointing."[3]

Ella's letter mostly had its desired effect. Within two weeks, she received three royalties checks from Asch. Yet the total amount still fell well short of what she had requested, leading Moe to send her an additional $500 as a loan.[4] These gestures were in line with Asch's practices with most Folkways artists, but most of them sold very few copies of their albums, whereas Ella, selling untold thousands, kept him in business. And so Ella burned with resentment at being treated as Folkways' golden goose. As she knew well from Odetta's old song "The Fox," the fate of the goose was always to be someone else's dinner.

Since declaring herself a freelance "rhythm specialist" in 1956, Ella had been rigorously protective of her creative labors. In many ways, owning her work and being justly compensated for it were at the core of her professional identity, going back to her rejection of Albert Grossman and her original contract negotiation with Asch. And yet now, in the third decade of her career, she was unexpectedly embroiled in conflicts over compensation with two parties whom she regarded not as enemies, but as creative allies. The aggravation of this in-fighting depleted her energy for new projects. Of the seven albums she had excitedly pitched to Asch, none would come to fruition.

The strain on Ella was complicated by the fact that the two disputes carried distinct emotional shadings. Understanding herself to be part of Ailey's wide circle of artist-friends, Ella was flummoxed by the Ailey organization's neglect of her petitions. Eventually, her frustration soured into feelings of personal injury and disrespect. "I can no longer speak in pleasant language as I have not been treated pleasantly," she wrote to William Hammons, the Ailey company's executive director, in 1980. "I feel quite disappointed as a composer, a Black, a woman and as a friend of the Alvin Ailey Dance Theater, which I've supported for over twenty years."[5]

Ella's conflict with Asch was also personal, but in a different way. He had always been an unreliable figure whose promises could quickly curdle into disappointments. But Ella always forgave his eccentricity because of a deep sense of indebtedness to him as the person who had given her "little record" a chance. By early 1981, however, Ella's tolerance had worn thin. Against the backdrop of the conflict with the Ailey company, and in the face of bitter disputes over royalties from a Folkways partnership with the Scholastic label, Asch and Ella's relationship fell apart. In February she wrote to inform him that she would be taking her future projects to Activities Records (later Educational Activities), a label that catered to the educational market.[6]

> I'm very sorry that we have come to such an uncomfortable place in our relationship and I do hope one day it can be resolved—I hope that you will keep your word and try to compensate some of the past errors regarding my payments and new royalty considerations. Moe, I have made Folkways a lot of money over the years—everywhere I go people—bookstores, teacher stores, other countries speak of selling my records but my royalties never measure up to more than a few thousand—I should be receiving much more than 8 to 9 thousand a year.

As ever, Ella could not end her letter without extending an olive branch. "Moe, I felt very hurt after our last meeting—perhaps you did too—and I could not compose for awhile but now I have come up with two nice albums," she assured him. "I'm looking forward to hearing from you this month and let's do our best to have better rapport." The letter was signed, "Understandingly, Ella."[7]

Drafting a response on Valentine's Day, Asch drew a tiny Cupid's heart in the upper right-hand corner—an uncharacteristically tender gesture for a man who was famously gruff. He took the news of her "new record venture" in stride, but he also enclosed a statement of royalties and a check, and wrote encouragingly of a group that had invited Ella to Japan.

Their mutual attempts at a rapprochement continued through the end of the year, when Ella and her attorney visited the Folkways office, now located at 632 Broadway. This space had the ambiance of a shambolic museum of African art, stuffed with sculptures, masks, and other objects. To Linda Mensch, these were the manifestations of the income Ella had generated for Asch, and she was fully prepared to get Ella her fair share. A trailblazing woman in entertainment law, Mensch viewed the Folkways owner as a "type," in the mold of the workaday Jewish peddlers she remembered from her childhood. "Moe was a yeller. He yelled. I told myself, just think of this as a fish wharf. I'm selling fish," she recalled. "And so I kept up with him." Ella was so disturbed by their yelling that she fled the office.[8]

Ella and Asch continued their argument through letters. Ella pressed for royalties; he pointed to his own difficulties getting a proper accounting of Ella's sales from Scholastic. But eventually Asch waved a white flag, conceding the point if not all of the money. "I do want to end this nonsense of bickering and unhappiness. There is too much of that in today's world."[9] It was a point on which he and Ella could agree. They could not solve the problems of the world, but she hoped that, with a bit of time, they could repair their relationship.

In the midst of this rancor—and to work through her turbulent feelings—Ella recorded new material for Activities Records on themes of harmonious co-existence. On *I Know the Colors of the Rainbow* (1981), she cut through lingering Cold War static by humanizing Chinese children in the song "In the People's Republic of China." (In the liner notes, Ella included Bernadelle's snapshots from their trip, showing Chinese preschoolers looking like their American equivalents.) In "A Train Ride to the Great Wall," she taught children how to say "very good," "no good," and "how are you?" in Mandarin. And on "Chotto Matte, Kudasai" (a phonetic rendering of "Just a moment, please" in Japanese), she produced a wistful and lovely "farewell" song by rhyming the title phrase with "Please wait before you say goodbye."

A pair of Activities recordings from 1983, *Hopping Around from Place to Place*, volumes 1 and 2, similarly used song to invite children to "travel" with Ella to places including Egypt, Australia, Hawaiʻi, and a Seminole reservation near Okeechobee, Florida. In the volume 2 liner notes, she reflected on her own extraordinary history of travel, and made a promise: "My next big travel ADVENTURE, hopefully, will be the ANTAR[C]TICA, completing the SEVEN CONTINENTS."[10]

Ella and Bernadelle made good on this promise with an arduous trip in the winter of 1983. The had to travel first to the southernmost tip of Argentina, and from there ride the rough seas of the Drake Passage to the "white continent." Once ashore, they navigated the perils of frigid waters and crevasses formed by shifting ice. To be able to say that she had not merely visited all seven continents but *performed* on them, Ella sang with the children of scientists stationed there. She even serenaded a group of penguins, joking that the birds in their feathered tuxedos were her most "formal" concert audience.

The Antarctica trip was not just about boasting rights, however. In 1940, when Ella was in high school, George Washington Gibbs Jr. achieved a minor notoriety as the first African American person to visit the southernmost point on Earth. The *Defender* carried word of his achievement, which symbolized Black American freedom in an age of Jim Crow constraints. As a Black man, Gibbs had needed to sweep floors and peel potatoes to join a US Navy expedition to Antarctica. Although Ella arrived there as a tourist, she also looked at Antarctica as an emblem of how far she had traveled from humble beginnings. "When I was a little girl growing up on the South Side of Chicago I never thought that one day I would visit the South Pole, Antarctica," she wrote in a personal document she titled "Things to Remember." The trip was not the manifestation of a dream, then, but the realization of possibilities that had once been beyond dreaming.[11]

Perhaps because of the deep satisfaction she took from that trip, Ella regained her professional equilibrium, reaching truces both with the Ailey company and with Asch. In June of 1983 Moe mailed her a clipping of a flattering *New York Times* profile titled "How a Recording Pioneer Created a Treasury of Folk Music." "Today, Folkways Records, which Mr. Asch founded more than 30 years ago, boasts the largest catalogue of folk music recordings in the world," wrote music critic Robert Palmer. "More than any other single individual, Mr. Asch has educated his fellow Americans to this country's bounteous wealth of vernacular music."[12] Ella's response was equally flattering. "Today I sat down in a comfortable chair and read that most stimulating article about you and the beginning of Folkways. . . . I shall keep and treasure this article for always—thank you for sending it to me," she wrote, before pivoting to discuss her missing mechanical royalties from Scholastic.[13]

Within a few years the future of Folkways would be in doubt, after Asch suffered a series of strokes that left him unable to mind the label's day-to-day business. When it became clear that neither Moe's wife Frances nor his son Michael, an ethnomusicologist, had any interest in taking over, Moe began to vet prospective buyers.

Eventually the Smithsonian Institution emerged as the most likely candidate to purchase Folkways. But first Ralph Rinzler, the musician and folklorist who led the Smithsonian effort, had to convince Moe, who had survived McCarthyism, that an institution under the guardianship of the federal government could be entrusted with his life's work.[14] Ella also worried about the future of her catalog in the hands of the culturally conservative, bureaucratic Smithsonian. To convince holdouts within the institution, Rinzler was touting Folkways as an important archive of vernacular and traditional music, giving short shrift to the children's music that was central to it. Ella doubted that the Washington "folk intelligentsia" would care about her interpretations of Black folk tradition for young listeners, or care that sales of *You'll Sing a Song and I'll Sing a Song* had helped to keep Folkways in business for the previous two decades.

Ella's concerns were grounded in personal experiences, going back to the devaluation of her work by self-declared guardians of American folk tradition. Over the years, moreover, she had seen too many "ballad catchers" exercise a racial power of eminent domain over Black musical traditions. In the celebration of Folkways recordings of "We Shall Overcome," she saw the potential erasure of the song's roots in a composition by Charles Tindley, one of the founding fathers of gospel music. Her years-long struggles with Asch over royalties expressed her resistance to such "theft"—not only to her personal exploitation, but also to the very history of white profiteering from Black music.

Ella saw Moe Asch for the last time in the fall of 1986, as negotiations between Folkways and Smithsonian continued. "Hope you're feeling better, Moe," she wrote in an October 13 postcard from Zurich, Switzerland. But Moe died on October 19—the day before she returned to the States.

Ella and Bernadelle arrived early for the private funeral at Gramercy Chapel at Tenth Street and Second Avenue. To pass the time, they stopped in at the bustling nearby Second Avenue Deli. Ella saw some diners who looked to her like "folk people," and asked whether they too were in town to pay respects to Asch. Rinzler and Bess Lomax Hawes, the sister of Alan Lomax, asked how Ella had known. "I don't know, you just looked 'folky,'" she responded. The look of annoyance on their faces reinforced Ella's sense of permanent outsidership within elite folk circles.[15]

Asch, she felt, had never approached her as though she were lesser. The day before the funeral, the *New York Times* eulogized him as a preeminent sonic archivist of the twentieth century. "By documenting traditional music and sounds from around the world, Folkways established an invaluable library—one that was hugely influential during the folk and blues revivals of the 1960s as well as a continuing resource of musicians and listeners," wrote Jon Pareles.[16] No one could doubt the truth of this description, but it was not the whole story. As much as Asch valued documentation, he also supported invention. In 1956 he recognized the simple brilliance and originality in Ella's rough recordings of call-and-response chants, and he never wavered in his commitment to her or to her children's music.

Moe Asch died without ever having seen Ella perform. But even if he had opportunities to see one of her concerts or rhythm workshops,

FIGURE 12.1. A rare photograph of Ella and Moe Asch, ca. 1970s.
Unknown photographer.

he may simply have not felt the need, knowing everything he needed
to know from the music and from their emotionally charged relationship. They were an odd couple, Ella and Moe: forever fighting, forever
making up, in a rhythm that extended over thirty years. She would
miss him.

Asch's passing marked the end of an era in Ella's life, coinciding with
changes in the US children's music industry that affected the ways
Ella would do business. Ella had never hired a publicist or a booking
agent, instead relying on word-of-mouth and the support of independent sellers, such as the Children's Music Center in Los Angeles.

Grassroots networks were effective because, outside of Disney block-busters and other high-profile projects, children's music was mostly an afterthought of commercial record labels.

That indifference began to fade in the mid- to late 1970s, as commercial labels came to recognize an untapped market in children's recordings. The success of musical spin-offs of *Sesame Street* and *The Electric Company* fanned industry speculation that children's music was finally on the verge of making it big. Marketers took note of the spending power of baby-boomers-turned-parents, while sales professionals devised novel ways of connecting adult buyers to children's products—for example, through eye-catching displays of LPs and cassettes at grocery stores. Most important, a new generation of artists was stepping in to the fold of children's performance. Among them were Greg Scelsa and Steve Millang, California-based music teachers who, as Greg & Steve, made rock and roll for kids, and the folk musicians Cathy Fink and Marcy Marxer, solo artists who performed as the children's duo Cathy & Marcy.[17]

The relatively sedate children's music ecosystem was shaken up in 1985 when the first six albums of Canadian children's music star Raffi Cavoukian were made easily available to US audiences. The same year, Raffi embarked on a US tour that drew sellout crowds everywhere. Within two years he would be on the front page of the *Wall Street Journal* and the subject of *New York Times* speculation about "the Raffi industry"—whose young audiences turned over every three years.[18]

Raffi's sound and repertoire were rooted in Anglo-American tradition. Like many an aspiring male folk troubadour, he frequently cited Woody Guthrie and Pete Seeger as influences. But Raffi and his folksinger friends in Toronto also knew Ella's songs, including "You'll Sing a Song, and I'll Sing a Song," which was the lead track on his 1979 album, *Corner Grocery Store*. "She was one of the pioneers in music for children, someone we admired and learned from," he said. "I certainly learned from her simple, direct and respectful approach in making music for young ones."[19]

Outside of Raffi's cover of Ella's most famous song (for which he paid her royalties, Bernadelle noted), their careers did not tangibly intersect, and they spent time together only once, over dinner in Quebec in the late 1980s. But Raffi's unprecedented commercial success in North America changed the public perception of children's music. After he demonstrated that independently produced children's music could sell millions of albums—and at the price-point of pop recordings, not the discounted commercial children's fare—"everybody and their brother and sister thought they could make music for children," said Moira McCormick, a music journalist who covered children's media at the time for *Billboard*.[20]

Ella, too, was swept up in the "discovery" of a mass market for children's music. She hired Nancy Rosenbacher, a Hyde Park promoter, to book her on a national tour of prestigious auditoriums and performing arts centers. Kicking off in December 1985 and extending through May 1986, "Ella Jenkins: A Live Theatre Concert Tour for Children" covered eighteen cities and included a four-day run at New York's 92nd Street Y Theatre. The following year, Ella played in thirty-three cities, including five afternoon shows at the New York Y.

With healthy ticket prices and "no free chaperones," the Raffi-style tour helped to sustain Ella through a period of transition. But the pace was grueling, and Ella missed the intimacy of her work in schools and community centers. "This schedule is typical of what my situation has been since seeing you last," she scribbled on an "Ella Jenkins" publicity flyer that may have been intended for her brother Tom. The glossy illustrated color handbill contained the sort of hyped-up language that, while commonplace in the entertainment world, clashed awkwardly with Ella's folksy sincerity. "How would you like to take your children on a field trip where they are taken through the colorful streets of New Orleans, across the seas to the mysterious Orient, and returned with a better understanding of the beauty to be found in their own backyards?," one 1985–86 poster asked. Ella eventually managed to get such overheated sales pitches and retrograde language replaced with more sober endorsements from respected educators.

FIGURE 12.2. Ella outside of the Ninety-Second Street Y, New York City, March 1968. Photo by David Gahr.

Around this time Ella hired Lynn Orman, a former Head Start teacher and mentee of her lawyer Linda Mensch, as a promoter, and independently struck a deal with Rhythm Band, a Texas-based supplier of the educational market, to manufacture, sell, and distribute "Ella Jenkins"-branded musical instruments. The Rhythm Band products, which resembled Orff instruments, included an Ella Jenkins Rhythm Set (with guiros, castanets, claves, maracas, a cowbell, and a tambourine), an Ella Jenkins baritone ukulele and kazoo, and an Ella Jenkins limbertoy—a wooden figure that could be made to dance on the head of a tambourine. For teachers, Rhythm Band offered *Ella Jenkins' Rhythm Fun*, a sixteen-page instructional pamphlet.

Ella had long been interested in the production of instruments to support the classroom use of her music. As early as 1957, she had pitched the possibility of a tie-in with Peripole, another supplier of school instruments, to Moe Asch. But in the 1980s it also served to reassert the participatory quality of her work, distinguishing it from the performance-oriented approach of Raffi, Greg & Steve, and others. The instructional booklet, which used language that directly echoed *Adventures in Rhythm*, also marked a return to more familiar cadences.

Ella brought her red Rhythm Band kazoos with her on her last guest appearance on *Mister Rogers' Neighborhood*, in 1992, leading Fred Rogers through a kazoo duet to the tune of "London Bridge." When they finished, Rogers raised his head to look at her. "You know I was just thinking as I was playing this [kazoo], I wonder why I love to learn things with you so much," he said. "Well, you know, it's always great to learn—and share," Ella replied. "It's because there's so much sharing being done."

But Rogers would not allow Ella to deflect the compliment. "I guess so," he answered, "but it just dawned on me, whatever you taught me I'd probably learn it because I like you so much."[21] After the taping Rogers kept the red kazoo with Ella's name on it as a testament to their friendship.

The Smithsonian finalized its purchase of Folkways while Ella was on her "Ella Jenkins, Live in Concert" tour. To publicize the acquisition,

Rinzler commissioned a poster featuring a grid of thirty-two album covers, intended to display the richness of Folkways' holdings. They included albums featuring the voices of Eleanor Roosevelt and Margaret Mead, narrative reenactments of the poems of Ovid and the speeches of Frederick Douglass and Sojourner Truth, and collections of field recordings, such as *Healing Songs of the American Indians* and *Roots of Black Music in America.* Children's music was represented through ethnographic collections of youth from Africa, Mexico, and the Caribbean. Titles by Pete Seeger, Woody Guthrie, and Lead Belly attested to Folkways' seminal role in the folk revival.

Ella's name was nowhere to be found—either on the poster or in any of the Smithsonian's press releases about the Folkways deal. She saw the omissions as an indifference to children's music, and although she would never say it publicly, as indifference to her contributions as a Black woman who had made it possible for Asch to pursue recordings that would never sell more than a handful of copies. In the terms offered by Langston Hughes's poem "I, Too," Ella felt as though she had been sent to the Folkways "kitchen," while others were invited to the Smithsonian table to dine on a meal she herself had prepared.

Over time, the wounds Ella suffered in the earliest days of the Smithsonian acquisition of Folkways healed, particularly after Rinzler appointed ethnomusicologist Anthony Seeger to head the new label, dubbed Smithsonian Folkways. A veteran summer-camp song leader, Seeger understood the power of group singing in children's lives and recognized Ella's importance as a financial pillar of Moe Asch's enterprise.[22] As the nephew of Pete Seeger, he also came highly recommended. Without his knowledge, Pete's wife Toshi Seeger had arranged to have dinner with Ella and Bernadelle to vouch for him.

Tony Seeger worked to ensure that Ella stayed on with Smithsonian Folkways. He prioritized her most popular recordings for vinyl reissues and oversaw their conversion to compact discs, after she pointed out that cassettes, then a favored format, were deeply impractical for teachers of small children. Through a new distribution deal with Rounder Records, a respected Americana and bluegrass label, he also managed to reverse an earlier distributor's decision that had priced Ella out of the educational market. Most crucially, he initiated discussions with Ella about new material, recognizing that she remained vibrant and energetic in her sixth decade.

Ella rewarded Seeger's attentiveness with a burst of creativity during which she produced some of the most critically acclaimed work of her career. Between 1991 and 1999, a period that also her increasingly referred to as the "First Lady of Children's Music," she released two videotapes and five albums, of which three featured new material.[23] The videotapes, *Ella Jenkins Live at the Smithsonian* (1991) and *Ella Jenkins For the Family* (1991), translated her minimalist aesthetic to a visual medium. *Ella Jenkins Live at the Smithsonian*, recorded with preschoolers at the institution's daycare facility, captures her skillful work with a group of unrehearsed three- and four-year-olds. On *Ella Jenkins for the Family*, she appears against a plain white background, addressing the camera in the manner of Fred Rogers. In the first ten minutes, she conducts a deceptively simple master class in folkloric tradition, sharing different versions of "Miss Mary Mack," each associated with a different social or geographic setting.

Also released in 1991, *Come Dance by the Ocean*, Ella's first album for Smithsonian Folkways, assembles songs about environmentalism and environments, both built and natural. "Our oceans, cities, and peoples face difficult problems of pollution, violence, and cultural intolerance," she wrote in the liner notes, expressing a forward-thinking concern with environmental racism.[24] Bernadelle supplied the cover photograph, a portrait that Ella counted as a personal favorite. It showed her standing in front of a large body of water—it was actually Lake Michigan, not an ocean—holding a conga drum, a breeze blowing through her earrings and hair. The presence of the drum connected the new work to her earliest work *Call-and-Response Rhythmic Group Singing*, evoking the rhythms that traveled over oceans with enslaved Africans.

Ella's other original recordings include *Holiday Times* (1996), a collection of songs for celebrations including Christmas, Chinese New

Year, St. Patrick's Day, Hanukkah, and Kwanzaa, and *Ella Jenkins and a Union of Friends Pulling Together* (1999), an album expressing support for labor unions. The latter, which earned Ella her first Grammy nomination (in the category Best Musical Album for Children), appeared at a time when popular support for US organized labor was at a historic ebb and had a nostalgic tinge, looking back to the mid-century heyday of Popular Front–inspired folk music, even as it looked forward to post-industrial-era labor solidarities.[25] Ella took the "union" metaphor seriously, emphasizing collaborations and including previously recorded performances by Pete Seeger ("If I Had a Hammer") and Josh White Jr. (singing his father's hit "One Meat Ball"). And through versions of the Almanac Singers' "Union Train" and Woody Guthrie's "Union Maid," she invoked the figures of her Uncle Flood, a steelworker and union man, and her mother Annabelle, a domestic servant.

While both albums of original recordings were critical successes— with *Holiday Times* earning Ella a rare A+ from *Parenting* magazine— Ella's 1995 anthology album, *Multicultural Children's Songs*, had the most enduring and widespread impact of her 1990s work. Tony Seeger came up with the idea of organizing and marketing Ella's music under the banner of "multiculturalism," a term that had become a commonplace in US education, as well as in government and corporate spheres. By the time the album appeared, *multiculturalism* had shed its politically radical roots in mid-century democratic pluralism, movements for Black, Mexican/Chicano, Native American, Asian American, and "Third World" liberation, and 1970s grassroots projects advancing integration and racial justice. Yet Ella signed on to Seeger's idea, knowing that "multiculturalism" remained an important tool for teachers, especially in an era that purported color blindness as a national ideal.

She and Seeger were correct in discerning a need for such a collection. "The children's music industry has not kept up with children's book publishers in providing multicultural resources," noted the *School Library Journal*, in reviewing *Multicultural Children's Songs*. "In a time when there is still a scarcity of quality multicultural sound recordings for children, this is a very rich treasure." *Parenting* magazine rewarded

Ella with another A+, noting that although the world had changed in the forty years since she started recording, her voice was still relevant and necessary.[26]

Multicultural Children's Songs framed the pluralist principles of Ella's career for a new generation of listeners; "multiculturalism" was in this sense an old idea garbed in new clothes befitting a more conservative era in American history. "Ella Jenkins was singing for children long before it was the cool thing to do, and was espousing music from many cultures long before diversity became a buzzword," asserted one review. And yet even children's folk songs could encode a xenophobic fear of the Other. Back in 1971, the coordinator of early childhood programs for Duluth, Minnesota, public schools had reached out to Ella to suggest that "John Brown Had a Little Indian," from her 1965 Folkways album *Counting Games and Rhythms for the Little Ones*, was "dehumanizing to the American Indian." On the 1997 Smithsonian Folkways CD reissue of the same title, the song no longer appeared.[27]

Seeger's initial intuition about the commercial potential of *Multicultural Children's Songs* was borne out by sales that matched or exceeded those of *You'll Sing a Song and I'll Sing a Song*, riding a wave of popular 1990s children's offerings with "multicultural" elements. For example, in hearkening back to "Tah-boo," her Africa-inspired chant and to tracks from her *Jambo* album of 1974, the record presented children with an alternative to Walt Disney's 1994 *The Lion King* soundtrack, which won the Grammy for best children's album. It also coincided with the release of *World Playground*, the first album of a new division of Putumayo World Music called Putumayo Kids. Even Barney, the friendly purple TV dinosaur whom Ella visited in 1993, was tapping into the market for multiculturalism, with *What a World We Share*, a video that found Barney and Friends journeying "from the highest mountains in Canada to the streets of Mexico and France."[28]

While delighted by the album's success in bringing her old songs to new audiences, Ella worried about cosmetic projects of diversity, just as she had been sensitive to an earlier vogue for Black history. "I have been to every continent," she told one reporter. "And everywhere I go

I try at the very least to learn how to say hello in the native language. People get caught up in multiculture this and multiculture that, but if we aren't out there trying to get to know one another, we're missing the point." The point was not merely to celebrate "difference," but to create conditions for connection and change.[29]

Ella rode out the last years of the twentieth century on an extended high note. On August 6, 1994, she blew out the candles on a seventieth birthday cake from the stage of the Pavilion at the Ravinia Festival as the audience sang "Happy Birthday." In 1996 she received the Zora Neale Hurston Award from the National Association of Black Storytellers. Ella "was adamant that she was not a storyteller," recalled Shanta Nurullah, a Chicago musician who pursued storytelling with Ella's encouragement. But Nurullah and others in the group recognized Ella's stories of her own childhood as integral to her work as a musician. "Every time she spoke she would say, 'When I was a little girl' or 'We used to play this game,'" Nurullah said. Without knowing it, "She was a proponent of the tradition of Black storytelling."[30]

Ella brought children's games and Black folkloric tradition to a "Folkways at 50" concert fundraiser on May Day of 1998 at Carnegie Hall, where she took the stage alongside old friends including Pete Seeger, Theodore Bikel, and Bernice Johnson Reagon, whom Ella first met in the early 1970s, when Reagon's a cappella ensemble Sweet Honey in the Rock visited Chicago. When it was her turn to perform, Ella made audience members play the English clapping game Pat-a-Cake with their neighbors, led them through call-and-response songs, and finished by playing "Go Down, Moses" on harmonica. The audience's warm response confirmed her centrality in the Folkways story. As the *New York Times* noted, "Ms. Jenkins's albums for children helped keep Folkways solvent and, judging by a sing-along, nurtured many audience members."[31]

In August 1999 the Ravinia Pavilion was once again the stage for Ella's birthday celebration—her seventy-fifth. But this time the cake and candles were accompanied by the presentation of a Lifetime Achievement Award from the ASCAP Foundation. The award came with $5,000 and was "offered as a tribute to veteran music creators who, over the years, have made significant contributions to our nation's music culture." Ella was particularly cited for her efforts on behalf of music education, at a time when more and more school districts were slashing budgets for elementary school music programs.[32]

To be honored by ASCAP was particularly poignant for Ella, because it recognized her deep desire to serve children through composition. She wanted to give them songs that delighted them in the present, but could be carried with them as they aged—perhaps even shared with future children. As Pete Seeger, talking about Ella's craft as a composer, observed, "Like all good songs, even a simple children's song can mean different things at different times. The song bounces back new meanings as life gives you new experiences."[33] Ella accepted the award gracefully and gratefully, as she accepted all expressions of love.

EPILOGUE
FIRST LADY
2000–2024

In November 2000, more than 30,000 teachers, childcare professionals, academics, and policy specialists descended on Atlanta for the annual meeting of the National Association for the Education of Young Children (NAEYC), North America's largest and most important gathering of professionals focused on the education of three- to eight-year-olds. They came to attend seminars and presentations, to network and socialize, and to browse a vast exhibit hall filled with offerings from publishers, professional organizations, and manufacturers of classroom supplies. They wore lanyards with name tags and carried tote bags bulging with swag.

The conference was a first for Daniel Sheehy, a musician and ethnomusicologist who had recently taken charge of Smithsonian Folkways after Tony Seeger stepped down. He had come to observe Ella, who was giving a keynote, and to get a sense of the educational market for Smithsonian Folkways recordings. Yet although Sheehy knew of the success of her 1995 album *Multicultural Children's Songs*, he was unprepared for the intense devotion her presence generated. When she appeared in the exhibit hall, a throng of people—mostly women—quickly formed around her. At the Smithsonian Folkways booth, they queued up in long lines to purchase her CDs, LPs, books, harmonicas, and rhythm sticks, hoping for a chance to greet her, perhaps even get a photograph or a hug. Teachers who had used Ella's music in their classrooms for decades approached Ella as an old friend; some welled up when they told her what her work had meant to them. Ella patiently greeted everyone, obliging requests for autographs with a version of the stylized signature she had worked out in the 1950s: a whimsical face made out of the letters of her first name.

Sales were like nothing Sheehy had seen. "It took two credit card machines just to keep up," he said. When Ella had to leave, he and another person had to carve out an exit path for her. "Those of us who were there were like bodyguards, like for Bruce Springsteen," Sheehy remembered. "You couldn't walk ten steps across the conference room with her before she was stopped. She was a rock star."[1]

But Ella was conspicuously lacking in rock-star attitude. Once, while he was still easing into his new role, Sheehy met Ella and Bernadelle for lunch in Chicago. While they ate, four women at a nearby table eyed Ella. Eventually, they came over to say hello. Each told a story about Ella's music over three generations. Each had learned Ella's songs as children, and now each was teaching these same songs to grandchildren. "It was just a beautiful testimony to Ella," Sheehy said.[2]

While the Atlanta NAEYC conference illustrated Ella's national status, the lunch spoke of Chicagoans' particular veneration for Ella. She routinely got stopped at stores and restaurants, while walking one of her dogs or dropping off mail at the post office. Yet it was inevitable that as Ella approached eighty, people would begin inquiring gently about retirement. Ella responded by pointing out, "You don't really retire from children." As she told Moe Asch's son Michael, "As soon as I step on that stage, I [feel I] should produce, because these children, I owe it to them, and there's a call and response, there's a relationship that we have with one another."[3]

Christian Science also gave her reasons to carry on without thought of retirement. As she told a reporter, "I don't count the years too much. If I have something to give and others have something to give me, we have a fair exchange."[4] To outsiders to the faith, her words might have been unremarkable. But to Christian Scientists the phrase "count the years" recalled Mary Baker Eddy's exhortations against the use of human metrics, such as time, to measure lives created in God's immortal image. "Never record ages," wrote the woman who launched the *Christian Science Monitor* newspaper when she was eighty-eight. "Chronological data are not part of the vast forever. Time-tables of birth and death are so many conspiracies against manhood and womanhood."[5]

Ella had long since ceased to belong to a Christian Science church. Yet she had never abandoned its precepts. In particular, the faith's teachings about the bondage of "self-imposed materiality" remained alive in her cultivation of a "positive" outlook as a form of spiritual armor against racism and other social ills. Now Ella found solace in Eddy's teachings about health and aging. They helped Ella ignore the false mathematics of years and continue her work.[6]

Ella's attitude toward aging helps to explain a remarkable burst of late-career creativity that lasted through her early nineties. It kicked off in 2003 with *Sharing Cultures with Ella Jenkins*, a Grammy-nominated album of new material recorded with children from Chicago's LaSalle Language Academy and a roster of guest performers. The album's twenty-nine tracks included songs, chants, and stories from a variety of cultures and in several languages, especially Spanish. While directed at twenty-first-century children, the album once again found Ella mining childhood memory and revisiting freedom songs ("Guide Me," "I Want to Be Ready," "I'm on My Way to Canaan Land") that remained relevant forty years after the March on Washington. Influenced by the art of rapping, Ella offered two spoken-word pieces: "A Taxi Ride," about a conversation with a Nigerian taxi driver, and "Walking Around in Bronzeville" a memoir of the 1940s Black city-within-a-city, with shoutouts to the Regal Theater, the South Side Community Center, and "thousands of the sisters and the brothers working and playing and loving one another." She dedicated the album to Fred Rogers and her musical idol Celia Cruz, both of whom had died earlier in the year.

Sharing Cultures with Ella Jenkins had only been out for a few weeks when Ella learned that she was to receive a 2004 Grammy Lifetime Achievement Award, given to "individuals who during their lifetimes have made creative contributions of outstanding artistic significance to the field of recording." She, Bernadelle, and her promoter Lynn Orman traveled to Los Angeles for the ceremony on February 7, joining fellow honorees Van Cliburn, the Funk Brothers, Sonny Rollins, Artie Shaw, and Doc Watson. Jazz musician Kurt Elling presented Ella's award, recognizing her for "a lifetime of service to children's music and the high quality of her work throughout all of these years." "She's been a huge influence on musicians of many different genres, since she's reached so many young people when they were young," he said.[7]

Ella came up to the stage, where Grammy honorees Marian McPartland and Carole King stood, to receive the award. She was asked whether she wanted a chair. "No," she said, "because I stand for children." And then, instead of a conventional acceptance speech, she invited the audience, which included Lyle Lovett and Tony Bennett, to join her in singing "Did You Feed My Cow," complete with hand gestures. "She had all the industry heavies (including, so help me, Van Cliburn) milking the cow. Nobody but Ella," recalled her friend, folk musician Tom Paxton, who would go on to receive the award five years later.[8]

The end of the year brought more celebrations of Ella's career—but with a more familiar cast of characters. A raft of Ella's longtime friends, including Odetta, Frank Hamilton, and Betty Nudelman, showed up for an eightieth-birthday tribute that October at the Old Town School of Folk Music. The evening included performances of "Who Fed the Chickens?" and "Wake Up Little Sparrow." Juan Díes, who had recently contributed to Ella's *Sharing Cultures* album, serenaded her with "Bésame Mucho," honoring her love of Latin music; and old friends Cathy Fink and Marcy Marxer contributed "Red River Valley," which

Ella learned from her Uncle Flood. Hamilton and Odetta closed out the evening, with Hamilton contributing songs including "A Neighborhood Is a Friendly Place" (from her 1976 album *Growing Up with Ella Jenkins*), and Odetta performing soulful versions of "This Little Light of Mine," "Ain't Gonna Let Nobody Turn Me Around," and the anti-apartheid anthem "Something Inside So Strong." In between songs Odetta addressed Ella from the stage. "Getting up there, honey!," she joked at one point, before redeeming herself with a compliment: "And then she looking *good*, oh!" Later, the folk icon offered her own tribute. "I'm grateful for the fact that Ella has been working for these years with many children. Through her working with them, her effort, her dream, she has helped," she said. "Opening up children with music is one of the best callings upon the face of this Earth, and I celebrate Ella for doing that."[9]

Before the end of the year Smithsonian Folkways released its own birthday tribute to Ella, an album aptly titled *cELLAbration!* Produced by Fink and Marxer, it gathered acclaimed children's artists to cover her original compositions in styles ranging from Western swing to ragtime to mariachi. The tracks included Pete Seeger presenting "The World Is Big, The World Is Small," and Sweet Honey in the Rock performing Ella classics including "Did You Feed My Cow?" and a "Miss Mary Mack" medley. Reaching back to *Call-and-Response Rhythmic Group Singing*, Fink did "Toom-Bah-El-Lero" to the accompaniment of a conga drum.

At the 2005 Grammy Awards, *cELLAbration!* took home the award for Best Musical Album for Children, beating out Ella's own *Sharing Cultures with Ella Jenkins*. To some observers, it was unfair that Ella, who had altered the course of twentieth-century children's music, had never won a Grammy award for one of her albums. But Ella was indifferent to most formal accolades. "I don't think awards ever hit her the way they would with some other people. Even the Grammys," Bernadelle said. "She was more moved by the children." A telling bit of evidence came at the finale of the Old Town School birthday tribute. As she approached the stage to accept a bouquet of flowers, Ella called out, "Three cheers for children!" But everyone was too busy clapping for her to take her up on it.

Ella took the opportunity to reflect on her life in *Ella Jenkins: A Life of Song* (2011), an album that grew out of a commission from the National Museum of African American History and Culture, spearheaded by Lonnie Bunch.[10] A memoir in song and story enlivened by the earnest voices of children from Chicago elementary schools, *A Life of Song* collects material that represents aspects of Ella's life, from her memories of Southern kin ("Pick a Bale of Cotton") to the sounds of the Black Metropolis (the play song "Little Sally Walker"), to her civil rights activism (" I'm on My Way to Canaan Land"). And it pays tribute to significant figures in Ella's life, including Odetta, Tom, Uncle Flood, and, through a version of George Gershwin's "Summertime," Billie Holiday.

Specific but universal, focusing on African American music but drawing from diverse sonic traditions, *Ella Jenkins: A Life of Song* was a fitting offering for children growing up during the historic first term of the nation's first Black president, who frequently talked on the campaign trail of his formative years as a Chicago community organizer. Once, when he was still a US senator, Ella ran into Barack Obama as he walked through Chicago's McCormick Place convention center with future White House Chief of Staff Rahm Emanuel. She asked for his autograph and the future president obliged, but not before correcting her, saying, "I should be asking for *your* autograph."

Chicago Public Schools graduate Michelle Obama was also a fan. In 2015, when Ella was honored with a Fifth Star Award from the Chicago Department of Cultural Affairs, the First Lady paid her tribute via video. "For decades, you've been enriching our young people with music from around the world, inspiring them to lift their voices in song and teaching them not just to appreciate music, but to appreciate each other," Obama said. "So today I'm proud to honor a fellow First Lady, someone who is such a wonderful ambassador for my hometown and for our entire country."[11]

FIGURE E.1. Ella on stage with Pete Seeger, 1996. Tony Seeger of Smithsonian Folkways is seated on the left. Photo by Jeff Tinsley.

In her ninth decade, Ella continued to make music, overseeing three new Smithsonian Folkways compilations, including *Get Moving with Ella Jenkins*, a 2013 collection that tapped into the momentum generated by Michelle Obama's "Let's Move" campaign, and *More Multicultural Children's Songs* (2014), a follow-up to her 1995 bestseller. A 2013 appearance at the Lollapalooza music festival (on a children's stage) confirmed her relevance for a new generation of children, a grandmotherly figure who could nevertheless command the attention of digital natives. With her snow-white hair and colorful ensembles, she had the aura of a revered elder.

Yet there were signs that Ella was slowing down. In the terms offered by Christian Science, although her "immortal spirit" remained young, her "material body" manifested its years. Her knees troubled her, requiring her increasingly to perform from a chair. She also had begun to experience signs of cognitive decline—memory lapses and moments of confusion—that occasionally surfaced in front of audiences.

One story from April 2013 vividly illustrates the duet of age and vitality in Ella's performances from this period. Ella was giving the keynote at the family-entertainment industry event known as Kindie-Fest, held at the Brooklyn Academy of Music. Wearing a canary yellow jacket and black pants, she sat on a chair at the front of the stage, next to a small table holding water and a harmonica, telling stories. The room was filled with reverent musicians—artists who, following her pioneering example, hoped to create their own careers as children's artists and educators. When Ella began repeating herself, they silently willed her on, in an inverse of the manner of loving adults who do not want to see a child fail at a music recital. Things got better when Ella reached for her harmonica and spoke in the language of her simple songs. The audience listened with awe. As professionals in the family-music industry, they understood that they were privy to something both precious and sacred.

When she finished, Ella called out a request: "For the next song, I'm going to need some help. Are there any kids out there?" She tried to see through the glare of the spotlights. But the room contained no kids, only adults who made music for them. As the seconds ticked by, audience members began to fidget nervously. A child was not going to magically materialize and walk to the stage. Ella, unaware of their dilemma, sat quietly waiting.

That's when Sarah McCarthy, an arts administrator who was looking to form a family-music booking agency, realized that her infant daughter Calla was the only "child" in the room. But the baby was fussing—so much so that McCarthy had been considering whether to take her outside. With Ella waiting and the room growing increasingly awkward, however, McCarthy felt that she had no choice.

As she stepped onto the stage with Calla, McCarthy told Ella, "This is my daughter but I don't think she's going to help you very much! She's just six weeks old." People in the crowd chuckled nervously. But Ella, unfazed, reached out for Calla. Then, as McCarthy remembered,

Ella led the room through "London Bridge" with variations, singing, humming, then la-la-ing. In the room of musicians, everyone was breaking out into soft harmonies. My fussy baby got very quiet. Calla went into this moment of bliss, baby bliss . . . and everyone was kind of connecting with each other through this communal singing. Especially because there was this focus now who was Calla.[12]

The KindieFest organizers had been very clear: No photography during Ella's performance. But a friend handed McCarthy a cell phone and, with the moderator's permission, she was able to snap one photo, as Ella held Calla and she and the audience serenaded her. The baby, sitting comfortably and clear-eyed, would never remember the moment. But McCarthy and the other adults, many of them now openly weeping, would carry the image with them as a source of future inspiration.

In retrospect, McCarthy was delighted to help create a moment for Ella to demonstrate her remarkable powers of forming community through music. Yet she and the other attendees could not forget Ella's vulnerability in asking for a child-volunteer from an audience of adults.

FIGURE E.2. Ella and Bernadelle at the Admiral at the Lake, Chicago, 2014.
Photo by Tim Ferrin.

Such vulnerable moments became more and more common
as Ella approached ninety and began using a wheelchair, making
it impossible for Bernadelle to care for her without help. In 2014
Bernadelle found a spot for her at the Admiral at the Lake, a Chicago retirement and assisted-living facility a few miles from their
home on North Mohawk Street. Bernadelle imagined that Ella's
stay there would be temporary, until she regained her strength.

But the arrangement took on an air of permanence, with Bernadelle settling into a routine of regular visits.

Ella was living at the Admiral when Tom died on April 11, 2016. A few years earlier, after surviving an accident that totaled his car, he had moved into Glenmont Christian Science Home in Hilliard, Ohio. In their subsequent phone calls, following Christian Science theology, Ella and Tom never brought up the question of Tom's health. Neither did Bernadelle, even though by early spring 2016 she took his weakening voice to be a sign that the end was near. Tom was ninety-three when he passed away. Per its practice, Glenmont offered no medical cause of death.

Ella was no longer able to travel, so Bernadelle and her cousin Jane made the trip to Cincinnati for a small service at Tom's Christian Science church; after that they gathered at the home of one of Tom's church friends. Until the accident slowed him down, Tom had been as vibrant and busy as his sister. In addition to being a pioneering Black urban planner with master's degrees from both the University of Chicago and Harvard, he was a world traveler, a prolific writer of poetry (most of it unpublished, and more formal and conventional than Ella's), and, with his sister, a tennis fanatic, who attended Grand Slam tournaments at every venue except the Australian Open. Like Ella, he closely followed the rise of the talented Williams sisters, Venus and Serena, the most famous Black women in the game since the 1950s star Althea Gibson.

Tom was also proud of Ella—so much so that in a Harvard alumnus profile from 2005 he wrote of his "famous sister, Ella Jenkins, who has taught and performed in children's music worldwide—every continent!"[13] Another time, after seeing a 1997 Smithsonian Folkways catalog that contained the formal photograph of Ella and Tom from the 1930s, he wrote excitedly to her:

> What a *great* treat! The cup of goodness runneth over! I dropped everything, sat down on the stairs and went through that Smithsonian Folkways catalogue of recordings and videotapes—especially the many

pages with all those "Ella Jenkinses" on them. I AM SO VERY PROUD OF YOU!

The true measure is that you are in the same measure and frame of Lead Belly, Langston Hughes, Mary Lou Williams, Woodie Guthrie, Mayalou herself and Pete Seeger, *et al*!! Egads![14]

Following the practice of their childhood, he almost always addressed his letters to "Sis" or "Sister" and signed them "Bro" or "Brother." This one he had signed "Peace, Brother."

After his death Ella sometimes spoke of Tom as though he were still alive. In these moments Bernadelle would sometimes leave her mistake uncorrected, unsure whether Ella was having difficulty coming to terms with the loss or whether, within the Christian Science framework, she still experienced his immortal presence. As her time at the Admiral stretched to years, Ella invested more and more in the faith of her childhood. In addition to personal mementos, her room came to include tokens of her career—an etching of children playing by Margaret Burroughs; a picture of Chicago mayor Rahm Emanuel giving her an award—as well as an audio version of *Science and Health with a Key to the Scriptures.*

Just as she never retired from children, so Ella never stopped making music. In the 2010s she powered through several more performances, awards, and celebrations. In October 2016 the Chicago Lawyers' Committee for Civil Rights honored her with its Edwin A. Rothschild Award for Lifetime Achievement in Civil Rights. "In her trailblazing role in children's music, Ella broke gender and color barriers, and she fought in the Civil Rights Movement and Women's Movement," read the citation.[15] In 2017 Smithsonian Folkways released *Camp Songs with Ella Jenkins and Friends,* Ella's fortieth album of original material. That same year, she watched the livestream of the ceremony in which she was named a National Heritage Fellow by the National Endowment for the Arts (NEA), with Claudia Eliaza and Dan Zanes performing in her honor. Later, NEA chair Jane Chu, a former elementary school music teacher, gave Ella the award in person. "Sometimes as adults, we forget to honor these natural abilities that bring out our purest and most authentic selves," Chu said. "But Ella's songs remind children that their ability to express themselves through singing and rhythms comes naturally. . . . She has always known that music is an equalizer which belongs to everyone."[16]

On August 4, 2024, Ella celebrated her one hundredth birthday at a party hosted by community members at Ella Jenkins Park, an attractive brick and concrete plaza adjacent to the Church of the Three Crosses at the corner of Wisconsin and Sedgwick Streets in Old Town. There were tributes from local dignitaries and musicians to lead the group in Ella's songs. But of course Ella was the main attraction. As she sat in a wheelchair, a Kente cloth-inspired blanket draped over her legs for warmth, people lined up to greet her. Bernadelle tried to keep the line moving, but the well-wishers took their time. Some were adults who wanted their children or grandchildren to meet a Chicago icon; others wanted a chance to tell Ella their memories of having seen her perform. Almost everyone snapped pictures. Friends from the Old Town School of Folk Music stopped by. Aquanetta White-Olive came to greet Ella fifty-four years after she agreed to include "Go, Aquanetta, Go" on the *Seasons for Singing* album. Middle-aged people reminisced about learning Ella's songs in elementary school. Church members like Frank Alan Schneider, who had grown up with Ella's music, recalled what it meant to have sung with her, both at services and in the studio when she was recording *A Union of Friends Pulling Together*. The line was long, but Ella visited patiently with each person.[17]

Before Ella departed the Admiral for the party, her health aides made sure she traveled with an extra tank of oxygen, in case her supply ran low. But the singing and celebrating and socializing had the effect of oxygen, buoying and inspiring Ella. It had long been her practice to approach living as call and response. As she wrote in an unpublished memoir, "I always feel that each day I can learn more and what I try to benefit from experiences good as well as bad from people that I meet. When I am out sharing ideas, I feel I gain a great deal. Whatever it is, a workshop or a concert, sharing with children or adults, I always feel that the sharing always brings something back to me."[18]

Although Bronzeville and family nurtured her, in other ways the world Ella grew up in had threatened to choke her. But then through the music she discovered she could breathe and created a means of sharing her discovery with others. Her simple call-and-response songs and chants could not change the world, but they could and did model rhythm as an antidote to its cacophony. "It's not always the people that make the biggest contribution that get the most notoriety," educator Barbara Bowman once observed of Ella. Likewise, it's often the simple songs that leave the deepest imprint.

FIGURE E.3. Ella photographed by Bernadelle for the cover of *Come Dance by the Ocean*, 1991. Ella said this photo, taken in front of Lake Michigan, was one of her favorites.

ACKNOWLEDGMENTS

Meeting Ella Jenkins and Bernadelle Richter in 2017 was a gift that changed my life. I cannot thank them enough for their friendship and generosity and beautiful example.

Ella died while this book was in production, and I am sorry she did not get to hold it in her hands. Ella: I am immensely grateful that you entrusted me with the precious task of writing your biography. I wish I could know how you would have felt about it. I'm almost sure you would have cracked a joke about cramming one hundred years of living into a slender book. We would have cracked up at that one.

To Bernadelle: When we first met, you said this story was not about you, but of course it is, and it could never have been told without you. I am so grateful for your good will and patience through a long process, even while you bore the burden of being a caretaker. You answered every question I ever asked and more. This book is a testimony to your commitment to Ella's story and her legacy.

After Ella and Bernadelle, my thanks go to filmmaker Tim Ferrin. When we met, you were already working on *You'll Sing a Song*, your documentary about Ella, and you could have been territorial and mistrusting. Instead, you were welcoming and collaborative. I know this reflects your love for Ella, but mostly it reflects your generosity of spirit and your own commitments as a storyteller. It has been an honor and a pleasure to learn from and work alongside you. Thank you, too, to your beautiful family: Emily, Nora, and AJ.

Ella and Bernadelle's dear ones—Yoshi Atee, Leslie Fisher, and Lynn Orman—have become my friends as well. Thank you all for taking care of Ella and Bernadelle in your different ways.

I deeply appreciate everyone who took time to talk to me about Ella Jenkins. (The names of all of the people I interviewed are in an appendix.) Many of you responded to a cold call and miraculously stayed on the phone to talk. Even if I was not able to include quotations from all of you in this book, every memory, story, observation, and analysis that you shared is part of it. I especially want to thank Tony Seeger, Daniel Sheehy, and Michael Asch for supporting this project with your deep knowledge of Ella's recording career.

My friend, writer David Sax, was the first person to tell me to check out Ella Jenkins, knowing my interest in trailblazing Black women in American music. That tip was providential. When I first showed up to poke around the Ralph Rinzler Archives of the Center for Folklife and Cultural Heritage (CFCH) the curator, Jeff Place, suggested that "someone" should write a biography of Ella, planting another seed.

I have relied on the wisdom of many scholars, archivists, and librarians in writing this book. For their expert guidance, I wish to thank Robert Stepto, Raul Fernandez, Kyra Gaunt, Ron Radano, Jessica Phillips Silver, and Thomas DeFrantz. At the CFCH Greg Adams was unfailingly helpful. Maureen Loughran, director and curator of Smithsonian Folkways, immediately understood the importance of documenting Ella's life and—along with Logan Clark, Cecilia Peterson, and Will Griffin—was an eleventh-hour hero. Judith Gray helped me navigate the collections at the Library of Congress's American Folklife Center. Colby Maddox at the Old Town School of Folk Music let me have at the school's rich archive and shared occasional finds with me. Thank you to Allison Shein Homes and Michael McKee at WTTW/WFMT for their help locating Studs Terkel's interviews. Meredith Eliassen in Special Collections at San Francisco State University and Laura Mills, librarian at Roosevelt University in Chicago, helped me research Ella's time at both institutions. I benefited greatly from the advice and leads offered by Aaron Cohen, Stephen Wade, and Ian Zack.

Particularly during the period when COVID restrictions made it impossible to travel or to visit archives, I relied on the skills of various people who conducted research remotely for me. I thank Herbert Dittersdorf, W. Danielle Jones, Marla McMackin, and Esperanza Ortega-Tapia. There were areas of Ella's life that lie well beyond my expertise. Larry Hodges and Tim Boggan helped me with the history of table tennis, particularly its Black players. Educators Katie Palmer, Marie Ringenberg, Roberta Lamb, Lisa DeLorenzo, Melonee Burnham, Patricia Shehan Campbell, and Evelyn K. Moore helped me navigate the histories of US music education and early childhood education. Louise Dimiceli-Mitran and Deforia Lane helped me understand the field of music therapy. Kathryn Lofton directed me to scholarship to help me grasp aspects of Ella's experience as a Christian Scientist.

Lea Bradley and Oliver Bradley generously facilitated a lengthy interview with their remarkable father Harold Bradley Jr., who attended Christian Science church with Ella. Cece Fadope was a kind interlocutor at the Christian Science Reading Room on Sixteenth Street in Washington, DC.

Among the children's/family musicians I reached out to, Claudia Eliaza, Pierce Freelon, Divinity Roxx, Ashli St. Armant, and Dan Zanes deserve special mention as artists who are keeping Ella's flame burning through their own music. Sarah McCarthy gave me the gift of the amazing story of Ella and Calla. Making the "Ella connection" with Bonnie Thornton Dill was a special delight. And Bill Isler, Susan Linn, Hedda Sharapan, and Margy Whitmer, all of whom worked with the late Fred Rogers, were gracious in sharing their insights.

To my own dear ones: To my Black feminist music scholar posse of Daphne Brooks, Farah Griffin, Michelle Habell-Pallán, Maureen Mahon, Sonnet Retman, Sherrie Tucker, and Alexandra Vazquez. You are all role models and inspirations who keep me going. To Ann Powers, Gus Stadler, and David Suisman—close friends who all lent an ear to this project at various times. To the wonderful digital community that is PMBIP, Popular Music Books-in-Progress, an outgrowth of both the US branch of the International Association for the Study of Popular Music and the legendary PopCon (formerly "EMP conference"), for giving me a supportive audience for this project; thanks especially to Kim Mack, Francesca Royster, Eric Weisbard, and Carl Wilson for kicking it off and keeping it going. To Harry Weinger at Universal Music, who always comes through in a last-minute music "emergency." To Melani McAlister and Andrea Levine, longtime besties and most trusted interlocutors. To Loren Kajikawa and Lauren Onkey, my dream team of pop music collaborators at George Washington University. To Mora McLean, for a helpful last-minute tip, and to Samantha Silver and Ariel Pennington-Reyes for reading. To Justin Mann, Robb Yancey, (Uncle) Tony Barash, Terri Hanson, Jennifer Steinhauer, Jonathan Weisman, Tamar Newberger, and Andy Schapiro, who graciously hosted and/or fed me on my many trips to Chicago.

After Ella, Bernadelle, and Tim, this book would not have been written (or not been written in a timely manner) without the generous support of the National Endowment for the Humanities, in the form of a 2022–2023 Public Scholars grant. Thank you as well to The George Washington University, especially the Columbian College of Arts and Sciences, for financial support in the form of a University Facilitating Fellowship and Humanities Facilitating Fellowships. I am privileged to have received such funding at a time when resources for the humanities are scarce and the need great. I hope this will not always be the case.

The wonderful editor Nate Jung helped me get my thoughts in order and see through the fog of details to the hub of the story I wanted to tell. Marie Hellinger listened with unfailing empathy and insight.

Mika Tanner and Soyica Colbert graciously read late drafts of the book—Soyica as a fellow biographer, and Mika with her acute novelist's eye. Tim Ferrin did a painstaking edit of the submitted draft, mercifully catching mistakes before they made it to the printed page. I also thank Tim Mennel at the University of Chicago Press for taking this project on and working with me on it at such a granular level. He is responsible for recruiting the two extraordinary anonymous readers, who offered copious and incisive feedback.

I send love to my parents, Max and Marlene Wald, who moved to the DC suburbs as this book was being written, and to my remarkable sister Heidi Wald, brother-in-law Phil Weiser, niece Aviva Weiser, and nephew Samuel Weiser. It almost goes without saying that none of this would have been possible without the infallible support of my husband Scott Barash and our wonderful son Zachary Barash. They embody the loving dynamic of call and response in my life. I am so happy that they both got to spend precious time with Ella, and thus to understand my own drive to write this book.

A NOTE ABOUT INTERVIEWS AND PAPERS

This Is Rhythm relies on dozens of interviews and scores of casual conversations over the course of seven years with Ella Jenkins and her partner and manager Bernadelle Richter. My practice here is to reference with an endnote any quotations I use from interviews they gave to others (whether published or unpublished). The reader can assume that citations without an endnote are from my own interviews.

In writing this book, I liberally quote from and otherwise reference materials from Ella Jenkins's personal papers, courtesy of Bernadelle Richter. I thank Bernadelle for her permission to use and cite these materials while they were stored in Chicago. Many of these materials will be part of an Ella Jenkins collection at the Library of Congress.

APPENDIX A
INTERVIEWS

The following people (in addition to Ella Jenkins and Bernadelle Richter) kindly offered their time, guidance, and precious knowledge:

Kathie Anderson (with Rosalind Henderson Mustafa), phone, January 17, 2021
Ashli St. Armant, video call, March 15, 2022
Michael Asch, phone, October 10, 2023
Baba Atu (a.k.a. Harold Hampton Murray), phone, July 22, 2021
Nandini Bhattacharjya, phone, April 18, 2023
Amy Billingsley (with Eileen Cline), phone, January 10, 2021
Elvin Bishop, phone, March 25, 2021
Zoe Borkowski, phone, April 19, 2023
Barbara Bowman, in person, August 7, 2019
Harold Bradley, in person, October 11, 2019
Linda Bubon, phone, March 14, 2022
Lonnie G. Bunch III, phone, September 13, 2021
Patricia Shehan Campbell, phone, December 8, 2021

Richard Carlin, video call, October 17, 2023

Terri Lyne Carrington, video call, November 17, 2022

Raffi Cavoukian, video call, March 14, 2022

Mimi Brodsky Chenfield, phone, January 7, 2021

Jane Chu, email, December 9, 2022

Eileen Cline (with Amy Billingsley), phone, January 10, 2021

Diane Cohen, phone, January 4, 2021

Ronald Cohen, phone, June 4, 2021

Suzanne Courier, phone, December 9, 2022

Barbara Dane, phone, March 11, 2021

Lisa DeLorenzo, video call, January 13, 2023

Bonnie Thornton Dill, video call, February 16, 2023

Louise Dimiceli-Mitran, phone, May 27, 2021

Claudia Eliaza (with Dan Zanes), phone, March 13, 2020

Cathy Fink (with Marcy Marxer), in person, March 2, 2020

Pierce Freelon, video call, January 26, 2021

Annette Friedman, in person, August 7, 2019

Kyra Gaunt, video call, September 19, 2023

Guy Guilbert, phone, November 2, 2020

Frank Hamilton, phone, July 29, 2020

Allan Hirsch, phone, June 29, 2020

John Hobbs, phone, June 9, 2021

Richard Hunt, in person, January 9, 2020

William Isler, phone, September 2, 2023

Roberta Lamb, video call, January 9, 2023

Deforia Lane, phone, June 8, 2021

Susan Linn, phone, August 24, 2023

Peggy Lipshutz, in person, August 5, 2019

Beverly Lucas, phone, March 24, 2021

Steven Malk, phone, January 18, 2022

Marcy Marxer (with Cathy Fink), in person, March 2, 2020

Sarah McCarthy, video calls, February 25, 2022, and November 15, 2023

Moira McCormick, phone, September 5, 2023

Maria McCullough, phone, July 3, 2020

Linda Mensch, phone, June 7, 2021

Rosa Millang (with Steve Millang, Laurie Sale, and Greg Scelsa), video call, May 17, 2021

Steve Millang (with Rosa Millang, Laurie Sale, and Greg Scelsa), video call, May 17, 2021

Evelyn K. Moore, phone, February 2, 2023

Thomas Moore, video calls, August 17, 2021, and November 12, 2023

Rosalind Henderson Mustafa (with Kathie Anderson), phone, January 17, 2021

Shanta Nurullah, phone, November 14, 2023

Lynn Orman, in person, March 17, 2022

Katie Palmer, video call, February 28, 2023

Jimmy Payne Jr., phone, March 30, 2021

Jeffrey Place, video call, October 11, 2023

Eliza Powell, in person, October 12, 2019

Richard Powell, phone, September 17, 2019

Rosita Ragin-Saladeen, phone, April 19, 2021

Julieanne Richardson, video call, August 2, 2023

Shawnelle Richie, phone, March 29, 2023

Marie Ringenberg, video call, October 20, 2021

Renee Robbins, phone, August 2, 2022

Divinity Roxx, video call, May 2, 2021

Philip Royster, video call, December 1, 2022

Laurie Sale (with Rosa Millang, Steve Millang, and Greg Scelsa), video call, May 17, 2021

Greg Scelsa (with Rosa Millang, Steve Millang, and Laurie Sale), video call, May 17, 2021

Anthony Seeger, phone, February 19, 2018; video call, October 12, 2023

Daniel Sheehy, in person, April 3, 2023

Hedda Sharapan, phone, September 6, 2023

Jessica Phillips Silver, phone, January 12, 2021

Ronald Soffer, phone, January 29, 2023

Shelley Sutherland, phone, April 11, 2021

Devin Walker, phone, November 18, 2020

Aquanetta White-Olive, phone, July 21, 2023

Margy Whitmer, phone, September 13, 2023

Martin Yarbrough, phone, April 5 and 24, 2021

Dan Zanes (with Claudia Eliaza), phone, March 13, 2020

I also relied on the following archival interviews:

Louise Dimiceli, unpublished interview with Ella Jenkins, 1978. Come for to Sing archives, Chicago Public Library, Harold Washington Library Center, Music Information Center.

Tim Ferrin, unpublished interviews with Lillian Horowitz Osran, Ella Jenkins, Thomas Jenkins, Ella and Thomas Jenkins (joint interview), and Betty Nudelman.

National Visionary Leadership Project, interviews with Ella Jenkins and Odetta Holmes. National Visionary Leadership Project Oral History Collection (AFC 2004/007), Archive of Folk Culture, American Folklife Center, Library of Congress. Tapes are also available at https://www.youtube.com/user/visionaryproject.

The History Makers interviews with Barbara Bowman and Ella Jenkins. https://www.thehistorymakers.org/about-the-historymakers.

"Sound Sessions" with Sam Litzinger and Jeff Place, interview with Ella Jenkins. https://folkways.si.edu/sounds-sessions-radio -ella-jenkins-first-lady-of-childrens-music/music/podcast /smithsonian.

Studs Terkel interviews 1963, 1993. The Studs Terkel Radio Archives. https://studsterkel.wfmt.com/.

APPENDIX B
BIBLIOGRAPHIC ESSAY

In writing this book, I drew from and was influenced by the works of a great many others. Specific sources are mentioned in the notes. Below I provide a more general list of works I consulted and had in mind as I wrote, grouped according to topics of major concern to *This Is Rhythm*.

BRONZEVILLE AND THE BLACK METROPOLIS

There is an abundance of excellent scholarship on Black Chicago, particularly the Bronzeville neighborhood where Ella grew up. No scholar can talk about twentieth-century Chicago without referencing St. Clair Drake and Horace Cayton's *Black Metropolis: A Study of Negro Life in a Northern City* (1945; rpt., Chicago: University of Chicago Press, 2015). Davarian Baldwin's *Chicago's New Negroes: Modernity, The Great Migration, and Black Urban Life* (Chapel Hill: University of North Carolina Press, 2007) and Marcia Chatelain's *South Side Girls: Growing Up in the Great Migration* (Durham, NC: Duke University Press, 2015) approach Bronzeville as a destination for migrants.

For studies of Black women's community activism and cultural leadership, see Mary Ann Cain, *South Side Venus: The Legacy of Margaret Burroughs* (Evanston, IL: Northwestern University Press, 2018), and Anne Meis Knupfer, *The Chicago Black Renaissance and Women's Activism* (Urbana: University of Illinois Press, 2006). Although not centered on Chicago, Judith Weisenfeld's *African American Women and Christian Activism: New York's Black YWCA, 1905-1945* (Cambridge, MA: Harvard University Press, 1998) and Nancy Marie Robertson's *Christian Sisterhood, Race Relations, and the YWCA, 1906-46* (Urbana: University of Illinois Press, 2007) shed light on the role of the YWCA in the lives of post–World War II Black Chicago women.

Adam Green's *Selling the Race: Culture, Community, and Black Chicago, 1940-1955* (Chicago: University of Chicago Press, 2009) offers valuable insights into cultural entrepreneurship. In tracking the musical career of one musician, William Sites's *Sun Ra's Chicago: Afrofuturism and the City* (Chicago: University of Chicago Press, 2020) offers a granular history of Chicago's music scene at mid-century. Timuel D. Black Jr., *Bridges of Memory: Chicago's First Wave of Black Migration* (Evanston, IL: Northwestern University Press, 2003), is an invaluable collection of interviews. On the Black Left in Chicago, I recommend Bill V. Mullen, *Popular Fronts: Chicago and African-American Cultural Politics, 1935-46* (rpt., Urbana: University of Illinois Press, 2015). Kevin D. Greene's "'Just a Dream': Big Bill Broonzy, the Blues, and Chicago's Black Metropolis," *Journal of Urban History* 40, no. 1 (2014): 116-36, explores Chicago from the eyes of Ella's friend and mentor.

CHILDREN'S MUSIC AND CHILDHOOD

David Bonner's *Revolutionizing Children's Records: The Young People's Records and Children's Record Guild Series, 1946-1977* (Lanham, MD: Scarecrow Press, 2008) is an indispensable study of early and mid-twentieth century independent children's music and its relationship to commercial children's fare. While not about music, Julia Mickenberg's *Learning from the Left: Children's Literature, the Cold War, and Radical*

Politics in the United States (New York: Oxford University Press, 2006) is a model for thinking about music and the political left.

In writing this book, I consulted many mid-century children's songbooks, including Ruth Crawford Seeger, *American Folk Songs for Children: In Home, School and Nursery School* (New York: Doubleday and Company, 1948). On Crawford Seeger as a key figure in the dissemination of a children's folk canon, see Judith Tick, *Ruth Crawford Seeger: A Composer's Search for American Music* (New York: Oxford University Press, 1997), and Ray Allen and Elie M. Hisama, eds., *Ruth Crawford Seeger's Worlds: Innovation and Tradition in Twentieth-Century American Music* (Rochester, NY: University of Rochester Press, 2007). On Charity Bailey, a pioneering music educator and Folkways artist, see Dan Axtell's lovingly maintained website https://www.charitybailey .org/. Beatrice Landeck, who advised Moe Asch, is an underrecognized proponent of Black folk tradition as American tradition. See her *Songs to Grow On: A Collection of American Folk Songs for Children* (New York: Edward B. Marks Music Corporation, 1950). Bessie Jones and Bess Lomax Hawes, *Step It Down: Games, Plays, Songs, and Stories from the Afro-American Heritage* (New York: Harper and Row, 1972), assembles the sonic archive of Bessie Jones, a key figure of the "children's" folk revival.

Although the field of music education is vast, I found particularly helpful Michael L. Mark and Charles L. Gary's authoritative survey, *A History of American Music Education*, 3rd ed. (New York: Rowman and Littlefield Education, 2007). R. I. Dunham's PhD dissertation, "Music Appreciation in the Public Schools of the United States, 1897–1930" (University of Michigan, 1961), shed light on the concept of "appreciation" in US classrooms. Judith Tick, "The Legacy of Ruth Crawford Seeger," *American Music Teacher* 50, no. 6 (June 2001): 30–34, provided insight into Crawford Seeger's impact on music pedagogy. And I turned to Patricia Shehan Campbell, *Music, Education, and Diversity: Building Cultures and Communities* (New York: Teachers College Press, 2018), for an overview of multiculturalism in contemporary children's music education.

MUSIC AND THE LONG CIVIL RIGHTS MOVEMENT

The last twenty-five years have seen an outpouring of new scholarship on music and the long civil rights movement. Although I mostly do not cite directly from this body of work, it shapes my thinking about the relation between culture and politics. Farah Griffin's *If You Can't Be Free, Be a Mystery: In Search of Billie Holiday* (New York: Free Press, 2001) is a touchstone for my work and informs my approach to Black feminist biography. Daphne A. Brooks, *Liner Notes for the Revolution: The Archive, the Critic, and Black Women's Sound Cultures* (Cambridge, MA: Harvard University Press, 2021), includes a powerful critique of folkloric collection in the context of Black female musicians. For important books that explore music as an expression of civil rights, see Ruth Feldstein, *How It Feels to Be Free: Black Women Entertainers and the Civil Rights Movement* (New York: Oxford University Press, 2017); Ingrid Monson, *Freedom Sounds: Civil Rights Call Out to Jazz and Africa* (New York: Oxford University Press, 2007); Scott Saul, *Freedom Is, Freedom Aint: Jazz and the Making of the Sixties* (Cambridge, MA: Harvard University Press, 2003); and Matthew Frye Jacobson, *Dancing Down the Barricades: Sammy Davis Jr. and the Long Civil Rights Era: A Cultural History* (Berkeley: University of California Press, 2023).

Although they primarily focus on the music of the early twentieth century, Daphne Duvall Harrison, *Black Pearls: Blues Queens of the 1920s* (New Brunswick, NJ: Rutgers University Press, 1988) and Angela Davis, *Blues Legacies and Black Feminism: Gertrude "Ma" Rainey, Bessie Smith, and Billie Holiday* (New York: Pantheon, 1998) inform my understanding of the relation between Black women's popular music and the politics of Black freedom.

The literature on freedom songs of the 1950s and 1960s is also copious, but the standard for me remains Bernice Johnson Reagon, *If You Don't Go, Don't Hinder Me: The African American Sacred Song Tradition* (Lincoln: University of Nebraska Press, 2001).

Another touchstone is TV Reid's "Singing Civil Rights" chapter in *The Art of Protest: Culture and Activism from the Civil Rights Movement to the Present*, 2nd ed. (Minneapolis: University of Minnesota Press, 2019).

Finally, although it is not solely "about" civil rights, Thomas Turino's *Music as Social Life: The Politics of Participation* (Chicago: University of Chicago Press, 2008) informs my sense of Ella Jenkins as a "social" musician. So, too, has Martha Gonzalez's *Chican@ Artivistas: Music, Community, and Transborder Tactics in Los Angeles* (Austin: University of Texas Press, 2020).

FOLKWAYS, SMITHSONIAN FOLKWAYS, AND MOSES ASCH

Several excellent works have been indispensable to this project. Peter Goldsmith, *Making People's Music: Moe Asch and Folkways Records* (Washington, DC: Smithsonian Books, 1998), is a meticulous study of the founder of Folkways, and Goldsmith's research notes are part of the Ralph Rinzler Archives at the Center for Folklore and Cultural History in Washington, DC. Richard Carlin, *Worlds of Sound: The Story of Smithsonian Folkways* (Washington, DC: Smithsonian Press, 2008), is also superb and includes an excellent chapter on children's music. Izzy Young's interview with Moe Asch, "Moses Asch: Twentieth Century Man," is in *Sing Out!* 26, no. 1 (1977).

Smithsonian Folkways makes all of the liner notes of its releases publicly available as PDFs at https://folkways.si.edu/. These notes are both an expression of Moe Asch's "encyclopedia of sound" and a uniquely rich site for researchers of all ages. I have particularly benefited from liner notes of Jeff Place on Lead Belly and Big Bill Broonzy. Record catalogs are notoriously tricky beasts, and I found Frank Daniels's "Asch Records Discography 1941-1947," which can be accessed at https://www.friktech.com/labels/AschRecordings.pdf, to be immeasurably useful.

THE FOLK REVIVAL AND AMERICAN CULTURE

The mid-century US folk revival has received enormous scholarly attention, although much of the scholarship shortchanges (or overlooks) children's music and Ella Jenkins. Robert Cantwell's *When We Were Good: The Folk Revival* (Cambridge, MA: Harvard University Press, 1996) and Ronald D. Cohen's *Rainbow Quest: The Folk Music Revival and American Society, 1940–1970* (Amherst: University of Massachusetts Press, 2002) set the standards for the field. I also relied on Norm Cohen, *Folk Song America: A 20th Century Revival* (Washington, DC: Smithsonian Institution Press, 1990), William G. Roy, *Reds, Whites, and Blues: Social Movements, Folk Music, and Race in the United States* (Princeton, NJ: Princeton University Press, 2010), and Dick Weissman, *Which Side Are You On? An Inside History of the Folk Music Revival in America* (New York: Continuum, 2005).

Although it does not discuss the Chicago folk scene, I have benefited enormously from Stephen Petrus and Ronald D. Cohen's *Folk City: New York and the American Folk Music Revival* (New York: Oxford University Press, 2015), a simultaneously panoramic and detailed study, and Rachel C. Donaldson's *"I Hear America Singing": Folk Music and National Identity* (Philadelphia: Temple University Press, 2014), which contains an important chapter on Folkways and Cold War education, which is also available as "Teaching Democracy: Folkways and Cold War Education," *History of Education Quarterly* 55, no. 1 (February 2015): 58–81.

Michael Denning's *The Cultural Front: The Laboring of American Culture in the Twentieth Century* (New York: Verso, 1996) is an important source for anyone wishing to understanding musical expressions of Popular Front politics. Matthew Frye Jacobson's *Odetta's One Grain of Sand* (New York: Bloomsbury, 2019) contains the best discussion I have encountered on folk "café culture" and its relationship to antiracist politics. Sonnet Retman's *Real Folks: Race and Genre in the Great Depression* (Durham, NC: Duke University Press, 2011) informs my approach to the "folk" as a construction of American society and culture.

I turned to Benjamin Filene, *Romancing the Folk: Public Memory and American Roots Music* (Chapel Hill: University of North Carolina Press, 2000), and Grace Elizabeth Hale, *A Nation of Outsiders: How the White Middle Class Fell in Love with Rebellion in Postwar America* (New York: Oxford University Press, 2014), for critical takes on the folk revival in American culture.

BLACK DIASPORIC MUSIC

I cannot possibly hope to cover the field of Black diasporic music, only cite key texts that were beside me on my bookshelf as I wrote. They include Samuel A. Floyd, *The Power of Black Music: Interpreting Its History from Africa to the United States* (New York: Oxford University Press, 1995); Portia Maultsby, "Africanisms in African American Music," in *Africanisms in American Culture*, 2nd ed., ed. Joseph Holloway (Bloomington: Indiana University Press, 2005), 326–55; Paul Gilroy, *The Black Atlantic: Modernity and Double-Consciousness* (Cambridge, MA: Harvard University Press, 1993); Ronald Michael Radano, *Lying Up a Nation: Race and Black Music* (Chicago: University of Chicago Press, 2003); and Kofi Agawu *The African Imagination in Music* (New York: Oxford University Press, 2016), which contains helpful discussions of the "imagination" of Africa in the Black diaspora. Raul A. Fernandez, *From Afro-Cuban Rhythms to Latin Jazz* (Berkeley: University of California Press, 2006), guided my thinking about Afro-Cuban music. In many ways, Ella's work anticipates the influential scholarship of Christopher Small, whose concept of "musicking" has done much to change the field of music studies. See *Music of the Common Tongue: Survival and Celebration in African American Music* (1987; rpt., Middletown, CT: Wesleyan University Press, 1998), especially the chapters "Africans, Europeans and the Making of Music" (17–48) and "On the Ritual Performance" (49–79). On the application of "musicking" to education, see "Afterword: On Music Education" in *The Christopher Small*

Reader, ed. Robert Walser (Middletown, CT: Wesleyan University Press, 2016), 217–26.

TWENTIETH-CENTURY BLACK POLITICS

Because it points to modes of education that lie outside the scope of authorized curricula, I found inspiration for this project in Jarvis R. Givens, *Fugitive Pedagogy: Carter G. Woodson and the Art of Black Teaching* (Cambridge, MA: Harvard University Press, 2021). The following titles guided my understanding of Black politics and diasporic consciousness at mid-century, the fertile period when Ella developed her own political consciousness: Tiffany Patterson and Robin D. G. Kelley, "Unfinished Migrations: Reflections on the African Diaspora and the Making of the Modern World," *African Studies Review* (2000): 11–45; Brent Edwards, *The Practice of Diaspora: Literature, Translation, and the Rise of Black Internationalism* (Cambridge, MA: Harvard University Press, 2003); Keisha N. Blain and Tiffany M. Gill, eds., *To Turn the Whole World Over: Black Women and Internationalism* (Urbana: University of Illinois Press, 2019); Mary L. Dudziak, *Cold War Civil Rights: Race and the Image of American Democracy* (Princeton, NJ: Princeton University Press, 2011); Cheryl Higashida, *Black Internationalist Feminism: Women Writers of the Black Left, 1945–1995* (Urbana: University of Illinois Press, 2012); Bill V. Mullen, *Popular Fronts: Chicago and African American Cultural Politics, 1935–46*, 2nd ed. (Urbana: University of Illinois Press, 1999); Brenda Gayle Plummer, *In Search of Power: African Americans in the Era of Decolonization, 1956–1974* (New York: Cambridge University Press, 2013); and Ian Rocksborough-Smith, *Black Public History in Chicago: Civil Rights Activism from World War II into the Cold War* (Urbana: University of Illinois Press, 2018).

MULTICULTURALISM

"Multiculturalism" has a long and complex legacy in the United States, taking root in postwar liberal and left politics and then gradually being reimagined as a sanctioned project of the neoliberal state in the post–civil rights, postindustrial era. I document the ways that Ella Jenkins's songs and chants were reclassified as "multicultural" music beginning in the 1970s and 1980s and culminating in the release of her Smithsonian Folkways compilations *Multicultural Children's Songs* (1995) and *More Multicultural Children's Songs* (2014). For readers in search of critical studies of neoliberal multiculturalism, I recommend Stuart Hall, "The Multicultural Question," in *Un/settled Multiculturalisms: Diasporas, Entanglements, Transruptions*, ed. Barnor Hesse (London: Zed Books, 2000), Chandra Talpade Mohanty, *Feminism without Borders: Decolonizing Theory, Practicing Solidarity* (Durham, NC: Duke University Press, 2003), and Jodi Melamed, "The Spirit of Neoliberalism: From Racial Liberalism to Neoliberal Multiculturalism," *Social Text* 24, no. 4 (Winter 2006): 1–24. In my first attempt to write about Ella Jenkins, I grappled with and against the concept of multiculturalism in her music. See Gayle Wald, "'It's Awfully Important to Listen': Ella Jenkins and Musical Multiculturalism," *Current Musicology* 104 (Spring 2019), https://doi.org/10.7916/cm.v0i104.5391.

APPENDIX C
DISCOGRAPHY

Consistent with Moe Asch's desire to maintain the Folkways sonic archive in perpetuity, all of Ella Jenkins's recordings for Folkways and Smithsonian Folkways have been digitized and are available for purchase and downloading from Smithsonian Folkways Recordings, https://folkways.si.edu.

In most cases, the Smithsonian Folkways Recordings website also has downloadable digitized versions of Jenkins's original liner notes. In a few cases, however, the digitized notes reflect updates to Jenkins's originals. For example, the liner notes to the fiftieth anniversary reissue of *Call-and-Response Rhythmic Group Singing* combine Jenkins's 1998 reflections on the album, as well as a Curator's Introduction by Anthony Seeger, with her original 1957 text. The album originally issued in 1960 as *Negro Folk Rhythms* by Ella Jenkins and the Goodwill Spiritual Choir of Monumental Baptist Church (FW 7654) has been retitled *African American Folk Rhythms* (SFW 45003), reflecting post–civil rights changes in language. *Counting Games and Rhythms for the Little Ones*, originally issued as FW 7679 in 1965, contained a song called "John Brown Had a Little Indian." The current Smithsonian Folkways version (SFW 45029) of the album omits this song, in recognition of its objectifying representation of Native Americans.

Some of Jenkins's albums from the 1980s were originally issued on the Activities Records imprint (AR), later Educational Activities (EA), and were subsequently acquired by Smithsonian Folkways (SFS). The original booklets accompanying these recordings are not available through the Smithsonian Folkways website, but may be found through secondhand vendors.

A discography (organized by decade) is available at https://ellajenkins.com/discography.html.

The Grammy-winning 2004 album *cELLAbration! A Tribute to Ella Jenkins*, produced by Cathy Fink and Marcy Marxer, is available through Smithsonian Folkways (SFS 45059). It includes Jenkins's music performed by other artists, including Sweet Honey in the Rock and Pete Seeger.

A newcomer to Ella Jenkins's music may find her enormous catalog intimidating. I recommend starting with *Ella Jenkins: A Life of Song* (SFW 45067), released in 2011 as part of the Smithsonian Folkways African American Legacy Series, co-presented with the Smithsonian National Museum of African American History and Culture. Jenkins recorded it when she was in her late eighties, and she prefaces songs with brief remembrances. The compilation *Multicultural Children's Songs* (SFW 45045) is also excellent for getting a sense of the long arc of Jenkins's use of song to promote democratic pluralism.

Call-and-Response Rhythmic Group Singing, Jenkins's 1957 debut, still merits attention, especially the tracks "Tah-Boo," "Moon Don't Go," and "An American Chain Gang Chant." So, too, does Jenkins's 1960 album *African American Folk Rhythms* (originally *Negro Folk Rhythms*), which contains her composition/arrangement "Wade in the Water" (used by the Alvin Ailey Dance Theater).

Many teachers and fans of Jenkins's work know *You'll Sing a Song and I'll Sing a Song*, her best-selling album originally issued in 1966. It contains the popular title track, as well as one of Jenkins's recorded versions of her trademark chant "Did You Feed My Cow?" Less well known but equally worthwhile are *Play Your Instruments and Make a Pretty Sound* (SFW 45018), a delightful introduction to New Orleans jazz, and *A Long Time to Freedom,* Jenkins's moving tribute (with Brother John Sellers and Joseph Brewer) to Martin Luther King and the Black freedom struggle. Among other songs, it contains Jenkins's favorite spiritual/freedom song, "The Wilderness," as well as her original compositions "A Friendly Loan" and "A Long Time." *Rhythms of Childhood* (SFW 45008) contains "Wake Up, Little Sparrow," a song that has been lovingly interpreted by contemporary musicians including Lizz Wright, Devendra Banhart, and Leyla McCalla.

NOTES

INTRODUCTION

1. Jeanne Marie Laskas, "Zen and the Art of Make Believe," *Pittsburgh*, October 1985, 45.
2. Kyra Gaunt, interview by author. See also Gaunt's *The Games Black Girls Play: Learning the Ropes from Double-Dutch to Hip-Hop* (New York: New York University Press, 2006).
3. My definition of civil rights activism and use of the term "long civil rights movement" is derived from Jacquelyn Dowd Hall, "The Long Civil Rights Movement and the Political Uses of the Past," *Journal of American History* 91, no. 4 (March 2005): 1234.
4. See Ty-Juana Taylor, "Ella Jenkins, a Hidden Figure in the Fight for Civil Rights," *Folklife*, February 26, 2021. My understanding of Ella's fugitive civil rights pedagogy draws on Jarvis R. Givens's *Fugitive Pedagogy: Carter G. Woodson and the Art of Black Teaching* (Cambridge, MA: Harvard University Press, 2021).
5. Helen Haggie, "Music Means for Others' Travel," *Lincoln Journal Star*, March 6, 1976.
6. See the bibliographic essay in appendix B for an overview of scholarship on children's music.
7. Ella's practices anticipate the social and musical values and ideals expressed in Christopher Small's term "musicking." See Small, *Music of the Common Tongue: Survival and Celebration in African American Music* (Hanover, NH: University Press of New England, 1998).

8. V. Y. Mudimbe, *The Idea of Africa* (Bloomington: Indiana University Press, 1994). See also Kofi Agawu, *The African Imagination in Music* (New York: Oxford University Press, 2016), 2.

9. See the bibliographic essay in appendix B for an overview of scholarship on music and civil rights.

10. "Before Barney," *The Torch: A Monthly Newsletter for the Smithsonian Institution* 95, no. 4 (April 1995): n.p., Ella Jenkins papers, Chicago, courtesy of Bernadelle Richter.

11. Dan Zanes, interview by author.

12. Cathy Fink and Marcy Marxer, interview by author.

13. Sam Litzinger and Jeff Place, "Ella Jenkins, First Lady of Children's Music," *Sound Sessions* podcast, episode 14, FPD10029, https://media .smithsonianfolkways.org/audio/podcasts/sound_sessions/sound_sessions _14_EllaJenkins.mp3; Betsy Morris, "Do Sing Back to Ella," *Knoxville News-Sentinel*, October 4, 1974.

14. Interviews by author: Rosalind Henderson Mustafa and Katie Anderson ("very free"); Louise Dimiceli-Mitran ("didn't seem to get").

15. "A Singer of Folk Songs," track 13 on *Ella Jenkins and a Union of Friends Pulling Together*, SWF 45046, 1999, compact disc.

16. Frannie Kelley, "The Rhythm That's a Way of Living," *All Things Considered*, NPR, June 20, 2014, https://www.npr.org/2014/06/20/324008351 /the-rhythm-thats-a-way-of-living.

CHAPTER ONE

1. "Marriage Licenses," *St. Louis Star and Times*, August 11, 1922.

2. "The Massacre in East St. Louis," *The Crisis* 14, no. 5 (September 1917): 219–38.

3. William Ferris, *Give My Poor Heart Ease: Voices of the Mississippi Blues* (Chapel Hill: University of North Carolina Press, 2009), 2.

4. St. Clair Drake and Horace R. Cayton, *Black Metropolis: A Study of Negro Life in a Northern City*, with an introduction by Richard Wright (New York: Harcourt Brace, 1945), xvii.

5. Tom Jenkins, interview by Tim Ferrin, December 4, 2015 (hereafter Tom Jenkins interview).

6. Ella Jenkins, oral history interview by Renee Poussaint, November 3, 2011, National Visionary Leadership Project Interviews and Conference Collection (AFC 2004/2007), Archive of Folk Culture, American Folklife Center, Library of Congress, Washington, DC.

7. Sam Litzinger and Jeff Place, "Ella Jenkins, First Lady of Children's Music," *Sound Sessions* podcast, episode 14, n.d., 52:00, FPD10029, https://media .smithsonianfolkways.org/audio/podcasts/sound_sessions/sound_sessions _14_EllaJenkins.mp3.

8. "Chicago and St. Louis," typescript dated December 1993, Ella Jenkins papers.

9. Tom Jenkins interview.

10. Judith Weisenfeld, *New World A-Coming: Black Religion and Racial Identity During the Great Migration* (New York: New York University Press, 2017), 1–8.

11. As Judith Weisenfeld notes, "Neither African American participation in the Christian Science movement nor its institutions have received much scholarly attention." See Weisenfeld, "'The Secret at the Root': Performing African American Religious Modernity in Hall Johnson's *Run, Little Chillun*," *Religion and American Culture: A Journal of Interpretation* 21, no. 1 (2011): 55. See also "Christian Science: Despite Lack of Emotionalism, Church Makes Long Strides in Enlisting Negroes," *Ebony* 6, no. 1 (November 1950): 58–63.

12. "H. S. Hering Lectures at 8th Church of Christ," *Chicago Examiner*, June 27, 1911.

13. Ella Jenkins, oral history interview by Poussaint.

14. Ella Jenkins, unpublished typescript memoir, ca. 1982 (hereafter Ella Jenkins, typescript memoir), Ella Jenkins papers. See also "Mary Baker Eddy," *Chicago Defender*, December 31, 1932.

15. *God's Law of Adjustment and Other Articles* (Boston: CS Publishing Society, 1940), 8–11.

16. See Marcia Chatelain, *South Side Girls: Growing Up in the Great Migration* (Durham, NC: Duke University Press, 2015).

17. Evelyn Brooks Higginbotham, *Righteous Discontent: The Women's Movement in the Black Baptist Church, 1880–1920* (Cambridge, MA: Harvard University Press, 1993), 186.

18. Ella Jenkins, typescript memoir.

19. Ella Jenkins undated notes, Ella Jenkins papers. See also the liner notes for Ella Jenkins, *A Long Time to Freedom*, FW 7754, 1969, LP.

20. Ella Jenkins, interview by Diane Dunne, KNCT Central Texas College, September 1983, 21:47, https://www.youtube.com/watch?v=dF_u23pzcVw.

21. Litzinger and Place, "Ella Jenkins, First Lady of Children's Music."

22. Ella Jenkins, typescript memoir.

23. Ella Jenkins, unpublished Q&A notes, Ella Jenkins papers.

24. Ella Jenkins, liner notes, *A Long Time to Freedom*, Smithsonian Folkways FC 7754, 1969, LP, 2.

CHAPTER TWO

1. DuSable High School, Preliminary Summary of Information, Submitted to the Commission on Chicago Landmarks, December 2011, p. 1; accessed online at https://www.chicago.gov/dam/city/depts/zlup/Historic_Preservation/Publications/DuSable_HS_Prelim_Summ_report.pdf.

2. The quote is attributed to Phillips in the *Christian Recorder*, January 31, 1884; accessed online at http://www.accessible.com.proxygw.wrlc.org/accessible/preLog?LinkType=SERIALSSOLUTIONS&ArticleID=THECHRISTIANRECORDER.FR1884013133.131725.

3. David Roediger, "The Making of a Historian: An Interview with Sterling Stuckey," *Journal of African American History* 99, nos. 1–2 (2014): 92.

4. On DuSable's "Hi-Jinks" shows, see Timuel D. Black Jr., *Bridges of Memory: Chicago's First Wave of Black Migration* (Evanston, IL: Northwestern University Press, 2003), 166–67, 181–82.

5. "Table Tennis Champ Tells of Exciting Tournaments," *Billings Gazette*, January 29, 1943; Marshall Dann, "Table Tennis Has Abbott to Thank for Popularity," *Detroit Free Press*, December 21, 1941; Paul J. Malone, "Table Tennis Again 'Major' Indoor Sport," *Billings Gazette*, February 11, 1942; Glen Perkins, "Table Tennis He-Man's Game," *Times Record News* (Texas), June 30, 1943; "Women's Table Tennis Champ Feminine but Plenty Fierce," *Great Falls Tribune* (Montana), February 2, 1940.

6. William Fay, "Blind Referee Scores with Fans at Table Tennis Meet," *Chicago Tribune*, March 30, 1947.

7. "Ella Jenkins Is Chicagoland's Table Net Champ," *Chicago Defender*, March 20, 1948.

8. Amy Billingsley and Eileen Tate Cline, interview by author.

9. Fay, "Blind Referee Scores."

10. See Laura Burt, "Vivian Harsh, Adult Education, and the Library's Role as Community Center," *Libraries and the Cultural Record* 44, no. 2 (2009): 234–55.

11. See the bibliographic essay in appendix B for an overview of scholarship on Bronzeville.

12. George F. McCray, "12,000 in Chicago Voice Demands for Democracy," *Chicago Defender*, July 4, 1942.

13. Lillian Horowitz Osran, interview by Tim Ferrin, January 28, 2015 (hereafter Osran interview).

14. Osran interview.

15. Osran interview. Ella Jenkins to Lillian Horowitz, 1944; courtesy Lillian Horowitz Osran.

16. Obadiah Jenkins will, Ella Jenkins 1940s–1950s scrapbook, p. 5, Ella Jenkins papers.

17. Ella Jenkins, "A Father Is Dying," unpublished manuscript, Ella Jenkins papers.

18. Ella Jenkins, oral history interview by Renee Poussaint, November 3, 2011, National Visionary Leadership Project Interviews and Conference Collection (AFC 2004/2007), Archive of Folk Culture, American Folklife Center, Library of Congress, Washington, DC.

19. Annette (Haase) Friedman, interview by author.

20. On Roosevelt College, see Florence Hamlish Levinsohn, *Harold Washington: A Political Biography* (Chicago: Chicago Review Press, 1983), 43.

21. Roosevelt College, *The Vanguard: The First Yearbook of Roosevelt College, 1948*. *U.S. School Yearbooks, 1900–2016*, Ancestry.com, https://www.ancestry.com/search/collections/1265/

22. *Los Angeles Herald-Express*, January 19, 1948; quoted in "Communist Youth in America," California Digital Library, Online Library of California, https://oac.cdlib.org/view?docId=kt4w1003q8;NAAN=13030&doc.view=frames&chunk.id=d0e722.

23. On American Youth for Democracy (AYD), see Mari Matsuda, "Japanese American Progressives: A Case Study in Identity Formation," in *Trans-Pacific*

Japanese American Studies: Conversations on Race and Racializations, ed. Yasuko Takezawa and Gary Y. Okihiro (Honolulu: University of Hawai'i Press, 2016), 342–36. See *The Vanguard: The First Yearbook of Roosevelt College, 1948,* 70.

24. Matsuda, in "Japanese American Progressives," speaks of the "commonsense appeal" of communism to Nisei progressives (350).
25. Ella Jenkins, untitled typescript manuscript, Ella Jenkins papers.
26. "Try Funference Camp as New Experiment in Race Relations," *Chicago Defender,* September 2, 1944. On CORE see August Meier and Elliott Rudwick, *CORE: A Study in the Civil Rights Movement, 1942–1968* (New York: Oxford University Press, 1973).
27. Marion B. Campfield, "Mostly about Women," *Chicago Defender,* June 30, 1951.
28. Ella Jenkins, 1940s–1950s scrapbook, p. 8, Ella Jenkins papers.
29. Ibid., p. 7, 10.
30. Jenkins, oral history interview by Poussaint.
31. Tom Jenkins interview.
32. Osran interview.
33. See Tristan Cabello, "Queer Bronzeville," *Out History,* 2008, https://outhistory .org/exhibits/show/queer-bronzeville. On Black queer religious leaders in Chicago, see Wallace D. Best, *Passionately Human, No Less Divine: Religion and Black Culture in Chicago, 1915–1952* (Princeton, NJ: Princeton University Press, 2007).
34. See also Jenkins, oral history interview by Poussaint.

CHAPTER THREE

1. Berkeley Student Cooperative, "Our History," 2024, https://bsc.coop /about-us/our-history.
2. Zoe Borkowski, interview by author.
3. Tom Jenkins interview.
4. Emanu-El Residence Club (San Francisco, CA) Records, BANC MSS 2010/717, The Magnes Collection, Manuscripts Collection, UC-Berkeley Bancroft Library.
5. Diane Cohen, interview by author.
6. See John A. Lomax, *Adventures of a Ballad Hunter* (1947; rpt., Austin: University of Texas Press, 2017).
7. Maya Angelou, *Singin' and Swingin' and Gettin' Merry Like Christmas* (New York: Bantam Books, 1976), 79.
8. See David Rothkop, "The Way It All Began," *folknik,* n.d., http://old.sffmc .org/archives/jan10/folknik.html.
9. Christopher Lowen Agee, *The Streets of San Francisco: Policing and the Creation of a Cosmopolitan Liberal Politics, 1950–1972* (Chicago: University of Chicago Press, 2014).
10. Ella Jenkins's personal copies of *Poems by Emily Dickinson,* ed. Martha Dickinson Bianchi and Alfred Leete Hampson (Boston: Little, Brown, 1950) and *The Poems and Fairy Tales of Oscar Wilde* (1936; rpt., New York: Modern Library, 1950), Ella Jenkins papers.

11. Ella Jenkins, "The Codornices Recreation Center and Some of Its Problems" (manuscript), April 1951, p. 2, Ella Jenkins papers.

12. Ella Jenkins, "My Sensitive Soul" (manuscript), p 2. Ella Jenkins papers.

13. Louise Dimiceli, "Ella Jenkins: Chicago's Magical Pied Piper," *Come for to Sing* 4, no. 2 (Spring 1978): 6.

14. See Cary Cordova, *The Heart of the Mission: Latino Art and Politics in San Francisco* (Philadelphia: University of Pennsylvania Press, 2017), 35; John Storm Roberts, *The Latin Tinge: The Impact of Latin American Music on the United States* (New York: Oxford University Press, 1999), 127–28.

15. *San Francisco Examiner* advertisement, September 25, 1951; Jesse Varela, "Sonaremó el tambo: The Life and Times of Armando Peraza, part 2," *Latin Beat Magazine*, May 2004, 23.

16. Jesse Varela, "Sonaremó el Tambo: The Life and Times of Armando Peraza, Part Two," *Latin Beat Magazine*, May 2004, 23.

17. Agee, *The Streets of San Francisco*, p. 78, identifies the Cable Car Village as a "gay bar" and documents police surveillance of men dancing together there in 1959.

18. Raúl Fernández, *Latin Jazz: The Perfect Combination/La Combinación Perfecta* (San Francisco: Chronicle Book 2002), 76. Quote from Ivan Paul, "Around Town," *San Francisco Examiner*, March 4, 1962.

19. Dimiceli, "Ella Jenkins: Chicago's Magical Pied Piper," 6.

20. Ella Jenkins, interview by Louise Dimiceli, January 31, 1978 (audiotape) (hereafter Jenkins, interview by Dimiceli). See also Dimiceli, "Ella Jenkins: Chicago's Magical Pied Piper"; Zora Neale Hurston, "How It Feels to Be Colored Me," in *I Love Myself When I Am Laughing: A Zora Neale Hurston Reader*, ed. Alice Walker (1979; rpt., New York:The Feminist Press, 1993), 152–55.

21. Fernando Ortiz, "The Conga," in *Fernando Ortiz on Music: Selected Writing on Afro-Cuban Culture*, ed. Robin D. Moore, trans. Sarah Lahasky (Philadelphia: Temple University Press), 157.

22. Kofi Agawu, *The African Imagination in Music* (New York: Oxford University Press, 2016), 308. See also Ronald Michael Radono, *Lying Up a Nation: Race and Black Music* (Chicago: University of Chicago Press, 2003).

23. Jenkins, interview by Dimiceli.

24. Ella Jenkins, personal copy of *The Rubáiyát of Omar Khayyám* (New York: Thomas Y. Crowell Company, 1946), Ella Jenkins papers.

CHAPTER FOUR

1. Ella Jenkins, oral history interview by Renee Poussaint, November 3, 2011, 59, National Visionary Leadership Project Interviews and Conference Collection (AFC 2004/2007), Archive of Folk Culture, American Folklife Center, Library of Congress, Washington, DC.

2. "YWCA and Racial Justice," *YWCA*, 2023, https://www.ywca.org/what-we-do/racial-justice-civil-rights. On the YWCA and Black women's activism, see Judith Weisenfeld, *African American Women and Christian Activism: New York's Black YWCA, 1905–1945* (Cambridge, MA: Harvard University Press, 1997), and

Nancy Marie Robertson, *Christian Sisterhood, Race Relations, and the YWCA, 1906–46* (Urbana: University of Illinois Press, 2007).

3. Ella L. Jenkins, "Monthly Report on Teen-Age Clubs, September and October, 1953," 1, YWCA of Metropolitan Chicago Records, Series 1, Box 9, Center South Parkway 1953–54, University of Illinois at Chicago.

4. Ibid., 8.

5. Ella Jenkins, interview by Louise Dimiceli, January 31, 1978 (audiotape) (hereafter Jenkins, interview by Dimiceli).

6. Joanna Dee Das, *Dance and the African Diaspora* (New York: Oxford University Press, 2017), 121; Jimmy Payne Jr., interview by author (hereafter Payne interview).

7. Margaret Burroughs, "Poem on Africa," *Nommo* 21, no. 1 (March 8, 1990). The poem is dated December 9, 1963. Accessed online at https://archive.org/stream /nommo2119univ/nommo2119univ_djvu.txt. "Ella Jenkins Discusses Her Music and Her Influences," Ella Jenkins, interview by Studs Terkel, December 7, 1963, accessed online at the Studs Terkel Radio Archive, https://studsterkel .wfmt.com/programs/ella-jenkins-discusses-her-music-and-her-influences.

8. Raeburn Flerlage and Iola Flerlage, "Ella Jenkins: Sing Out Magazine," unpublished manuscript, Box 32, Folder 11, p. 5, Raeburn Flerlage Photographs and Papers, Chicago History Museum, Chicago.

9. Beverly Lucas, interview by author.

10. Dallas L. Browne to Ella Jenkins, May 22 [no year], Ella Jenkins papers.

11. "Ask Fighting $$$ at Till Funeral: 'Let People See What They Did to My Boy,' His Mother Cries," *Afro-American*, September 17, 1955.

12. "Instantaneous Disc 789: Jenkins 1: Ella Jenkins, "Oyez me Tambuo and Composite Pornography: Side 2" and "Instantaneous Disc 790: Jenkins 2: Ella Jenkins Yo Me Voy, Side 1," Billy Faier Collection #20380, Southern Folklife Collection, Wilson Library, University of North Carolina at Chapel Hill.

13. Ella Jenkins, interview by author ("You didn't even"); Jenkins, interview by Dimiceli ("you didn't stop").

14. "Duncan and Pupils Give Dance Program at 8:30 P.M. Today," *Chicago Tribune*, September 14, 1952; Payne interview.

15. For an example of the tour's reception see "Denman Kountze, Jr., "Beat of Drum, Bongos Casts Spell over 1,000," *Omaha Evening World-Herald*, February 21, 1957.

16. Martin Yarbrough, interview by author.

17. "Afro-Cuban Dancers to 'Complexes,'" *Chicago Daily Defender*, October 8, 1956. See Mark Guarino, *Country and Midwestern: Chicago in the History of Country Music and the Folk Revival* (Chicago: University of Chicago Press, 2023), 132–35.

18. Guarino, *Country and Midwestern*, 132.

19. On "I Come for to Sing," see ibid., 135–38. On Broonzy's participation, see Bob Riesman, *I Feel So Good: The Life and Times of Big Bill Broonzy* (Chicago: University of Chicago Press, 2011).

20. Ella Jenkins, interview by Tim Ferrin.

21. Riesman, *I Feel So Good*, 210.

22. Richard Powell, interview by author; Marion Campfield, "Mostly about Women," *Chicago Defender*, June 18, 1955.

23. "Seeger Returns to Mandel Tomorrow; Afro-Cuban Vocalist Is Also Featured," *Chicago Maroon*, April 2, 1954.

24. *Chicago Maroon*, caption of photograph of Pete Seeger, March 12, 1954.

25. Peter J. Baird, "Children's Song-Makers as Messengers of Hope: Participatory Research with Implications for Educators," Ph.D. diss., University of San Francisco, 2001, 81. On wood-chopping see Arlo Guthrie, "Arlo Guthrie Remembers Pete Seeger: 'He Brought Humanity Together with His Actions," *Billboard*, January 31, 2014, https://www.billboard.com/music/music-news/arlo-guthrie-remembers-pete-seeger-appreciation-5893661/.

26. "Folk Singer," *Chicago Daily Tribune*, March 28, 1954.

27. Mickey Stein, "Seeger Shines in Second Concert," *Chicago Maroon*, April 9, 1954.

28. "Drum Routine at NAACP Party," *Chicago Maroon*, March 5, 1955.

29. Roger Bowen, "Broonzy Outstanding in Concert," *Chicago Maroon*, May 13, 1955.

30. Rose Ethel Hill, "Percussion Club," *Y-Teener*, November 1955, p. 5, YWCA of Metropolitan Chicago Records, Series 1, Box 8, Folders 111–22, Special Collections and University Archives, University of Illinois at Chicago.

31. Photo of Ella with teens at the South Side Community Committee workshop, *Chicago Defender*, December 8, 1956, 16.

32. Ella Jenkins, interview by Larry Crowe, August 5, 2002, *The History Makers*, n.d., http://thehistorymakers.org/biography/ella-jenkins-39.

CHAPTER FIVE

1. Big Bill Broonzy to Ella Jenkins, 1956, Ella Jenkins papers.

2. Bob Gibson, *Bob Gibson: I Come for to Sing* (Gretna, LA: Pelican, 2001), 33.

3. "On the Town with Will Leonard," *Chicago Tribune*, March 11, 1956.

4. Ella Jenkins, interview by Tim Ferrin.

5. Greil Marcus, *Folk Music: A Bob Dylan Biography in Seven Songs* (New Haven, CT: Yale University Press, 2022), 1.

6. Matthew Frye Jacobson, *Odetta's One Grain of Sand* (New York: Bloomsbury Academic, 2019), 53.

7. See William Leonard, "The College of Cut-ups!," *Chicago Tribune*, May 13, 1956; "Vernon Duncan's Dancers to Play 'Complexes' Café," *Chicago Daily Defender*, November 29, 1956.

8. Judith E. Smith, *Becoming Belafonte: Black Artist, Public Radical* (Austin: University of Texas Press, 2014), 110–20.

9. Bob Dylan, *Chronicles, Volume I* (New York: Simon and Schuster, 2004), 97; Joan Baez, *And a Voice to Sing With: A Memoir* (New York: Summit Books, 1987), 58. See also Mark Guarino, *Country and Midwestern: Chicago in the History of Country Music and the Folk Revival* (Chicago: University of Chicago Press, 2023), 145–46.

10. Terri Lyne Carrington, interview by author.

11. Joyce Goodman, "Talent Came Naturally to Folksinging Artist," *Montreal Star*, April 27, 1963.

12. Mahalia Jackson, "Why I Turned Down a Million Dollars," *Tone*, May 1, 1960, 6–7.

13. Guarino, *Country and Midwestern*, 148.

14. Mary Schmich, "Children's Music Never Grows Old to Ella Jenkins," *Chicago Tribune*, August 31, 2014.

15. Ella has slightly varied the details of the story over the years. In one version, after she kissed Holiday, the singer said, "Oh, you fresh young thing!"

16. Ella Jenkins, personal copy of *A Pictorial History of Jazz: People and Places from New Orleans to Modern Jazz*, ed. Bill Brauer Jr. and Orrin Keepnews (New York: Crown, 1955), Ella Jenkins papers.

17. Ella Jenkins, interview by Larry Crowe, August 5, 2002, *The History Makers*, n.d., http://thehistorymakers.org/biography/ella-jenkins-39.

18. "On the Town with Will Leonard," *Chicago Sunday Tribune*, December 2, 1956.

19. Ian Zack, *Odetta: A Life in Music and* Protest (Boston: Beacon Press, 2020), 53.

20. Marion B. Campfield, "Mostly about Women," *Chicago Defender*, January 26, 1957; Lee D. Jenkins, "New Folk Singer Gets High Praise," undated clipping, Ella Jenkins personal papers.

21. Odetta Felious to Ella Jenkins, January 22, 1957, Ella Jenkins papers.

22. "Mostly about Folksingers" scrapbook, Ella Jenkins papers.

23. Richard Powell, interview by author.

24. Lonnie G. Bunch III, interview by author.

25. Ella Jenkins, personal copy of James Weldon Johnson, *The Book of American Negro Spirituals* (New York: Viking Press, 1929), 19, 21, Ella Jenkins papers.

26. Ella Jenkins, personal copy of Langston Hughes, *The First Book of Rhythms* (New York: Franklin Watts, 1954), 29, 33, 58, Ella Jenkins papers.

27. Langston Hughes, *Rhythms of the World*, Folkways FW07340, 1955, LP. See also Robert G. O'Meally, "Afterword" to Langston Hughes, *The Book of Rhythms* (New York: Oxford University Press, 2000), 50.

28. Hughes, *Rhythms of the World*.

29. Standalone photo (no title), *Chicago Defender*, December 8, 1956.

30. Linda Mensch, interview by author.

CHAPTER SIX

1. Ella Jenkins, interview by Peter Goldsmith, August 22, 1991 (hereafter Jenkins, interview by Goldsmith), Moses and Frances Asch Collection (hereafter Asch Collection), Box 6.3, Folder 34, Ralph Rinzler Archives, Center for Folklife and Cultural Heritage, Smithsonian Institution, Washington, DC.

2. According to Goldsmith's interview with Ella Jenkins, Ella understood Odetta not to be directing her comments to Asch specifically, but to music deals in general.

3. Ella Jenkins, liner notes, *Call-and-Response Rhythmic Group Singing*, Smithsonian Folkways SFW 45030, 1998, compact disc, 1.

4. Gene Bluestein, "Moses Asch, Documentor," *American Music* 5, no. 3 (Autumn 1987): 300.

5. Jenkins, liner notes, *Call-and-Response Rhythmic Group Singing*, 1.

6. Ella Jenkins, interview by author. See also Jenkins, interview by Goldsmith.

7. Ella Jenkins to Moses Asch, April 16, 1958, Asch Collection, Box 16, Folder 23.

8. Jeff Place, interview by author.

9. David Bonner, *Revolutionizing Children's Records: The Young People's Records and Children's Record Guild Series, 1946-1977* (Lanham, MD: Scarecrow Press, 2008), 30–40.

10. Ibid., 30; Richard Carlin, *Worlds of Sound: The Story of Smithsonian Folkways* (Washington, DC: Smithsonian Institution Press, 2008), 135.

11. Rachel C. Donaldson, "Teaching Democracy: Folkways Records and Cold War Education," *History of Education Quarterly* 55, no. 1 (February 2015): 70–71.

12. Charity Bailey, *Music Time with Charity Bailey*, Folkways FW07307, 1952.

13. Ella Jenkins, liner notes, *Call-and-Response Rhythmic Group Singing*, 6.

14. Ibid., 6–7.

15. Ibid., 4.

16. See the bibliographic essay in appendix B for an overview of twentieth-century Black politics.

17. Ella L. Jenkins, "Monthly Report on Teenage Clubs, September & October, 1953," 10–11, YWCA of Metropolitan Chicago Records, Series 1, Box 9, Center South Parkway 1953–54, University of Illinois at Chicago.

18. Reprint from *The Liberalist* 35, no. 7 (October 1958), published by the People's Church of Chicago, Ella Jenkins papers.

19. Ella Jenkins, liner notes, *Call-and-Response Rhythmic Group Singing*, 4.

20. Kofi Agawu, *The African Imagination in Music* (New York: Oxford University Press, 2016), 249, 307.

21. Ian Zack, *Odetta: A Life in Music and Protest* (Boston: Beacon Press, 2020), 54.

22. Ella Jenkins, liner notes, *A Long Time to Freedom*, Folkways FC 7754, 1970, LP, p. 4.

23. Ella Jenkins, liner notes, *Call-and-Response Rhythmic Group Singing*, 11.

24. See Jeff Place, liner notes, *Lead Belly: The Smithsonian Folkways Collection*, Smithsonian Folkways SFW 40201, 2015, compact disc, 14.

25. Renato Rosaldo, "Cultural Citizenship and Educational Democracy," *Cultural Anthropology* 9, no. 3 (1994): 402.

26. Ella Jenkins to Moe Asch, August 2, 1957, Asch Collection, Box 16, Folder 23.

27. *Call-and-Response Rhythmic Group Music* autograph party invitation, 1957, Ella Jenkins papers.

28. Margaret Burroughs to Ella Jenkins, November 20, 1957, Ella Jenkins papers.

29. Broonzy benefit audio, courtesy of Old Town School of Folk Music archives. Hoke Norris, "A Singing Man Sits Silent at His Rousing Benefit," *Chicago Sun-Times*, November 29, 1957; Don Gold, "Big Bill Broonzy Benefit Concert," *DownBeat* 25, no. 1 (January 1958): 37.

30. Ronald D. Cohen, *Rainbow Quest: The Folk Music Revival and American Society, 1940-1970* (Amherst, MA: University of Massachusetts Press, 2002), 117.

CHAPTER SEVEN

1. Barbara Gottesman, "Children's Records for Holidays," *New York Herald Tribune*, November 10, 1957; B. A. Botkin and William G. Tyrrell, "Upstate, Downstate: Folklore News and Notes," *New York Folklore Quarterly* 14, no. 1 (Spring 1958): 72; Don Gold, "Tangents," *DownBeat* 25, no. 6 (March 20, 1958): 8.

2. Theodore C. Stone, "Music and Musicians," *Chicago Defender*, August 16, 1958; "Reprint from 'The Liberalist,'" 35, no. 7 (October 1958), People's Church of Chicago, Ella Jenkins papers.

3. Ella Jenkins to Moe Asch, April 16, 1958, Moses and Frances Asch Collection (hereafter Asch Collection), Box 16, Folder 23, Ralph Rinzler Archives, Center for Folklife and Cultural Heritage, Smithsonian Institution, Washington, DC.

4. Ella Jenkins to Moe Asch, July 31, 1957, Asch Collection, Box 16, Folder 23.

5. Ella Jenkins to Moe Asch, September 5, 1961, Asch Collection, Box 16, Folder 24.

6. Ella Jenkins, oral history interview by Renee Poussaint, November 3, 2011, National Visionary Leadership Project Interviews and Conference Collection (AFC 2004/2007), Archive of Folk Culture, American Folklife Center, Library of Congress, Washington, DC.

7. Ella recalled that Broonzy appeared on *This Is Rhythm*, but I found no independent record of it. If so, he would have played guitar but not sung, since he was already ill.

8. "King Gets a Hearing," *Chicago Defender*, March 14, 1957; "M. L. King Meets Nixon in Ghana," *Pittsburgh Courier*, March 9, 1957.

9. Tom Jenkins to Langston Hughes, February 22, 1958, Langston Hughes Papers, JWJ MSS 26, Box 88, Folder 1679, Series 1, Personal Correspondence, James Weldon Johnson Collection in the Yale Collection of American Literature, Beineke Rare Book and Manuscript Library; "Do You Remember," WTTW broadcast 2005, video courtesy of Tim Ferrin.

10. Eliza Powell, interview by author.

11. "She Teaches Folk Rhythms on Television," *Hue* 5, no. 6 (April 1958): 4.

12. *Chicago Daily News*, November 17, 1960 ("television folk singer"); *Park Forest Star*, June 2, 1959 ("TV rhythm artist"); *Chicago Defender*, June 25, 1959 ("TV and recording personality").

13. Roi Ottley, "Ella Jenkins an Authority on Folk Music," *Chicago Defender*, January 17, 1959.

14. Philip Royster, interview by author.

15. Harriet Hahn, "Sing Up, Grow Up This Musician's Lesson," *The Pantagraph* (Bloomington, IN), April 1, 1979.

16. Ella L. Jenkins to Lorraine Hansberry Nemiroff, June 1, 1959, Ella Jenkins papers.

17. David Blake, "'Everybody Makes Up Folksongs': Pete Seeger's 1950s College Concerts and the Democratic Potential of Folk Music," *Journal of the Society for American Music* 12, no. 4 (2018): 397.

18. Ella Jenkins, liner notes, *Adventures in Rhythm*, Folkways FC 7682, 1959, LP, n.p.

19. Ibid.
20. Langton Hughes, *The Big Sea* (New York: Hill and Wang, 1940), 23.
21. Léopold Sédar Senghor, "What the Black Man Contributes," trans. Mary Beth Mader, in *Race and Racism in Continental Philosophy*, ed. Robert Bernasconi with Sybol Cook (Bloomington: Indiana University Press, 2003), 297.
22. Ella may have learned "Zum Gali Gali," a song popular with American Jews, from a 1957 YWCA song booklet titled *Sing Along* (New York: National Board, YMCA).
23. Herbert Mitgang, "Children 'Hear' Art," *New York Times*, February 21, 1960.
24. Ella Jenkins, liner notes, *Negro Folk Rhythms*, Folkways FC 7654, 1960, LP, n.p.
25. Bernard J. Hayes, "Social Scene," *The Bulletin*, February 23, 1961, 4; D. K. Wilgus, "Record Reviews," *Journal of American Folklore* 74, no. 293 (July–September 1961): 284.
26. Paul Nelson and Jon Pankake, "Editor's Column," *Little Sandy Review* 1 (n.d.): 2. Issues of the *Little Sandy Review* were not dated, but Cohen, in *Rainbow Quest, 164*, dates the first issue to March 1960.
27. Barry Hansen, review of Ella Jenkins and the Goodwill Spiritual Choir of Monumental Baptist Church, *Negro Folk Rhythms*, *Little Sandy Review* 13 (n.d.): 11–12.
28. See Greil Marcus, *Folk Music: A Bob Dylan Biography in Seven Songs* (New Haven, CT: Yale University Press, 2022).
29. Ella Jenkins, "A Lot of Singing Going On," undated typewritten manuscript, Ella Jenkins papers.
30. Review of Nancy Whiskey and Chas. McDevitt Skiffle Group (Chic 1008), *Cash Box*, April 20, 1957, n.p.; available at https://www.45cat.com/record/nc767299us.

CHAPTER EIGHT

1. Ella Jenkins to Bernadelle Richter, August 1961, Ella Jenkins papers.
2. Betty Nudelman, interview by Tim Ferrin.
3. Ella Jenkins, liner notes, *This Is Rhythm*, Folkways FC 7652, 1961, LP, 2.
4. Ella Jenkins, *This Is Rhythm* (New York: Oak Publications, 1961). The 1993 reprint of the book replaces Ella's original drawings with illustrations by Garrian Manning. See Jenkins, *This Is* Rhythm (Bethlehem, PA: Sing Out Corporation, 1993).
5. Deforia Lane, interview by author.
6. Barry Hansen, review of Ella Jenkins, *This Is Rhythm*, *Little Sandy Review* 19 (n.d.): 12.
7. Ella Jenkins, liner notes, *Songs, Rhythms, & Chants for the Dance*, Smithsonian Folkways SFW CD 45004, compact disc, 2.
8. The Editors, "The Second Annual University of Chicago Folk Festival," *Little Sandy Review* 21 (n.d.): 8.
9. Judith Tick, "The Legacy of Ruth Crawford Seeger," *American Music Teacher* 50, no. 6 (June/July 2001): 30.
10. Don Henahan, "Want Your Kids to Like Music? Here Are 12 Steps to Help Them Enjoy Classics," *Chicago Daily News*, April 7, 1962.

11. Mary Pakenham, "U. of C. Group Opens Folk Music Fest," *Chicago Daily Tribune*, January 22, 1961.
12. Ella Jenkins, "Rhythm for Children," *Sing Out!* 12, no. 1 (February–March 1962): 4.
13. See Robin Kaufman, "Demonstrators Released," *Chicago Maroon*, February 2, 1962. See also "10 Sit-Ins in U. of C. Area Draw $10 Fines Each; Sums Suspended," *Chicago Daily Defender*, February 1, 1962.
14. Alan C. Buechner, "The Folk Music Revival and the American Music Educator," *Sing Out!* 12, no. 1 (February–March 1962): 10.
15. Ella Jenkins, liner notes, *Negro Folk Rhythms*.
16. Rosemary D. Reinger, "Ella Jenkins: The Perennial Music Maker," *Teaching Music* 8, no. 1 (August 2004): 40–44.
17. See Andy Newman, "From Jumping Flea to Collegiate Craze," *New York Times*, April 10, 2000; Jim Tranquada and John King, *The Ukulele: A History* (Honolulu: University of Hawai'i Press, 2012), 142; Savage, "Tower Ticker," *Chicago Daily Tribune*, July 17, 1950.
18. Tranquada and King, *The Ukulele*, 152.

CHAPTER NINE

1. Ella recorded "I Woke Up This Morning" on *We Are America's Children* (Folkways FC 7666, 1976).
2. Ella Jenkins to Moe Asch, August 14, 1962, Moses and Frances Asch Collection (hereafter Asch Collection), Box 16, Folder 23, Ralph Rinzler Archives, Center for Folklife and Cultural Heritage, Smithsonian Institution, Washington, DC.
3. Murray appears as "Black Harold" playing flute and log drum on the 1964 album *Sun Ra featuring Pharoah Sanders & Black Harold* (ESP Disk ESP 4054).
4. Baba Atu (fka Harold Murray), interview by author.
5. Quotes from Baba Atu (fka Harold Murray) interview.
6. "Assembly Features Rhythms and Chants," *Preble Buzz* 8, no. 3 (1962).
7. School Assembly Service flyer, ca. 1962, Ella Jenkins papers.
8. Baba Atu (fka Harold Murray) interview.
9. Ella Jenkins, interview by Larry Crowe, August 5, 2002, *The History Makers*, n.d., http://thehistorymakers.org/biography/ella-jenkins-39.
10. Ibid.
11. Ella Jenkins to Bernadelle Richter, October 16, 1962, Ella Jenkins papers.
12. Ella Jenkins to Bernadelle Richter, October 7, 1962, Ella Jenkins papers.
13. Ella Jenkins to Moe Asch, October 8, 1962, Asch Collection, Box 16, Folder 24.
14. Betty Carlson to Ella Jenkins, April 5, 1963, Ella Jenkins papers.
15. Ella Jenkins to Bernadelle Richter, December 13, 1962, Ella Jenkins papers; Oscar A. Lundeen to Mr. B. L. O'Keefe, May 3, 1963, Ella Jenkins papers.
16. Ella Jenkins to Folkways Records, June 10, 1963, Ella Jenkins papers.
17. Scholar Alessandro Carrera places Dylan at Folkstudio in January 1963 and writes that "Dylan was not to return to Italy until 1984," but Bernadelle's

recollection suggests he was in Rome again in the summer of 1963. See Car-rera, "Oh, the Streets of Rome: Dylan in Italy," in *Highway 61 Revisited: Bob Dylan's Road from Minnesota to the World*, ed. Colleen J. Sheehy and Thomas Swiss (Minneapolis: University of Minnesota Press, 2009), 84.

18. Ella Jenkins to Moe Asch, July 20, 1963, Asch Collection, Box 16, Folder 25.

19. "Music for Children" flyer, Ball State Teachers College, 1963, Ella Jenkins papers.

20. Carl Orff to Ella Jenkins, July 29, 1963, Ella Jenkins papers; Ella Jenkins to Carl Orff, August 28, 1963, courtesy of Off-Zentrum München, Staatsinstitut für Forschung und Dokumentation.

21. See Emily Spitz, "From Idea to Institution: The Development and Dissem-ination of the Orff-Schulwerk from Germany to the United States," *Current Musicology* 104 (2019), https://doi.org/10.7916/cm.v0i104.5390.

22. James Baldwin, "Stranger in the Village," *Harper's Magazine* 207, no. 1241 (October 1953): 42–48.

23. "Ella Jenkins Discusses Her Music and Her Influences," Ella Jenkins, interview by Studs Terkel, December 7, 1963, accessed online at the Studs Terkel Radio Archive, https://studsterkel.wfmt.com/programs /ella-jenkins-discusses-her-music-and-her-influences.

24. Carl Orff to Ella Jenkins, July 29, 1963, courtesy of Off-Zentrum München Archive.

25. Ella Jenkins, undated letter to Bernadelle Richter, Ella Jenkins papers.

26. Ella Jenkins, liner notes, *Songs and Rhythms from Near and Far*, Folkways FC 7655, 1964, LP, 2.

27. Ibid., 5.

28. Ibid., 2.

CHAPTER TEN

1. Display advertisement, Lake Meadows Apartments, *Chicago Tribune*, January 18, 1959. On the development of the South Side, see Arnold R. Hirsch, *Making the Second Ghetto: Race and Housing in Chicago, 1940–1960* (New York: Cam-bridge University Press, 1983), 115–34.

2. Ella Jenkins, liner notes, *Counting Games and Rhythms for the Little Ones*, Folk-ways FC 7679, 1964, LP, 2.

3. The "imaginative worlds" of preschoolers were carefully observed by Vivian Gussin Paley. Paley refers to Ella's recording of "Did You Feed My Cow?" in *Wally's Stories: Conversations in the Kindergarten* (Cambridge, MA: Harvard University Press, 1981), 4, 20.

4. Patricia Shehan Campbell, interview by author.

5. Doris Geller, "Creativeness from Natural Rhythm," *Montreal Star*, May 11, 1964.

6. Ella Jenkins, liner notes, *Counting Games and Rhythms for the Little Ones*, 3.

7. Ibid.; Bonnie Thornton Dill, interview by author.

8. See Patricia Shehan Campbell, "Recording Reviews," *Ethnomusicology* 46, no. 2 (Spring–Summer 2002): 356–59.

9. Shawnelle Richie, interview by author.

10. See Jean Simpson, "Oneida Cockrell: Pioneer in the Field of Early Childhood Education," *Young Children* 67, no 5 (November 2012): 60–61.

11. Maris A. Vinovskis, *The Birth of Head Start: Preschool Education Policies in the Kennedy and Johnson Administrations* (Chicago: University of Chicago Press, 2005), 5–9.

12. Evelyn K. Moore, interview by author (hereafter Moore interview).

13. Whitney M. Young Jr., "To Be Equal," *Chicago Defender*, June 5, 1965.

14. Moore interview. See Samuel Y. Song and Shirley Mary Pyon, "Cultural Deficit Model," in *Encyclopedia of Educational Psychology*, ed. Neil J. Salkin (New York: Sage, 2008). Accessed online at https://doi.org/10.4135/9781412963848.

15. Ella Jenkins, liner notes, *A Long Time to Freedom*, Folkways FC 7754, 1970, LP, p. 2.

16. See "Mahalia Jackson Backs Boycott," *Chicago Daily Defender*, February 24, 1964.

17. Seymour M. Hersh, "70,000 in Chicago Hail Rights Bill," *Washington Post*, June 22, 1964; "57,000 Hear King Praise Legislation," *Chicago Tribune*, June 2, 1964.

18. Martin Luther King Jr., *Stride toward Freedom* (New York: Harper and Row, 1958), 80, 87.

19. The charges were dropped when the friend's father intervened. Ella Jenkins, interview by author.

20. See Ella Jenkins, "Freedom Singers: Two New Records," *Community* 22, 11 (July 1963), n.p.

21. *Free at Last: A Musical Tribute to Dr. Martin Luther King, Jr.*, January 14, 1985, accessed online at https://www.youtube.com/watch?v=uE1b-5UStYE&t=1116s.

22. Ella Jenkins, *The Ella Jenkins Songbook for Children* (New York: Oak Publications, 1966), 7.

23. Ella Jenkins to Moe Asch, January 19 and March 2, 1966, Moses and Frances Asch Collection (hereafter Asch Collection), Box 16, Folder 25, Ralph Rinzler Archives, Center for Folklife and Cultural Heritage, Smithsonian Institution, Washington, DC.

24. Ella Jenkins, liner notes, *You'll Sing a Song and I'll Sing a Song*, Folkways FW 07664, 1966, LP, n.p.

25. Ibid.

26. See "National Recording Preservation Board," Library of Congress, n.d., https://www.loc.gov/programs/national-recording-preservation-board/recording-registry/.

27. Ella Jenkins to Moe Asch, August 14, 1967, Asch Collection, Box 16, Folder 26.

28. *A Child's Introduction to Jazz*, Riverside RLP 1435, 1961, LP.

CHAPTER ELEVEN

1. June Sawyers, "With Summer Came Opera at Ravinia Park," *Chicago Tribune*, July 3, 1998.

2. "School assembly" is from Nany Maes, "After 40 years, Ella Jenkins Still Teaching the World to Sing," *Chicago Tribune*, July 5, 1998. "Everyone Has a Chance" from Ella Jenkins, interview by Diane Dunne, KNCT Central Texas College, September 1983, 21:47, https://www.youtube.com/watch?v=dF_u23pzcVw.

3. Tom Jenkins, interview by Tim Ferrin; "Hootenanny to Be Repeated at Ravinia," *Roselle Register* (Illinois), August 2, 1968.

4. "No One Model American: A Statement on Multicultural Education," *Journal of Teacher Education* 24, no. 4 (December 1973): 264–65; Robert A. Choate, ed., *Documentary Report of the Tanglewood Symposium* (Washington, DC: Music Educators National Conference, 1968), n.p.

5. Ella Jenkins, liner notes, *A Long Time to Freedom*, Folkways FC 7754, 1970, LP, 3.

6. Ella Jenkins, unpublished manuscript, ca. 1970, Ella Jenkins papers.

7. John Cohen, "Chicago Festival," *Sing Out!* 18 (June–July 1968): 65, qtd. in Ronald D. Cohen, *Rainbow Quest: The Folk Music Revival and American Society, 1940–1970* (Amherst: University of Massachusetts Press, 2002), 281; Happy Traum, "The Swan Song of Folk Music," *Rolling Stone*, May 17, 1969, 7–8.

8. John H. Johnson, "Why Ebony Jr?," *Ebony Jr!* 1, no. 1 (May 1973). Available online at https://books.google.com/books?id=yL4DAAAAMBAJ. Ella was featured several times in *Ebony Jr!* See Shirley Searcy, "Ella Jenkins: The Music Magician," *Ebony Jr!* 5, no. 5 (November 1977): 38-40.

9. *Water Is Wet*, dir. Gordon Weisenborn (1969); accessible online at Chicago Film Archives, https://collections.chicagofilmarchives.org/Detail/objects/3403.

10. Aquanetta White-Olive, interview by author; Al Monroe, "Sepians as Whites on Stage, Screen 'Common,'" *Chicago Daily Defender*, October 14, 1958.

11. White-Olive interview.

12. Ibid.

13. Ella Jenkins, liner notes, *A Long Time to Freedom*, 1.

14. Ibid.

15. Odetta, quoted in Greil Marcus, *Folk Music: A Bob Dylan Biography in Seven Songs* (New Haven, CT: Yale University Press, 2022), 25.

16. Ella Jenkins, liner notes, *A Long Time to Freedom*, 3.

17. Raymond Lowery, "3 Folk Albums Explore Rural and Urban Rags," *Raleigh News and Observer*, April 18, 1971; L. Weingarten, "Anti-War Ballad Is Rated Prine Album's Best," *Camden Courier-Post*, November 19, 1971.

18. Betsy Morris, "Do Sing Back to Ella," *Knoxville News-Sentinel*, October 4, 1974.

19. Ella Jenkins, liner notes, *Nursery Rhymes*, Folkways FC 7660, 1974, LP, 6.

20. Ella Jenkins, undated typescript memoir, Ella Jenkins papers.

21. Morris, "Do Sing Back to Ella."

22. Ella Jenkins, *We Are America's Children*, track 1, Folkways, FC 7666, 1976, LP.

23. Susan Linn, Hedda Sharapan, and Bill Isler, interviews by author. See Maxwell King, *The Good Neighbor: The Life and Work of Fred Rogers* (New York: Abrams Press, 2018).

24. Hedda Sharapan, interview by author.

25. *Mister Rogers' Neighborhood*, episode 1335, March 1, 1974.

26. Nan Wheelock to Ella Jenkins, January 29, 1974, Ella Jenkins papers.

27. In 1993 she sang the "Bobbity Bop" song with Barney, the purple dinosaur namesake of *Barney and Friends*, 2, episode 18: "A Very Special Delivery!" (1993).

28. King, *The Good Neighbor*, 9. The video is available at https://www.misterrogers .org/videos/head-and-shoulders-with-ella-jenkins/.

29. Jan Baskin and Tom Compton, "Women's Music Festival Good Despite Absence of 'Names,'" *Daily Illini* (University of Illinois at Champagne-Urbana), June 12, 1974. See also "Women's Music Festival: No More 'Canaries,'" *Fifth Estate* 9, no. 5 (June 22–July 5, 1974): 12–13.

30. *Ladyslipper Music: Records and Tapes by Women* catalog (Summer–Fall 1978), 2. Linda Bubon, interview by author.

31. Richard Hunt, interview by author.

32. Ella Jenkins to Moe Asch, October 12, 1978, Moses and Frances Asch Collection, Box 16, Folder 28, Ralph Rinzler Archives, Center for Folklife and Cultural Heritage, Smithsonian Institution, Washington, DC.

33. Elisha B. Seeley, "The Christian Science Sanitorium," *Christian Science Journal*, April 26, 1924.

CHAPTER TWELVE

1. "Ping-Pong Diplomacy Hailed by U.S. as Peking 'Breakthru': Invited to Red China," *Chicago Tribune*, April 8, 1971.

2. EJ archives. Dated March 8, 1979. Enjoli commercial: https://www.youtube .com/watch?v=xRoGbiOGC54.

3. Ella Jenkins to Moses Asch, January 14, 1980, Moses and Frances Asch Collection (hereafter Asch Collection), Box 16, Folder 29, Ralph Rinzler Archives, Center for Folklife and Cultural Heritage.

4. Moses Asch to Ella Jenkins, January 23, 1980, Asch Collection, Box 16, Folder 29.

5. Ella Jenkins to Bill Hammons and the Board of Trustees, Alvin Ailey American Dance Theater, December 30, 1980, Ella Jenkins papers.

6. Ella recorded four albums in the early 1980s with Educational Activities: *I Know the Colors of the Rainbow* (AR 595, 1981), *Looking Back and Looking Forward* (AR 596, 1981), *Hopping Around from Place to Place, Vol. 1* (AR 613, 1983), and *Hopping Around from Place to Place, Vol. 2* (AR-614, 1983).

7. Ella Jenkins to Moses Asch, February 4, 1981, Asch Collection, Box 16, Folder 30.

8. Linda Mensch, interview by author.

9. Moses Asch to Ella Jenkins, January 11, 1982, Asch Collection, Box 16, Folder 30.

10. Ella Jenkins, liner notes, *Hopping Around from Place to Place, Vol. 2*.

11. Elizabeth Galbreath, "Typovision," *Chicago Defender*, August 2, 1941; Ella Jenkins, "Things to Remember," unpublished manuscript dated December 29, 1984, Ella Jenkins papers.

12. Robert Palmer, "How a Recording Pioneer Created a Treasury of Folk Music," *New York Times*, May 29, 1983.

13. Ella Jenkins to Moses Asch, June 20, 1983, Asch Collection, Box 16, Folder 31.

14. On Smithsonian's purchase of Folkways, see Richard Carlin, *Worlds of South: The Story of Smithsonian Folkways* (New York: Smithsonian Books, 2008).

15. Peter Goldsmith recounts the same story in *Making People's Music: Moe Asch and Folkways Records* (Washington, DC: Smithsonian Books, 1998), 416. Rinzler did not see himself as a member of the folk aristocracy, according to Richard Carlin, *Worlds of Sound: The Story of Smithsonian Folkways* (Washington, DC: Smithsonian Press, 2008), 254. According to Tony Seeger, Bess Lomax Hawes spoke highly of Ella's work. Tony Seeger, interview by author (hereafter Tony Seeger interview).

16. Jon Pareles, "Moses Asch, Who Founded Folkways Records, Dies at 81," *New York Times*, October 21, 1986.

17. See Jeff McLaughlin, "A Bright New Day Is Dawning in Kids' Music Market," *Boston Globe*, May 25, 1986. Other prominent children's musicians of the era included Peter Alsop and Hap Palmer.

18. Constance Rosenbaum, "A Young Children's Concert with Raffi" (review), *New York Times*, October 18, 1987; Alan Freeman, "For Young Groupies, the Who Is 'What?' and Raffi Is the King," *Wall Street Journal*, June 29, 1987.

19. Raffi Cavoukian, interview by author.

20. Moira McCormick, interview by author.

21. *Mister Rogers' Neighborhood*, episode 1652, August 25, 1992. See http://www.neighborhoodarchive.com/memorabilia/other/kazoo_jenkins/index.html.

22. Tony Seeger interview.

23. Ella was referred to in print as the "First Lady of Children's Folk Music" (or variations thereof) as early as 1991. By the mid-1990s, print outlets had begun to shed the word "folk," referring to her simply at the "First Lady of Children's Music."

24. Ella Jenkins, liner notes, *Come Dance by the Ocean*, Smithsonian Folkways, SFW 45014, 1991, compact disc, n.p.

25. It lost to *The Adventures of Elmo in Grouchland*, the soundtrack of a 1999 film based on the *Sesame Street* character.

26. Rob Reid, review of *Multicultural Children's Songs*, *School Library Journal* (May 1966): n.p.; review of *Multicultural Children's Songs*, *Parenting* (June/July 1996): n.p. From Folkways publicity materials, Ella Jenkins papers.

27. Martin F. Kohn, "Multicultural Children's Songs," *Parents* 71, no. 12 (December 1996): 256–57 ("Ella was singing"); T. V. Churchill, Coordinator, Early Childhood Programs, Board of Education of the City of Duluth to Folkways Records and Service Corp., January 11, 1971, Asch Collection, Box 16, Folder 27.

28. *Barney: What a World We Share* (Universal Studios Home Entertainment, 1999). Available on YouTube, https://www.youtube.com/watch?v=gLsGcidxcd4.

29. Alisa Valdes, "A Diverse Turn for Kids' Music," *Boston Globe*, August 7, 1992.

30. Shanta Nurullah, interview by author.

31. Jon Pareles, "Banjo Tunes, Bombas and the Sounds of Tree Frogs in a Community Sing," *New York Times*, May 4, 1998.

32. Marilyn Bergman to Ella Jenkins, May 26, 1999, Ella Jenkins papers.
33. "Ella Jenkins—cELLAbration Live!," Smithsonian Folkways publicity film, https://www.youtube.com/watch?v=SvYKPCsNbQI.

EPILOGUE

1. Daniel Sheehy, interview by author.
2. Ibid.
3. Meredith Moss, "Folk Singer Shares Love of Music with Children," *Dayton Daily News*, February 7, 2001; Ella Jenkins, interview with Michael Asch and Atesh Sonneborn, February 2003, https://folkways.si.edu/ella-jenkins-conversation /african-american-childrens/music/video/smithsonian.
4. "Someone You Should Know: Musician Ella Jenkins," CBS 2 News with Harry Porterfield, August 8, 2014, CBS 2 Chicago YouTube channel, https://www .youtube.com/watch?v=cPZTs1aHeYk.
5. Mary Baker Eddy, *Science and Health with Key to the Scriptures*, 244:23, 245:17; accessed online at https://www.christianscience.com /the-christian-science-pastor/science-and-health.
6. Ibid., 191:16–17.
7. Neil Portnow to Ella Jenkins, December 19, 2003; qtd. in Lynne Heffley, "A Big Reputation for Entertaining Little Listeners," *Los Angeles Times*, February 2, 2004.
8. Lynn Orman, interview by author; Paxton quote from liner notes, *cELLAbration! A Tribute to Ella Jenkins*, Smithsonian Folkways SFW45059, 2004, compact disc, 8.
9. Audio recording, Ella Jenkins 80th Birthday Party Concert, Old Town School of Folk Music, October 30, 2004. Courtesy Old Town School of Folk Music Archives.
10. Lonnie G. Bunch III, interview by author.
11. Michelle Obama, video message to Ella Jenkins, Fifth Star awards ceremony, September 16, 2005, Chicago. Courtesy of Tim Ferrin.
12. Sarah McCarthy, interview by author.
13. Tom Jenkins to Ella Jenkins, March 18, 2005, Ella Jenkins papers.
14. Tom Jenkins to Ella Jenkins, June 5, 1997, Ella Jenkins papers.
15. Citation for Ella Jenkins, Edwin A. Rothschild Award for Lifetime Achievement in Civil Rights, Chicago Lawyer's Committee for Civil Rights Under Law, Inc., October 20, 2016.
16. Jane Chu, interview by author.
17. See Laurel Graeber, "How 100-Year-Old Ella Jenkins Revolutionized Children's Music," *New York Times*, August 7, 2024.
18. Ella Jenkins, undated typescript memoir, ca. 1982, Ella Jenkins papers.

INDEX

Page numbers in italics refer to figures. All unattributed songs and albums are performed by Ella Jenkins.